Forfeits and Successful
Protested Games in
Major League Baseball

Forfeits and Successfully Protested Games in Major League Baseball

A Complete Record, 1871–2013

DAVID NEMEC *and* ERIC MIKLICH

Foreword by PETE PALMER

McFarland & Company, Inc., Publishers

Jefferson, North Carolina

ALSO OF INTEREST:
David Nemec: *The Rank and File of 19th Century Major League Baseball: Biographies of 1,084 Players, Owners, Managers and Umpires* (McFarland, 2012)

Except where noted, all photographs are from the Library of Congress.

LIBRARY OF CONGRESS CATALOGUING-IN-PUBLICATION DATA

Nemec, David.
  Forfeits and successfully protested games in Major League baseball : a complete record, 1871–2013 / David Nemec and Eric Miklich ; foreword by Pete Palmer.
      p.   cm.
  Includes bibliographical references and index.

  ISBN 978-0-7864-9423-1 (softcover : acid free paper) ∞
  ISBN 978-1-4766-1629-2 (ebook)

  1. Baseball—Records—United States.   2. Baseball—United States—History.   I. Title.
  GV877.N45 2014
  796.357'64—dc23   2014012217

BRITISH LIBRARY CATALOGUING DATA ARE AVAILABLE

On the cover: Philadelphia Athletics catcher Ira Thomas (left) and Boston Braves infielder Johnny Evers with the umpires in the 1914 World Series (Library of Congress)

Printed in the United States of America

McFarland & Company, Inc., Publishers
  Box 611, Jefferson, North Carolina 28640
  www.mcfarlandpub.com

To all my fellow long-suffering
Cleveland sports fans
—David Nemec

To my mother Dorothy,
who gave me the love of history
—Eric Miklich

Acknowledgments

We would like to thank the many members of the Society for American Baseball Research (SABR) whose invaluable research on forfeited and protested major league games is reflected on the SABR Retrosheet web site, www.RetroSheet.org, and we offer special thanks to Dave Smith, Retrosheet's web master extraordinaire, and Tom Ruane. In addition, we want to offer special thanks to Bob Tiemann, one of the foremost authorities on forfeited and protested major league games, and to Pete Palmer for generously sharing his overall expertise on baseball with us by fact checking our book as well as writing its foreword.

Table of Contents

Foreword
by Pete Palmer

This book offers a fresh angle on the history of baseball by delineating the events surrounding all the forfeited and successfully protested major league games since 1871, the year the first all professional league was formed. Because the majority of these disputatious games occurred in the nineteenth century and the early part of the twentieth century for reasons that the authors analyze in some depth, a distinctive picture of our national pastime in its embryonic years is presented, particularly in regard to how and why certain rules evolved as they did and the growth and development of the craft of umpiring. There are also intriguing glimpses into the lives of many of the players and umpires involved in fractious events.

A fascinating example of a forfeited game that demonstrates how much baseball's early rules differed from those we know today occurred on August 23, 1884. When the dropped third strike rule first appeared in the game, there was no requirement to have first base open or two outs, so that a catcher could deliberately drop a third strike with the bases loaded and none out and get an easy double play or sometimes even a triple play by going swiftly around the horn. In the August 23, 1884, game between Detroit and Boston of the National League, the Detroit captain, Frank Cox, called into question the efficacy of this rule and was made to look foolish for doing so when his unrelenting argument, which seems to make perfect sense to us today but was met only with ridicule at the time, led to his team's forfeiting the game. Yet less than three years later, in the winter of 1886–87, rules makers suddenly heard the cries in the wilderness of Cox and others like him and removed the benefit of deliberately dropping a third strike with the bases loaded from a catcher's repertoire.

An outstanding aid in identifying most of the games covered in this book was the work of Bob Tiemann. In his personal notebooks Tiemann meticulously jotted down the results of every major league game from 1871 to the present from the newspaper account in a matrix by team and date, including details on such things as forfeits and protests. Arnie Braunstein computerized Tiemann's notebooks, which served as the foundation for the game logs that are posted on www.retrosheet.com. This site, which is operated by the Society of American Baseball Research (SABR), is a rich source for baseball data, particularly for those searching for play by play accounts of almost every game going back to 1950 and many from even earlier, as well as box scores for all games from 1914 to 1949 (and counting). Efforts in recent years have added box scores reaching all the way back to 1872. Dave Smith is the proprietor of the site and Tom Ruane played a major part in the game logs. The authors acknowledge their debt to both of these extraordinary researchers along with Tiemann.

My favorite protested game story centers on a play involving Stan Musial on June 30, 1959. The authors highlight this game in their introduction to protested games as well as several other protested games in the body of their study that will be new even to readers who are familiar with SABR's Retrosheet site.

Now, prepare yourself for a most entertaining and ground-breaking trip through the history of forfeited and successfully protested major league games.

Pete Palmer is the editor of Who's Who in Baseball, a coauthor of The Hidden Game of Baseball and a coeditor of The ESPN Baseball Encyclopedia. He introduced the on-base average statistic for the American League in 1979 and invented on-base plus slugging, now widely used. His baseball data are used in the SABR Encyclopedia and by MLB.com, Retrosheet, ESPN, and Baseball-Reference.com. In 2010, he was among the inaugural group of nine to receive SABR's Henry Chadwick Award.

Preface

Even if you're a dyed-in-the-wool baseball fan, the chances are strong that you've never seen either a forfeited or a successfully protested major league game on TV, never mind in person. If you're under 50 the odds are even longer, and if you've not yet reached voting age by the time you read this book, there's simply no chance at all.

Why then do we need a book dealing solely with forfeited and successfully protested major league games? How can there even be enough material to assemble one if they're such a rare occurrence? Ah, but these dinosaurs in our time haven't always been so rare. For a great many years scarcely a month would go by, let alone an entire major league season, without there being at least one forfeited or successfully protested game.

The reason that was so is that baseball even in its pre-professional days was rife with both on-field and off-field disputes between contesting clubs over the eligibility of players, umpires' decisions and the interpretation of the myriad of yearly rules changes. These same issues only intensified in 1871 when the National Association of Professional Base Ball Players (NA), the first openly professional league, was formed, continued vigorously until the mid–1920s, and after that began rapidly to dwindle to a point where 2014 marks the nineteenth season since there was either a forfeited or successfully protested major league game.

Why the sharp drop off starting in the mid–1920s? For one, the last forfeited or successfully protested game in big league history that centered on the use of an ineligible player had occurred some ten years earlier in 1915. Secondly, the rules by then had stabilized to a large degree. Indeed, while there continue to be rule amendments, additions to the game like instant replay and clarifications and refinements on fan and catcher's interference and similar matters, in the past twenty years the lone major revision in the actual playing rules occurred in 1995 when the lower level of the strike zone became a line at the hollow beneath a batter's kneecap rather than a line at the top of his knees. Consequently, the Rules Committee, which once upon a time met annually and had conferences that often lasted deep into the night for the better part of a week in order to thrash out all of the many proposed rules changes, has not met as a full body now since January 30, 1996.

Prior to 1920, and especially prior to 1900, the constantly changing playing rules triggered protracted debates in the midst of games during which nerves frayed, tempers flared, epithets flew and all too often were followed by spat wads of chewing tobacco and even fisticuffs. The rules makers' main objective during the nineteenth century was to achieve a balance between the pitching and hitting. However, other aspects of the game were also constantly being tested and circumvented, forcing numerous yearly revisions even after the beginning of relative rules stability when the current pitching distance was established in 1893. With each new rule change, unless it was worded with razor-sharp precision on its first appearance in the rule book how it was interpreted had a strong potential to instigate disagreements. Too, even veteran umpires were taxed heavily each year to memorize the rules changes during the offseason so as to incorporate them in their technique of officiating. As but one example: In 1887 the hit batsman rule was universally adopted by every professional league. The rule was changed in 1892 so as not to give a batsman his base if he was hit by a pitch on the hand or forearm. Five years later it was again changed to read as it had in 1887, awarding a batsman his base if he was hit anywhere on his person but only if he did not, in an umpire's judgment, allow himself to be hit deliberately. Then, in the winter of 1900–1901, the National League decided to dispense with the hit batsman rule entirely, only to reinstall it when its absence during preseason training that spring was taken as license by several National League pitchers to target particularly dangerous batsmen at will. Pity the poor umpire who in a 14-year span had to make four adjustments in how he enforced what was essentially the same rule while a multitude of other rules were constantly "adjusted" as well.

A second and even more important reason for the sharp drop off in forfeited and successfully protested games by the mid–1920s is that during that decade both major leagues went to a three-umpire system, which has since grown to four and now expands to a total of six in postseason games. In 1871, when the National Association of Professional Base Ball Players (NA), the first openly professional league, was formed, the game allowed for only one umpire and made no stipulations as to what credentials he needed to have for the job beyond that he had to be acceptable to both teams. What's more, he was often picked by lot and then not until minutes before a game was scheduled to begin. Games as a result might be umpired by almost anyone, ranging from a player not in uniform that day to a passerby who looked and talked the part. As might be expected, this haphazard system made for many abuses. Even player-umpires struggled at times. Not until the early 1880s did professional leagues begin to hire a regular staff of umpires prior to the start of a season and subject applicants to at least a modicum of a peer review. But games still remained in the hands of a lone official, putting him often at the unmitigated mercy of either an unruly player, a bellicose manager or an openly hostile crowd—and sometimes all three! Although there were periodic experiments in both the National League and the American Association with a two-umpire system during the 1880s, it was not until the Players League took up the cudgel in 1890 that a major circuit regularly employed two umpires in every game for a full season. Unfortunately the Players League breathed its last after only a single season in operation and the visionary two-umpire experiment died with it.

In 1898, the National League and American Association of Professional Base Ball Clubs (NLAAPBBC), an amalgam of the National League and its arch rival, the American Association, that was more commonly known in the media both then and now as simply the National League, revived the two-umpire system, but again, for a variety of reasons, it failed to take hold. The two-umpire system did not come to stay in the game until the latter part of the first decade in the twentieth century. But umpires working even in pairs remained vulnerable in ways that current umpires are not to constant assaults verbally, mentally and physically from players, managers and spectators that could not help but influence their decisions at times and contribute to situations appearing in this book that will be unimaginable to many of today's fans.

Equipment changes, the quirks of field specific rules owing to strange field configurations brought about by the confining properties on which the fields were built (often in only a matter of days), and weather also continued to provoke quarrels that could erupt at any moment in an umpire pulling out his watch and putting a disputant on the clock or a manager yanking his team off the diamond. While many of the forfeits and successfully protested games presented in these pages are clear cut even by today's standards, not understanding the progression of baseball rules and the changing conditions, particularly in the nature of crowd control, can make some of them seem incomprehensible from a twenty-first century standpoint.

As often as possible, a detailed storyline has been presented for each forfeited and successfully protested game. This we trust will provide readers with a better understanding of the circumstances and the reasoning behind the decisions rendered. When the reported events of a game were at variance among our sources, we have tried whenever possible to consult what we consider to be the most logical primary source and, in all, to present the most likely scenario that occurred when the variances in our sources were at odds with one another.

In addition, some forfeited games that were later overturned and protested games that were not thrown out or else ordered to resume from the point where the protested incident occurred have been included to illustrate that those empowered to make decisions on disputed contests were not always rocket scientists and, too, that there is still room for more research with regard to the field of forfeited and protested games in general. Our intention is not only to produce the first definitive source on the subject of forfeited and successfully protested major league games but to help educate readers on the rules and prevailing styles of play when each forfeit or protested game occurred.

Forfeited Games

The vast majority of forfeited games in major league history have radiated from a lapse of one sort or another. Oftentimes, especially in the early days when games were almost always officiated by a single umpire or a player serving as an umpire, the forfeit resulted from a lapse in patience either with the official or else by him. Throughout history, right up to the last forfeited major league game to date, there have been serious and sometimes outright dangerous lapses in the home team's ability to maintain adequate crowd control. On rare occasions the negligence has been created by the home team's failure to either provide ample equipment (such as enough new balls) or else to utilize its equipment properly and expeditiously so as to prevent its field from becoming needlessly unplayable. There have also unhappily been instances when a lapse has been in the fortitude of an umpire compounded by the decision of a faint-hearted league official to uphold his spineless forfeiture.

Statistics from forfeited and successfully protested games are a minefield for serious researchers endeavoring to make each major league player's career and season statistics as correct as humanly possible. It would have been ideal if an enduring rule had been drafted prior to 1871 to guide record-keepers on how to determine which statistics from disputed games should count and which should not, but instead there have been lengthy stretches when record-keepers have been entirely on their own. As a result, there continue to be major discrepancies among reference works. In 1920 a rule was adopted to count statistics from all protested games that went at least five innings, but prior to then there appears to have been no comprehensive rule. The lack of one has led to such vagaries as continuing to exclude statistics from all protested games between 1911 and 1918 while including some from earlier games that did not go five innings and restoring those from games in the nineteenth century that were declared no-decisions. As for forfeited games, the outlook is only slightly rosier. Throughout most of major league history the present practice of awarding pitching wins and losses has generally been followed. That rule assigns a win to a pitcher whose team was ahead at the time the forfeit occurred and a loss to the pitcher whose team was behind provided the game was forfeited to the team that was leading at the time. However, there were periods when this practice was not followed. To notate all the exceptions and exemptions along with the reasons for them would require a book in itself. Suffice it to say that we have worked to apprise the reader each time a meaningful statistic from a forfeited or a successfully protested game has either been included in, erased from or restored to the record book.

What follows is a report on each forfeited game in major league history, including the date on which it occurred along with the city, league and park where it took place, the two teams involved, and finally the umpire or umpires who participated in the forfeiture. The same template is employed in our reports on successfully protested games.

May 11, 1871

Place: Cleveland
League: National Association of Professional Base Ball Players (NA)
Field: Association Grounds
Clubs: Cleveland versus Chicago
Umpire: Henry Haynie

With the score tied 5–5 after five innings a disputed decision by Haynie led to five Chicago runs. By the top of the 8th inning Chicago was ahead 18–10 when Cleveland's captain, outfielder Charlie Pabor, was called out at third base. Morally certain he had been safe, Pabor, egged on by disgusted Cleveland club officials in attendance, decided he'd had his fill of Haynie's one-sided officiating. He grabbed the game ball in use at the time and angrily handed it to Chicago's captain and second baseman Jimmy Wood, an act that signified his team was quitting. The custom in the game's pre-professional era dictated that the final ball in play belonged to the winning nine.

Haynie was a former National Association of Base Ball Players Secretary in the pre-professional era and a sports writer with the *Chicago Times* who had accompanied the team to the Forest City. Wood prevailed upon Pabor to let Haynie officiate when the umpire the teams had mutually agreed upon earlier failed to appear. The following day the *Brooklyn Daily Eagle* depicted Haynie as "a man utterly unfit for the base ball positions he has occupied," and he never worked another ML game. The *Eagle* added that Haynie had umpired a game in 1870 in Chicago and the Athletic Club of Philadelphia left the field in protest.

The use of Haynie as the umpire was in accordance with the decision agreed upon at the National Association convention, which was held in New York City at 840 Broadway on March 17, 1871. Resolved during this meeting was the issue of selecting an umpire: *"that the question of selecting an umpire between contending clubs be arranged by the visiting club presenting the names of five persons to the local club to select one of their number, and that sufficient time be given before the day of play to make such arrangements. The persons named for selection shall be known and acknowledged as competent men for the position, and shall be chosen from three or more clubs. In the case the umpire selected should fail, for some unknown cause, to appear on the day of the game, then the umpire shall be selected by the two captains of the contesting nines."*

Haynie had served throughout the Civil War as a member of the first infantry regiment raised in Chicago and entered the newspaper business after mustering out. Departing Chicago in 1876, he served briefly as an editor on the *New York Times* staff, then left for Europe and spent 20 years as the Paris correspondent for several American papers while serving as president of the association of correspondents in that city. Late in the nineteenth century he returned to the U.S. and continued reporting for a few years before turning to purely literary work. He is entirely forgotten now, but in his own time Haynie was well known as the prolific author of works ranging from books about European celebrities to an essay on the art of carving meat. None of his large output, so far as we know, had anything at all to do with baseball.

SOURCES

Brooklyn Daily Eagle, April 12, 1871.

Nemec, David. *The Rank and File of 19th Century Major League Baseball* (Jefferson, NC: McFarland, 2012), 282.

Proceeding of Convention of the National Association of Professional Base Ball Players, Beresford, 1871.

Ryczek, William. *Blackguards and Red Stockings* (Wallingford, CT: Colebrook Press, 1999), 104–105.

May 17, 1871

Place: Rockford
League: National Association of Professional Base Ball Players
Field: Agricultural Society Fairgrounds
Teams: Rockford versus Washington
Umpire: Jimmy Wood

Despite losing on the playing field to Rockford, 15–12, Washington was subsequently declared the winner by forfeit, a verdict that was officially upheld at the final league meeting of the year on November 3, 1871, overriding a protest by Rockford catcher and captain Scott Hastings that he was not in violation of the league's mandate that no player under contract to another club could play with an NA team until a period of 60 days had elapsed since he had left his former club. The rule had been drawn up to put a stop to "revolving" or jumping from team to team, a practice that became rampant in the 1860s when some players began being paid to play and were eager to sell their services to the highest bidder.

Hastings had played with the Rockford club in 1870 but was with the independent Lone Star club of New Orleans when it faced the Chicago White Stockings on April 16, 1871, during Chicago's southern tour prior to the start of the NA season. It was Hastings's last appearance with the Lone Stars, and the NA contended that he was therefore ineligible to join any of its member clubs until June 16. Hastings argued to no avail that he had not been under a formal contract while with the Lone Stars but had simply gone south in the winter of 1870–71 to earn extra money. He had previously played in an NA game at Cleveland on May 6, but no formal protest was lodged then because the Forest City club won. The Washington game was the first of four forfeit losses Rockford would sustain before Hastings became an eligible team member.

The NA rule on a player's eligibility was as follows, Rule 5, Section 2: *"In playing all matches, nine players from each club shall constitute a full field; and they must be members of the club which they represent. They also must not have been members of any other club, in or out of the National Amateur Association—college-club nines, composed of actual students, excepted,—for sixty days immediately prior to the match. Positions of players and choice of innings shall be determined by captains previously appointed for that purpose by the respective clubs. Every player taking part in the regular match game, no matter what number of innings are played, shall be, in the meaning of this section of the rules, considered a member of the club he plays with."*

Significantly, playing center field in the same game for Washington on May 17 was George Hall, whose eligibility would also be called into question before the season was out.

Hall played for the Atlantic of Brooklyn Club in 1870 and was elected captain of the Atlantics in an 1871 spring meeting. The Judiciary Committee felt he was a member of the famed club, which had chosen to remain independent rather than join the fledgling National Association. Hall claimed he was not at the meeting where he was elected captain, but others in attendance testified that he was. Hall, realizing he was caught in a lie, then argued that the gathering was not a legal assembly.

Hall signed with Washington before playing any matches with the Atlantics and at the NA league meeting on November 3, 1871, all of Washington's matches were declared legal. The reasoning was that the rules of eligibility referred to playing for a club and not being elected to or holding an officer's position for a club (**SEE the NA rule above in italics**). Six years later, while playing for Louisville of the National League, Hall would be expelled from baseball for life along with three other players, the maiden permanent expulsion from the professional ranks for throwing games.

Wood, the umpire for the first Hastings forfeit game, was the playing captain of the Chicago club, which had the day off, and agreed to make the journey to nearby Rockford to officiate. Ironically, his team suffered heavily in the final standings as a result of the Athletics' undeserved forfeit win.

Sources

Charles Mears Base Ball Scrapbook, vol. II, 1871.
De Witt's Base Ball Guide for 1871.
Nemec, David. *Major League Baseball Profiles: 1871–1900* (Lincoln: University of Nebraska Press, 2011), 1: 243–244 and 2: 283–284.
New York Times, May 11, 1871.
Ryczek, William. *Blackguards and Red Stockings* (Wallingford, CT: Colebrook Press, 1999), 45–47.

May 23, 1871

Place: Fort Wayne
League: National Association of Professional Base Ball Players
Field: The Grand Duchess (on the grounds of Hamilton Field)
Teams: Fort Wayne versus Rockford
Umpire: Joe Simmons

Fort Wayne played this match under protest after learning that catcher Scott Hastings was in the Rockford line-up. Although the Indiana club lost, 17–13, it was officially declared the winner by forfeit at the league meeting on November 3, 1871. This was the second of the four forfeit losses Rockford suffered for using Hastings before the 60-day period had passed since his last appearance with his former team, the Lone Star club of New Orleans. Hastings's contributions to Rockford's victory on this day were mixed. He tallied three runs but allowed five of Cherokee Fisher's pitches to elude him and also made a throwing error.

Simmons in 1871 was the right fielder for the Chicago club. Like Jimmy Wood and many players in the NA era, he was occasionally called on to umpire in games in which his team was not involved and was expected to provide impartial and expert service and be well acquainted with the rules of the day. In most cases those expectations were met, at least to a tolerable degree.

Joe Simmons forfeited the first major league game he umpired. He later became a regular American Association umpire in 1882, the loop's inaugural season as a major league.

SOURCES

Charles Mears Base Ball Scrapbook, vol. II, 1871.
New York Times, May, 24, 1871.
Ryczek, William, *Blackguards and Red Stockings* (Wallingford, CT: Colebrook Press, 1999), 45–46.

June 5, 1871

Place: Philadelphia
League: National Association of Professional Base Ball Players
Field: Jefferson Street Grounds
Teams: Philadelphia versus Rockford
Umpire: Al Halbach

The Athletic club's demoralizing one-run loss to Rockford was later wiped out when the end-of-the-season league meeting brought a vote to overturn the 11–10 defeat and declare the Athletics the winner by forfeit. This was the third of the four forfeit losses Rockford suffered due to using catcher Scott Hastings before the 60-day period had elapsed since his last appearance with his former Lone Star club of New Orleans. As was true in each case that Rockford forfeited a game in which he stood accused of playing illegally, Hastings protested. None of his protests were ever subsequently honored.

One might wonder why Rockford persisted in using Hastings when each of its victories with him in the lineup before his 60-day waiting period elapsed was protested and ultimately forfeited. We can't provide a definitive answer except that Rockford had him under contract and was paying him whether or not he played. The team was not strong enough to win consistently without him and even with him in the lineup was never a serious contender. It would seem that Rockford had little to lose by playing him throughout his contentious 60-day waiting period and a fair amount to gain if his case that he was no more in violation of the "revolving" rule than, say, George Hall was won when the final verdict was returned.

SOURCES

Brooklyn Daily Eagle, June 6, 1871.
Charles Mears Base Ball Scrapbook, vol. II, 1871.

June 15, 1871

Place: Philadelphia
League: National Association of Professional Base Ball Players
Field: Jefferson Street Grounds
Teams: Philadelphia versus Rockford
Umpire: Theodore Bomeisler

The Athletics' second loss to visiting Rockford in a 10-day period was also erased at the end-of-the-season league meeting and was the fourth of the four forfeit losses handed to Rockford for using catcher Scott Hastings illegally, and arguably the most crucial. Rockford's 10–7 win came only one day before Hastings's 60-day waiting period expired and he became eligible to play for Rockford. Had it occurred on June 16, the 10–7 verdict would have stood and Boston, according to the rules of the time, would have tied Philadelphia for the NA's inaugural pennant, as both clubs would have finished the season with 20 wins.

Be aware that the current calculations of the final standings in 1871 differ in various reference works, depending in part on whether certain games are considered official or merely exhibition contests. Authorities as yet have not come to a meeting of the minds and may never do so, as there are numerous issues to be resolved before a consensus can be reached. One thing that is certain is that Scott Hastings had a hefty impact on the 1871 season; erasing the two losses to his team was essential in keeping the Athletics' pennant hopes alive. Chicago was 3–0 against Rockford, Boston was 3–0 and the Athletics were 1–2 before the forfeit situation was finally sorted out. Too, the Athletics were only 1–4 against Boston and 2–2 against Chicago, leading many historians to believe that Chicago and Boston were actually the NA's two best teams in 1871.

Less influential but of considerable interest to historians is the umpire who officiated the game that ultimately decided which club won the inaugural NA pennant. The son of a wealthy family, by the late 1860s Bomeisler had moved to the New York area from Philadelphia. Baseball was never his true calling. Census reports and city directories in that era list him as working in the liquor business, and early baseball records reflect that he was associated with the Eureka club of Newark. He continued to umpire in the professional NA in the early 1870s, but worked only one game in 1875 and never umpired in the NL after it was formed in 1876. In the late 1880s Bomeisler was living in East Orange, New Jersey, where he is buried, although he died in Philadelphia.

Sources

Charles Mears Base Ball Scrapbook, vol. II, 1871.
Nemec, David. *Major League Baseball Profiles: 1871–1900* (Lincoln: University of Nebraska Press, 2011), 2: 201.
New York Tribune, June 6, 1871.

June 19, 1871

Place: Troy
League: National Association of Professional Base Ball Players
Field: Rensselaer Park
Clubs: Troy versus Fort Wayne
Umpire: Isaac Leroy

According to nineteenth-century historian and author William Ryczek, the Fort Wayne team was acutely aware of the Troy club's penchant for a lively ball and cunningly supplied a ball of their own that "was of dubious quality and had no regulation markings on it bearing only the stamp "White Stockings." The *Charles Mears Base Ball Scrapbook* said it "was one of the most miserable specimens for a base ball that was ever thrown onto the field." By the 7th inning Fort Wayne led 6–3 and the ball was badly battered. During that frame it came apart at the seams. Troy captain and second baseman Bill Craver asked umpire Leroy to put a new ball into play and Leroy agreed one was in order. The rules at the time allowed for a ball to be replaced only at the end of an inning so that neither team would enjoy an advantage by obtaining an additional at-bat against a new ball. When the Kekionga Club could offer no alternative sphere, Craver produced a "Ryan's" dead white ball, which was a misnomer as the ball was actually of the lively sort that Troy favored. Fort Wayne captain and catcher Bill Lennon refused to accept it, claiming the ball his club had furnished was still serviceable. Craver then fished a handful of balls out Troy's ball bag and offered Lennon his choice of any of them, but Lennon rejected them all.

Troy's Lip Pike, the first batter due up in the 7th inning, remained standing at the plate while the debate fulminated around him. Leroy finally called for Fort Wayne to return to the field and commence pitching to Pike and, after waiting the necessary 15 minutes demanded by NA Rule 7, Section 3, declared the game forfeited to Troy when the Kekiongas still refused to comply. Reportedly, before taking his team off the field, Lennon appealed to the partisan Troy crowd to judge whether the ball was ripped or not in the hope they would want the game completed so they could get their full money's worth but received only jeers and hisses. Fort Wayne club officials subsequently took their case to the league's Judiciary Committee where the reception was no less unfriendly.

This was the first forfeited game not played to its completion in which no pitchers were charged with either a win or a loss because the guilty team was leading at the time action ceased.

It is vital to note here that major league baseball did not adopt an official ball maker until the 1873 season. Ball weights and sizes were specifically addressed in the playing rules beginning in 1854 and changed as the game progressed, but there was no rule on the "activity" of the baseball.

Stemming from the non-professional era, in the 1850s and 1860s, the visiting club was required to supply the ball for a contest prior to 1873. With this requirement came strategy. If the visiting club was playing a hard hitting team, they would have their ball maker reduce the core, which was supposed to be India rubber. This would result in a "dead" ball and allow the weaker hitting team more of a chance to compete. The opposite was done when the home club was a weak hitting team. More core and a livelier ball was then the visitors' choice.

John Ryan and Co., located at 121 Nassau Street, New York, received the first endorsement in professional baseball history at the March 3, 1873, National Association convention, held in the St. Clair Hotel in Baltimore, Maryland. Although his company was presented with this honor, as per the NA rules, no team was considered to be in violation of the rule of the championship code by using another ball as long as the non–Ryan match ball was of regulation dimensions.

SOURCES

Brooklyn Daily Eagle, June 21, 1871.
Charles Mears Base Ball Scrapbook, vol. II, 1871.
New York Times, June 20, 1871.
Ryczek, William. *Blackguards and Red Stockings* (Wallingford, CT: Colebrook Press, 1999), 44–45.
Troy Whig, June 21, 1871.

August 31, 1872

Place: Philadelphia
League: National Association of Professional Base Ball Players
Field: Jefferson Street Grounds
Clubs: Philadelphia Athletics versus Brooklyn Eckfords
Umpire: Tom Pratt

The Eckfords were a miserable team in 1872, finishing with a 3–26 record and came to Philadelphia with every expectation of being badly thrashed, but in the top of the 9th inning the score, to the Athletics' shock, was knotted at five all. After outfielder Ned Cuthbert led off by making an out, the Athletics' pitcher-manager Dick McBride doubled off George Zettlein. McBride then tagged up on Al Reach's fly ball to the Eckfords' rookie center field Candy Nelson and attempted to advance to third but met with a surprise when Nelson's throw beat him to the bag, where Frank Fleet stood in wait. Nelson's throw was slightly off line, however, forcing Fleet to catch the ball to the inside of the bag and then attempt a sweeping tag on McBride.

When umpire Pratt, a member at the time of the Philadelphia Olympic club but a former player and official with the Athletics, called McBride safe in the conviction that Fleet's hand had fallen short of touching McBride with the ball, the Eckfords stormed around him, led by right fielder Fahney Martin, serving as the Eckfords' captain that day in place of Jimmy Wood who had not accompanied the team to Philadelphia. When Martin was unable to convince Pratt to reverse his decision after he "and the rest of the team carried on the discussion for a full ten minutes," Martin "then coolly pulled his team off the field, packed the bats and left the park." Pratt, given no choice, awarded the game to his old team by forfeit.

Pratt's position at the time he made his contested call may not have afforded him the best view as to whether the ball in Fleet's hand made contact with McBride. Just so, his decision was inarguable once Martin had questioned it and been rebuffed. The 1871 DeWitt's Guide; Section VII, Section 5 said: *"No decision given by the Umpire shall be reversed, except for a palpable error in interpreting the rules, nor shall any decision be reversed upon the testimony of any player; and neither shall the Umpire be guided in his decision by any such testimony. The captains of each nine shall alone be allowed to appeal for a reversal of the decision of the Umpire."*

SOURCES

Charles Mears Base Ball Scrapbook, vol. II, 1872.
De Witt's Base Ball Guide for 1871.
New York Times, September 1, 1872.
Ryczek, William. *Blackguards and Red Stockings* (Wallingford, CT: Colebrook Press, 1999), 81–82.

September 28, 1874

Place: Philadelphia
League: National Association of Professional Base Ball Players
Field: Jefferson Street Grounds
Clubs: Philadelphia Athletics versus Chicago
Umpire: Billy McLean

In one of the most sloppily played games in the NA's history, the score was 7-all after eight completed innings and had already consumed over two hours. Chicago captain Jimmy Wood, whose playing career had ended abruptly a year earlier when he lost a leg after an accidental self-inflicted knife wound became infected, wanted the affair stopped at that point due to darkness. McLean, the leading umpire in his day, demurred. After Philadelphia tallied two runs in the top of the 9th, Chicago all but quit in disgust. Eventually Chicago pitcher George Zettlein tossed the ball to McLean and reputedly said, "No use playing anymore. We give up." The score by then had mounted to 15–7 in the Athletics' favor with only one out.

Of the 15 runs charged to Zettlein only two were earned. None of the seven runs Athletics hurler Dick McBride surrendered were earned as the two teams combined to make 21 miscues and numerous passed balls.

SOURCES

Nemec, David. *Major League Baseball Profiles: 1871–1900* (Lincoln: University of Nebraska Press, 2011), 1: 386–87 and 2: 213–14.
Orem, Preston. *Baseball 1845–1881: From the Newspaper Accounts* (Aldena, CA: privately published, 1961), 202.

May 29, 1875

Place: Washington
League: National Association of Professional Base Ball Players
Field: Olympic Grounds
Clubs: Washington versus New Haven
Umpire: Pliny Hough

New Haven had fallen behind 3–0 and was batting in the bottom of the first inning with one out when trouble first began as Washington pitcher Bill Stearns faced New Haven right fielder John McKelvey. Umpire Hough, a member of the Nationals club of Washington, called two balls on Stearns and then called the next three pitches balls but still did not issue McKelvey his base on called balls as expected. As per the rules in 1875, the third of three consecutive pitched balls that were "unfair," not over home base and not at the height called for by the batter, had to be called a ball.

New Haven center fielder Johnny Ryan ran to home base and alerted Hough, incorrectly, that the third pitch must be called a ball or a strike. The two began to quarrel as Hough was apparently not familiar on the calling of balls and strikes. Washington center fielder Holly Hollingshead was called to home base, where New Haven captain and first baseman Charlie Gould insisted that McKelvey should be given first base or else Gould would suspend play. The quartet came to a mutually acceptable conclusion and McKelvey was sent to first base.

According to the *National Republican*, "The balls were counted with care by players on either side during the entire game, and the same point raised a dozen times when it did not apply."

As the game experienced frequent stops and starts due to Hough's confusion regarding the calling of balls and strikes, the crowd became nearly as irritated as the players. After two innings and numerous errors, New Haven held a 6–3 edge. In the Washington half of the third inning, a fly ball to center fielder Jim Tipper was caught and he threw to second baseman Studs Bancker to double off Hollingshead. However, Hough called the runner safe and the grumbling began again and all the while the error totals for both clubs mounted.

A foul tip off of the bat of New Haven pitcher Henry Luff in the fifth inning found the eye of catcher Bill McCloskey and the game was halted for 30 minutes before New Haven would acquiesce that McCloskey was too disabled to continue. Washington second baseman Steve Brady went behind home base and substitute Lew Say came off the bench to play second.

After Washington scored four runs in the top of the seventh to tie the score at 9-all, left fielder Bill Parks replaced Stearns in the box, with Stearns taking Parks's place in left field. Parks immediately allowed New Haven to take the lead by one run.

In the top of the ninth, Washington scored two runs to take an 11–10 lead. After the first two batters for New Haven were retired in the bottom of the frame, Gould demanded that Hough rule Parks's delivery was illegal. Hough refused and Gould withdrew his club from the field. As Gould and Hough argued, the crowd spilled onto the field, engulfing the two debaters. At that point Hough forfeited the game to Washington.

Gould was excoriated in the papers for his actions. "The Umpire must be sustained or an end will soon come to all contests in the arena," admonished the *Brooklyn Daily Eagle*. According to the *National Republican*, Gould had made no protests of Parks's delivery in the two previous innings. Neither mentioned that Hough, a Baltimore native and a member of the National Club of Washington, was umpiring his first professional game. He was never asked to do another.

Parks was awarded the victory and his New Haven counterpart, Henry Luff, the loss because Washington was ahead when the forfeit occurred.

The pitching rules of 1875 required a hurler to release the baseball while within the six foot square pitchers box marked on the playing field and with the ball passing below the "line of the hip." The pitcher was allowed to bend his elbow, inward or outward and was not limited to how high the ball could be reached prior to releasing the ball, as long as it was released below the hip. A round arm swing, as in cricket, was prohibited. This evidently was what Gould was protesting about Parks's delivery.

SOURCES

Brooklyn Daily Eagle, May 31, 1875.
De Witt's Base Ball Umpire Guide. Edited by Henry Chadwick. 1875.
Hartford Courant, May 31, 1875.
National Republican, May 31, 1875.
Nemec, David. *Major League Baseball Profiles: 1871–1900* (Lincoln: University of Nebraska Press, 2011), 1: 309–10, 592.
Nemec, David. *The Rank and File of 19th Century Major League Baseball* (Jefferson, NC: McFarland, 2012), 113–114.
Orem, Preston. *Baseball 1845–1881: From the Newspaper Accounts* (Aldena, CA: privately published, 1961), 216.

August 3, 1876

Place: Louisville
League: National League (NL)

Field: Louisville Base Ball Park
Clubs: Louisville versus Chicago
Umpires: Charlie Hautz

Under threatening skies, Louisville, the home team, batted first and scored its lone run in the top of the first inning. Chicago countered with a run in the bottom of the frame off Louisville hurler Jim Devlin and then scored three runs in the 3rd inning to take a 4–1 lead that still held after Louisville had taken its at-bats in the top of the 5th inning. But unlike today, the game was still not official even though Louisville, the trailing team, had had five innings worth of at-bats. The rule at the time required Chicago to complete its fifth round of at-bats before the game was washed out in order to win.

With rain already beginning to fall, the bottom half of the 5th inning quickly became farcical as "the Louisvilles were bound not to have another game added to the Chicagos' long list of victories if they could help it." Louisville second baseman Ed Somerville opened matters by booting two consecutive easy ground balls, and soon Chicago batters were swinging wildly at every pitch regardless of how far from the strike zone Devlin threw it. Nonetheless "a thousand runs might have been scored before a man would have been put out." After an unknown number of runs actually were tallied, umpire Hautz, a marginal professional player who officiated at times when he was between teams, "became vexed at these proceedings and, seeing that there was no hopes of finishing the inning, decided the game in favor of the Chicagos by the score of 9–0." But the *Chicago Tribune* correctly predicted that Chicago would waive off the decision of the umpire and accede to the wishes of Louisville and play the game off on Monday, three days hence, "rather than have a litigation before the league about it." On Monday, August 7, which had been a scheduled off day, Chicago won 9–2 when the game was replayed in its entirety.

We are including this game for two reasons. The most significant one is that it met all the criteria for a forfeit to be declared by Hautz and therefore, if not for Chicago's unexplained beneficence in agreeing not to accept a forfeit, would have been the first forfeited game in National League history. At the time the game occurred Chicago had already made such a rout of the initial NL pennant race that it had all but clinched first place, and it may have been willing to play the game off instead simply because it meant an extra day's worth of gate receipts. The second reason is that by 1879 Chicago's on-field fortunes had taken a 180-degree turn, leading it to attempt to snare a game to which it had no right via forfeit. On August 13, 1879, some two hours before a scheduled Chicago match at Cincinnati a heavy rain fell, rendering the Cincinnati field "very soft and muddy." Afterward "a short interlude of bright weather came between 2 and 3 o'clock, and the clubs and 175 spectators went to the grounds." But the rain then began to fall again as the two teams were practicing, not ceasing until nearly 4 p.m. the scheduled game time. Cap Anson, then in his first of 19 consecutive seasons as Chicago's player-manager, insisted on playing; Cincinnati player-manager Cal McVey, a teammate of Anson's on the 1876 Chicagos, refused, claiming the field was unplayable. "No umpire having been agreed on, Anson appointed John A. Brown, an employee of the Chicago club, and sent his men to their positions. The ball was pitched a few times, and Brown announced the game won by Chicago, 9–0, to the amusement of the Cincinnati players." Anson then wanted McVey "to play at least one inning

Cap Anson played only a cameo role in the first successfully protested major league game in 1872 but would receive top billing in a multitude of protested and forfeited games in the years to come.

so that the ticket money might be held, but [McVey] refused to treat the spectators this shabbily, and the tickets were returned."

Preposterous as it might seem given all this background knowledge, the 1880 Spalding guide, under the auspices of Al Spalding, a former Chicago pitcher who was now a club official, claimed that it had been resolved at a meeting of the NL Board of Directors on December 3, 1879, chaired by Will Hulbert who was president of both the Chicago club and the National League, that Brown's forfeit declaration on August 13 would stand. Notwithstanding the guide's report, the non-game of August 13, 1879, has long since been disregarded by all reference works and rightly so. Anson, the visiting team's manager, had no authority to declare the field playable, nor did Brown, who was not accepted as an umpire by Cincinnati, have the authority to declare a forfeiture.

These two games, both involving Chicago, offer a study in contrast. The 1876 contest should by rights have been a forfeit win for Chicago but was not as per the choice of Chicago, the league's kingpin at the time both on and off the field in that it was by far the most talented team and had in addition as its club president Hulbert, who had founded the National League just a few months earlier. The 1879 affair was not even considered a game by the *Chicago Tribune*, which headlined its report on the episode: "Jangle Growing Out Of an Unplayed Game at Cincinnati," and yet the Chicagos, having descended by then to mediocrity on the field, were willing to go to any lengths to claim victory in it. Why? There is at least one good reason. If Chicago is ever credited with that ersatz forfeit win, it will finish in third place in the final 1879 National League standings with one victory more than Buffalo.

This episode was also the first public demonstration on a national scale of Anson's overbearing nature that would only grow increasingly intolerable over the years ahead.

The following year, with the addition of several key minor league acquisitions, namely infielder Tom Burns and pitchers Larry Corcoran and Fred Goldsmith, Chicago under Anson's leadership bagged its first of three consecutive NL pennants entirely on the legit.

SOURCE

Chicago Tribune, August 4, 1876, August 14, 1879.

August 21, 1876

Place: St. Louis
League: National League
Field: Grand Avenue Park
Clubs: St. Louis versus Chicago
Umpire: William Walker

With the score tied 6–6 in the bottom of the 9th, St. Louis second sacker Mike McGeary led off the Brown Stockings' final at-bat by hitting a pop fly that got him safely to first base when it fell between two Chicago infielders who were unable to decide which of them should take it. He then went all the way to third when Chicago's Cal McVey, on one of the rare days he was used as a hurler, sailed a pitch over catcher Deacon White's head. After Joe Battin was retired on a routine fly, the next batter, Ned Cuthbert, engaged in "much whispering and consultation among the nine" and then bunted down the third base line, enabling McGeary to score the go-ahead run. But Chicago's Cap

Anson, playing third base after several lineup switches during the game, heatedly contended that the ball not only hit McGeary but was then deliberately kicked away so that Anson could not make a play on it. Umpire Walker, a young Cincinnati man who was characterized by the *Chicago Tribune* the following day as having "about as much backbone as a clam," ruled that McGeary had made contact with the rolling ball accidentally, however, although the whispering made it seem the play had been planned for the ball to be bunted toward McGeary so that his foot could redirect it. When Chicago captain Al Spalding pulled his league-leading nine off the field in protest, Walker awarded the game to St. Louis.

Note that while the game would have ended according to today's rules when McGeary scored the seventh run that was not the case until 1880. Since the inception of the "New York" game in 1845 and until the end of the 1879 season, both teams were required to bat for a full nine innings, even if the winning run was scored in the bottom of the ninth before the third hand (out) was made.

SOURCES

Brooklyn Daily Eagle, August 22, 1876.
Charles Mears Base Ball Scrapbook, vol. II, 1876.
Chicago Tribune, August 22, 1876.
New York Times, August 22, 1876.

September 10, 1880

Place: Buffalo
League: National
Field: Riverside Grounds
Clubs: Buffalo versus Cincinnati
Umpire: Fred Skelley

In an error-filled game—there were a total of 33 by both sides—Cincinnati's workhorse pitcher, Will White, who in 1879 hurled an all-time record 680 innings despite being the first major leaguer to wear glasses on the playing field, held an 11–9 lead when Buffalo came to bat in its half of the 9th inning. According to the *New York Times*, Buffalo had loaded the bases with one out in the 9th when Cincinnati player-manager John Clapp, who was also the Reds' catcher, protested that it was too dark to play and first threatened to remove his club from the field. Cincinnati had already asked umpire Skelley to stop the game due to darkness prior to the start of the inning, a plea Clapp took up again in more earnest after his club went scoreless in its last at-bats and then pursued almost nonstop on every pitch once Buffalo came to bat.

After the Bisons pushed across two runs in the bottom of the 9th to tie the count at 11-all and had Joe Hornung on second and Jack Rowe on third with still only one out and shortstop Mike Moynahan at bat, Clapp, who had just let a pitch from White go by "to demonstrate that he could not see to catch," had White challenge Skelley to try to catch one of his pitches in the dimming light. "The umpire was not about to be stumped by any four-eyed youth and throwing off his coat he braced himself for the effort. [White] took his position and gathering himself up he called on every ounce of muscle and hurled the sphere with all the strength he could command. The umpire checked it and was satisfied the game should go on." Clapp by that point was willing to accept a tie, but Buffalo, smelling victory, declined the offer. When Clapp made good on his threat to take his team off the field, Skelley, an amateur umpire from the Buffalo area, forfeited the game to his hometown team.

Even though the forfeit was later overruled by NL president Will Hulbert and the game declared an 11–11 tie, we are including it because all the statistics were counted including those compiled in Buffalo's partial half of the ninth inning. We also believe that Hulbert would not have overruled this forfeit if Skelley had been an umpire whose work he knew and trusted, for Skelley's ruling that there was sufficient light to continue has traditionally been the type of judgment call that league officials routinely support in the absence of incontrovertible evidence to the contrary. Furthermore, Skelley appears to have more than adequately proved his point if the report from the *Buffalo Commercial Advertiser* that he smothered one of White's fastest pitches is not exaggerated. Yet we are also aware that if indeed Skelley did rise to White's challenge in the manner the *Advertiser* described, in Hulbert's eyes he might have been viewed as one who could be baited into making something of a mockery of the game and thus not fit to umpire at the major league level.

SOURCES

Buffalo Commercial Advertiser, September 11, 1880.
Charles Mears Base Ball Scrapbook, vol. III, 1880–1883.
New York Clipper, September 16, 1880.
New York Times, September 11, 1880.

July 4, 1883

Place: Philadelphia
League: National League

Field: Recreation Park
Clubs: Philadelphia versus Providence
Umpire: Frank Lane

Scheduled to play a morning and afternoon Decoration Day double-header in two different cities—New York and Philadelphia—as was a holiday custom at that time when the cities lay within close proximity to one another, Providence, which had been staying in New York, left the Gotham by train at 8 a.m., seemingly with time to spare for its 10 a.m. morning game in Philadelphia. A delay in Trenton, where the Grays had to catch an "accommodation" train, got them to Philadelphia an hour late, however, and they had to depart at 1 p.m. after only seven innings had been played to catch a return train to New York for their afternoon game with the newly formed New York NL club, which had topped Boston 10–7 in their morning match behind Tip O'Neill.

Given no option, umpire Lane, a stage actor and wannabe dramatist by profession, forfeited the game to Philadelphia even though the Grays led 11–9 at the time of their forced departure. Further train delays caused the Grays to arrive at New York's Polo Grounds barely in time for their scheduled 4:30 p.m. start. Frazzled, given no time to warm up, they then lost 1–0 to New York's Mickey Welch in a contest played in "excessive heat" with an estimated crowd of over 7,500 in attendance. The forfeit in Philadelphia, given that Providence was ahead when it occurred and the Philadelphia club was a dreary tail ender unlikely to catch up, probably deprived the Grays' Charlie Sweeney of a win and in all likelihood spared Philadelphia's John Coleman from adding yet another blotch to his all-time season-record total of 48 losses.

SOURCES

Charles Mears Base Ball Scrapbook, vol. III, 1880–1883.
Nemec, David. *Major League Baseball Profiles: 1871–1900* (Lincoln: University of Nebraska Press, 2011), 2: 211.
New York Times, July 5, 1883.
Sporting Life, July 8, 1883.

August 1, 1883

Place: Cleveland
League: National League
Field: Kennard Street Park
Clubs: Cleveland versus Boston
Umpire: Foghorn Bradley

Boston was up 10–3 after five innings when Cleveland manager Frank Bancroft attempted to replace his beleaguered veteran pitcher Hugh "One

Arm" Daily with rookie Will Sawyer. Boston objected to the substitution, its right at the time since only an injured player could be replaced without the opposing team's approval if in the umpire's judgment the injury was serious enough to merit removal from the game, while Bancroft pleaded that Sawyer, a local Cleveland boy, had been scheduled to pitch all along but was simply late getting from his home to the park. Umpire Bradley dithered over which side had the better case, until Cleveland walked off the field in protest. The matter was referred to league secretary Nick Young, later the senior loop's president, who gave the game to Boston, the ultimate pennant winner, via forfeit.

Cleveland was in hot contention at the time this forfeit occurred and Sawyer was not only its best pitcher that season apart from injury-plagued Jim McCormick but the National League leader in fewest hits per nine innings (7.6). Sawyer's presence at the start of the game might have had some bearing on the way the NL pennant race played out especially since Charlie Buffinton, Boston's starter that day had hurled a complete game the previous afternoon and was likely to tire as the contest progressed.

Bradley, a former National League pitcher, should never have hesitated in rendering the forfeit. The 1883 NL rules were extremely clear on the subject of substitutions. Rule 47 stated: "A Substitute shall not be allowed to take the place of any player in the game, unless such player be disabled in the game then being played, by reason of illness or injury."

Sources

Nemec, David. *Major League Baseball Profiles: 1871–1900* (Lincoln: University of Nebraska Press, 2011), 1: 17 and 2: 445–446.
New York Daily Tribune, August 2, 1883.
New York Times, August 2, 1883.
Spalding's Official Base Ball Guide, 1883.

May 31, 1884

Place: Washington
League: American Association (AA)
Field: Athletic Park
Clubs: Washington versus Cincinnati
Umpire: Terry Connell

Washington had two men on base with a count of six balls and two strikes to the batter, center fielder Ed Trumbull, in the fourth inning when Cincinnati hurler pitcher Will White threw an inshoot. Trumbull leaped backward to avoid being hit, but umpire Connell nonetheless called him out on strikes. In the fifth inning Cincinnati had White and outfielder Tom Mansell on base with two out. Left fielder Charley Jones then hit a routine ground ball to third baseman Buck Gladmon and was apparently thrown out at first base. As the Washington club started off the field, Connell belatedly called Jones safe, and White and Mansell both scored. In the following frame, "after the home team had been retired without a run and [Charlie] Snyder had been put out, [Jimmy] Woulfe was on second base when [Chick] Fulmer hit a fair ball in the direction of third [and would have been an easy out], but Mr. Connell decided it foul."

At that juncture the crowd, having had its fill of Connell, erupted and Washington owner Lloyd Moxley stepped down from his box seat behind the Washington bench and instructed manager Holly Hollingshead to pull his team from the field, giving Cincinnati, who was leading at the time 6–0, the victory. Connell, who had been having trouble all season when he umpired in Washington, had to be escorted from the field by two policemen. Prior to the season he had been hired as a regular AA umpire, but he was gone from its ranks by midsummer. From time to time, however, he continued to umpire games on a substitute basis in both the AA and the NL until 1890.

Note that the count on Trumbull was full at the time he struck out, as in the AA in 1884 a batter received seven "called balls" before being given his base on balls. Since this game had gone the requisite number of innings to be an official contest, all the statistics have been tabulated, most importantly White's win, although he did not receive credit for a shutout even though he was leading 6–0 when play was stopped.

Connell is credited with having caught a major league game for Chicago in 1874, but we are skeptical that the game belongs to him. He was a patronage Mint worker until the Republicans took office in 1881 and then became a police sergeant while continuing to umpire as a sideline.

SOURCES

Nemec, David. *Major League Baseball Profiles: 1871–1900* (Lincoln: University of Nebraska Press, 2011), 2: 203.
New York Times, June 1, 1884.
Washington Post, June 1, 1884.

July 5, 1884

Place: Baltimore
League: Union Association (UA)
Field: Belair Lot

Clubs: Baltimore versus Cincinnati
Umpire: Dave Sullivan

When Sullivan had not arrived at Belair Lot by the scheduled game time, the two teams started an exhibition affair with Cincinnati's Dick Burns, who had pitched the previous day at Washington, serving as the umpire. After Baltimore jumped off to a 2–0 lead in the first inning, Sullivan appeared and declared that the game was official and would continue as is. Cincinnati refused to play a regulation game claiming that Sullivan's jurisdiction ceased once the exhibition game began. Sullivan then proclaimed that the regular game was forfeited in favor of Baltimore, to which Cincinnati player-manager Dan O'Leary immediately declared it was his club's intention to protest. The two teams then continued the game as an exhibition contest, Baltimore winning 13–3. The forfeit to Baltimore was upheld by UA president Denny McKnight, although Cincinnati had a strong case for it to be rescinded and further research as to why this protest was not honored would be worth pursuing. It would also be of interest to know the crowd's reaction to being jerked around after having paid to watch a regulation game, then learning to their disappointment that it would be an exhibition contest and finally discovering that their day would culminate with them having witnessed both a forfeited regulation game and a one-sided exhibition affair. Refunds would seem to have been in order for those fans that requested them.

This game was but the first of several disputed contests that swirled around the work of Sullivan, who umpired to the cacophony of his own music.

SOURCES

Sporting Life, July 16, 1884.
Washington Post, July 6, 1884.

August 11, 1884

Place: Chicago
League: National
Field: Lake Front Park
Clubs: Chicago versus Buffalo
Umpire: Stewart Decker

In the opening frame with Chicago center fielder George Gore on first, Mike "King" Kelly hit a grounder to Buffalo second baseman Hardy Richardson. Richardson stepped on second for the force, but Gore kept running and flung his arms around Richardson to prevent him from throwing the ball to first baseman Dan Brouthers for a double play. Umpire Decker properly called both the runner Gore and the batter Kelly out. Chicago player-manager Cap Anson argued that Kelly should not be out because it couldn't be certain a throw would have gotten him and also because Kelly, according to the rules, could not be declared out if he himself had been guilty of no infraction. When Anson refused to continue play, Decker then declared the game forfeited to Buffalo. After a lengthy debate "while the spectators ... got into a riotous frame of mind over being cheated out of a game they had paid to see," Buffalo captain and left fielder Jim O'Rourke, agreed to play a postponed game of June 2 so the crowd would not have to be refunded its money but only on the condition that Chicago paid Buffalo $200 to play an exhibition game that Thursday, three days hence and a scheduled off day for both clubs.

When that game ended in a 6-all tie, O'Rourke reportedly was denied his "pound of flesh" because the two teams were then compelled to play an official makeup game on Thursday, which Chicago won 17–10.

Anson was not unwarranted in disputing Decker's interpretation of Gore's actions. The 1884 NL rules only partially addressed the Gore-Richardson incident and still awaited refinement.

Rule 69. For the special benefit of the patrons of the game, and because the offenses specified are under his immediate jurisdiction, and not subject to appeal by players, the attention of the Umpire is particularly directed to possible violations of the purpose and spirit of the Rules, for the following character:

Section 4. "...if he hold a Fielder's arms so as to disable him from catching the ball, or if he knock the Fielder down with his fist for the same purpose."

While Gore's actions were not specifically detailed in the playing rules, corralling Richardson could be interpreted as interference and therefore within an umpire's province to rule the play as he felt appropriate. Decker was ahead of his time.

SOURCES

Chicago Tribune, August 12, 1884.
Spalding's Official Base Ball Guide, 1884.

August 22, 1884

Place: Kansas City
League: Union Association
Field: Athletic Park
Clubs: Kansas City versus St. Louis
Umpire: George Seward

Seward was a notorious drunk and a frequent source of both merriment and disdain when he worked a Union Association game while under the influence. During the game of August 22, Kansas City fans put him under constant siege. The catalytic event came in the 9th inning when Kansas City right fielder Taylor Shaffer seemingly threw out St. Louis's Jack Brennan at home on light-hitting Milt Whitehead's single to right. From the fans' viewpoint their catcher Kid Baldwin had the plate cleanly blocked and the ball in his hand when he tagged Brennan, but Seward gave the safe signal, cutting Kansas City's lead to 6 to 3. Kansas City president Americus McKim and the team's player-manager Ted Sullivan requested that the game continue with another umpire, but Seward refused to step aside and declared a forfeit in favor of St. Louis when Sullivan would not continue play unless he did.

There was speculation that Seward felt his job by then hung by a thread and could only be salvaged if he sucked up to St. Louis owner and UA founder, Henry Lucas. The game was hardly crucial, as St. Louis had the pennant firmly in hand by then. From outward appearances the St. Louis players were embarrassed to accept the victory, especially since they had beaten Kansas City the previous day only because "a doubtful decision by Umpire Seward in the tenth inning allowed St. Louis to score the two winning runs." If the game of August 22 had been played to its conclusion St. Louis's Perry Werden stood to be saddled with the defeat, dropping his record from a dazzling 12–1 to still admirable 12–2 in what was to be his final start of the year. Since the season still had some six weeks to run and he made no more appearances in the box, our surmise is that he probably injured his arm that day.

Note that many current reference works contend that Seward umpired his final ML game on August 8, 1884. They are incorrect in our view because the game of August 22 lasted into the 9th inning and was thus an official contest whose statistics counted.

SOURCES

Nemec, David. *The Rank and File of 19th Century Major League Baseball* (Jefferson, NC: McFarland, 2012), 284–285.
New York Times, August 23, 1884.
Sporting Life, August 27, 1884.

August 23, 1884

Place: Boston
League: National League
Field: South End Grounds

Clubs: Boston versus Detroit
Umpire: John Gaffney

Trailing 7–5, Detroit loaded the bases with one out in the 6th inning. Boston's Jim Whitney fanned Wolverines center fielder Ned Hanlon, but his catcher, Mike Hines, dropped the ball. After picking it up and stepping on home plate to force the runner on third base, Hines then chased Hanlon down the first base line before throwing to first baseman John Morrill to complete the double play and end the inning. Detroit's interim captain, shortstop Frank Cox (a relative of SABR's foremost authority on home runs, David Vincent), complained to umpire Gaffney that Hines had intentionally dropped the ball in order to execute an easy double play, which could well have been true but was then *de rigueur* for a catcher in Hines's situation. While the rest of the Detroit players took the field, Cox remained on the sidelines. Gaffney gave Cox five minutes to take his position and continue the game. When, at the end of that time Cox still refused to play, Gaffney forfeited the game to Boston. There is detailed coverage of this game in the *Boston Globe,* which chastised Cox for his protest and was incensed that his stubbornness had resulted in the first ML game ever forfeited on South End Grounds, then in its 14th season as a major league facility. After his ML finale on September 29, also at Boston, the *Boston Globe* jeeringly reported: "Cox, the fat shortstop, is knocked out by lameness." A week later the same paper noted that he was the only Detroit player not reserved for 1885 because he had been "no addition to the nine."

Current rules would prevent the play Cox contested, as the batter is automatically out when first base is occupied on a dropped third strike with less than two out; however, not until the 1887 season was the present rule instituted. The NL rules for 1884 were extremely specific on the incident that occurred and the following was presented in the annual Spalding Base Ball Guide, in an explanatory section on the playing rules: *"One of the advantageous amendments made by the League was that repealing the rule which decided the base-runner out for not running to first base. By this rule, if three men were on the bases when the third strike was called, all the base runner had to do was throw down his bat and stand still, that act alone putting him out, and at the same time preventing the runners on the bases from being forced off by the act of the base runner to first base. The amendment establishes the old rule which obliges the base runner to start for first base, and he cannot no be out on three strikes—if not caught out—unless touched by the catcher, fielder, or thrown out at first base. This amendment enables the catcher to affect a double or triple play, by not catching the ball on the third strike, but simply touching home base, and then throwing to third base, leaving the ball to be passed to second from third, or to first base to throw out the base runner from home. Last season this play was stopped by the batsman refusing to run."*

It is specifically written in Rule 57, Section 11.

The *Macmillan Encyclopedia* credited no pitchers with a decision in this game, but other reference works rightfully credit Whitney with a win and Detroit's Frank Meinke with the loss.

Sources

Boston Globe, August 24, 1884.
Nemec, David. *The Rank and File of 19th Century Major League Baseball* (Jefferson, NC: McFarland, 2012), 196.
New York Times, August 24, 1884.
Spalding's Official Base Ball Guide, 1884.

August 25, 1884

Place: Boston
League: Union Association
Field: Dartmouth Grounds
Clubs: Boston versus Wilmington
Umpire: Dave Sullivan

Boston had already been declared the winner by forfeit when Wilmington finally arrived at Dartmouth Grounds forty minutes late for a 3:30 p.m. outing owing to an unforeseen train delay, a violation Rule 40, section 1 of the UA playing rules. A game between Boston and a picked nine was about to begin after fans were informed they could get their money back since it would be pickup game not scheduled in advance as an exhibition. Reportedly the majority did so, and the rest lingered to see a contest played on the assumption that the league would accept it as an official contest, which it subsequently did. When Dupee Shaw blanked The Only Nolan 6–0 in a game Sullivan abbreviated due to encroaching darkness, Boston earned a doubleheader sweep on the day despite playing only six innings.

Sources

Boston Globe, August 26, 1884.
New York Times, August 26, 1884.
Wright and Ditson's Base Ball Guide, 1884.

August 30, 1884

Place: Toledo
League: American Association

Field: League Park
Clubs: Toledo versus St. Louis
Umpire: Billy Quinn

In the second game of a doubleheader (Toledo won the morning affair, 5–1), with Toledo ahead 2–1 in the top half of the 8th, umpire Quinn called St. Louis shortstop Bill Gleason out on a foul tip that was caught by Toledo's catcher, Moses Walker. Gleason insisted his bat had not touched the ball and was joined in his argument by St. Louis player-manager Charlie Comiskey. When Quinn stuck to his decision, Comiskey took his team off the field. The doubleheader loss to the second division Blue Stockings severely impaired the Browns' chances for the Association flag. The Browns had begun the day with a 50–29 record and a .633 winning percentage but finished the season below .600, far behind the first-place New York Mets.

In 1884 a foul tip caught by the catcher was an out regardless of the count at the time. That rule did not change until after the 1888 season.

SOURCES

New York Times, August 31, 1884.
Spalding's Official Base Ball Guide, 1889.
Sporting Life, September 10, 1884.

September 8, 1884

Place: Washington
League: Union Association
Field: Capitol Grounds
Clubs: Washington versus Pittsburgh
Umpire: Dan Stearns

When Pittsburgh failed to appear for unknown reasons, the game was awarded to Washington. There was no mention of the game in the *Washington Post* the following day, but note was made of it in that week's *Sporting Life*. Pittsburgh's last previous game had been in Boston four days earlier. There is no known excuse to this day for its nonappearance in Washington on time, as the club was on hand in full force for a game in DC the following afternoon. We are presuming that Stearns, an active player, presided over this forfeit since he had officiated the previous game in Washington.

SOURCE

Sporting Life, September 9, 1884.

September 20, 1884

Place: Washington
League: Union Association
Field: Capitol Grounds
Clubs: Washington versus Cincinnati
Umpire: Alamazoo Jennings

Cincinnati lingered in Boston an extra day to play an exhibition game on September 19 that was arranged at the last minute after its men thought their 13–7 win on September 18 concluded their stay in Beantown and then failed to make train connections to Washington in time for its scheduled match the following afternoon. After the forfeit was declared by Jennings, Washington manager Mike Scanlon scared up members of the recently disbanded Pittsburgh UA team he saw in the stands along with a couple of Baltimore players who were in attendance on their day off, including their captain Charlie Levis, and then staged an exhibition game, which Washington won, 7–4.

This game is no longer counted by most reference works, which makes for something of a puzzle and is why we're including it to encourage further study since it was counted at the time and for many years thereafter.

SOURCE

Washington Post, September 21, 1884.

September 24, 1884

Place: Pittsburgh
League: American Association
Field: Recreation Park
Clubs: Pittsburgh versus Baltimore
Umpire: Billy Barnie and Bill Traffley

When the assigned umpire, Billy Quinn, failed to show for the game, Pittsburgh manager Horace Phillips reluctantly agreed to let his counterpart, Baltimore manager Billy Barnie, officiate and soon regretted it. From the outset of the game Barnie made numerous calls that Pittsburgh complained strongly favored his own team. By the third inning the crowd was so rankled that Barnie ceded his umpiring duties to Baltimore catcher Bill Traffley, whom neither the Pittsburgh club nor its fans felt was an improvement. In the eighth inning, with Baltimore on top, 8–6, one of Traffley's calls so enraged the crowd that they poured over the railings "and but for the timely interference of the police" would have assaulted him. Fearful himself of the howling mob, Phillips had already resigned himself to a forfeit defeat as he watched the police hustle the entire Baltimore team to safety.

As late as 1884 it was still not unusual for the visiting team's manager or one of its players to be chosen to officiate in the absence of the scheduled umpire. Train schedules were erratic, accidents on lines were frequent, and in lieu of an absentee umpire, which was by no means an uncommon occurrence, choosing a participant in that day's game, if only in a bench role, was almost always preferable to picking someone out of the stands who professed to have umpiring experience but often as not had none in the presence of a highly partisan crowd.

Since Baltimore was leading when the game was stopped, its ace, Hardie Henderson, banked a win while "Stooping" Jack Gorman, an early-day submarine-ball hurler

Billy Barnie, who in 1884 became the only manager to umpire a major league game involving his own team (Baltimore of the American Association) that his club won via forfeit.

whose unique nickname was bestowed on him because his knuckles nearly scraped the ground on his delivery, took the loss.

SOURCES

Nemec, David. *The Rank and File of 19th Century Major League Baseball* (Jefferson, NC: McFarland, 2012), 180.
New York Times, September 25, 1884.
Sporting Life, October 1, 1884.
Washington Post, September 25, 1884.

September 24, 1884

Place: Toledo
League: American Association
Field: League Park
Clubs: Toledo versus Virginia
Umpire: "Honest" John Kelly

Rather than replay a 1–1 10-inning tie that occurred the previous day, the team from Richmond set out for home knowing in advance that Kelly would forfeit the game to Toledo. The Virginia club was already on the skids at the time and its manager, Felix Moses, no doubt foresaw that its share of the gate receipts for a replayed game against a team nearly as weak as itself would not defray the cost of putting its nine up in a Toledo hotel an extra night. There was otherwise no reason for it to hurry out of town. The team had three off days before its next scheduled game at home against St. Louis on September 27.

SOURCES

Sporting Life, October 1, 1884.
Washington Post, September 25, 1884.

October 11, 1884

Place: Cincinnati
League: Union Association
Field: Bank Street Grounds
Clubs: Cincinnati versus Boston
Umpire: Alamazoo Jennings

A rare forfeit in which the *home* team failed to appear was declared per-force by Jennings after Cincinnati traveled all the way to Memphis to play an exhibition game on October 10, an off day, after its 10–6 victory over the Bostons on October 9 and then found itself unable to return in time for its official contest with Boston on the 11th owing to train mishaps. There was no mention of this game in most newspapers, including *Sporting Life* and the *Boston Globe*. Cincinnati won the final two games of the series with Boston on October 12 and 13 by scores of 11–5 and 15–11, respectively.

The forfeit turned out to be Cincinnati's final loss of the season and inter-rupted what would otherwise have been a 14-game winning streak. Even though Cincinnati finished well behind the St. Louis Maroons in the final UA standings, after the Outlaw Reds pilfered shortstop Jack Glasscock, pitcher

Jim McCormick and catcher Fatty Briody from the Cleveland NL club in early August the two teams were close to equal in strength.

In 1884 Jennings was involved in two forfeits in a three-week period that were made necessary when one team failed to appear for a game. Six years earlier he had played in his lone major league game as a catcher with Milwaukee of the NL against Cincinnati and allowed a staggering total of 10 passed balls in a 13–2 loss.

SOURCES

Cincinnati Enquirer, October 12, 1884.
Nemec, David. *Major League Baseball Profiles: 1871–1900* (Lincoln: University of Nebraska Press, 2011), 2: 421–22.
Sporting Life, October 22, 1884.

October 11, 1884

Place: St. Louis
League: Union Association
Field: Palace Park
Clubs: St. Louis versus Washington
Umpire: Dan Devinney

With his club ahead 2–0 in the fourth inning, St. Louis pitcher Henry Boyle hit a foul ball out of the park. Washington captain Phil Baker called for a new ball, but the old ball was returned before the time limit expired for it to be ruled lost. When Washington refused to continue with the original ball, complaining that it was no longer in playable condition, Devinney, a former NL umpire with strong St. Louis connections who had been informally banned from that circuit for his actions during the scandal-ridden 1877 season, gave the game to St. Louis, which hardly needed it. In all likelihood, both the Maroons and their fans were resentful if anything that the game was stopped with their team ahead before it became official, meaning none of the statistics would count and the crowd would have to line up to have its ticket money refunded.

It is unclear whether the condition of the ball justified Washington's refusal. UA rules pertaining to the baseball during play stated: Rule 11, Section 4: Should the ball become out of shape, or cut or ripped, so as to expose the yarn, or in any way so injured as to be unfit for fair use in the opinion of the umpire, on being appealed to by either captain, a new ball shall be called for at once by the umpire. Rule 11, Section 5: Should the ball be lost during the game, the umpire shall, at the expiration of five minutes, call for a new ball.

SOURCE

Wright and Ditson's Base Ball Guide, 1884.

August 5, 1885

Place: Baltimore
League: American Association
Field: Oriole Park I
Clubs: Baltimore versus Philadelphia
Umpire: John Connolly

Needing three runs to tie in the bottom of the 9th, the Athletics tallied two of them on a single by outfielder Lon Knight that scored teammates Blondie Purcell and Ted Larkin, making the score 8–7. Just moments earlier Larkin, a right-handed hitter with good power, had driven a ball far over the left field fence but was given only a double when Connolly decided, after considerable debate that included both players and spectators, that it had cleared the short portion of the fence which earned only two bases as per the park ground rule. With Knight now on first with the tying run, A's third baseman Fred Corey sent a grounder to Orioles shortstop Jimmy Macullar, one of the last lefties to serve as a regular shortstop in the majors. Connolly ruled Knight forced out at second on a close play, bringing Larkin and other A's off the bench to protest. After his verbal efforts to get Larkin to stay off the field and remain on the bench failed, Connolly finally resorted to putting his hands on Larkin's chest in a calming manner and pushing him back. At that point captain Harry Stovey "called his men together and left the field." It seems in retrospect to have been a particularly foolish forfeit since the A's had the tying run at first and the winning run at the plate in the person of Sadie Houck.

Connolly was roasted by *Sporting Life* for the remainder of the 1885 season every time he umpired in Philadelphia. He officiated periodically throughout the 1880s in both the AA and the NL and is now believed by us to be the as yet unidentified outfielder, known as Red Connally in current reference works, who played two games for the St. Louis NL team in 1886. We think Connolly, who was in the St. Louis area at the time, donned a St. Louis uniform while between AA umpiring assignments, an action that would have been permissible in 1885 since he was a free agent and umpiring contracts did not forbid men in blue from playing in other leagues on their days off.

SOURCES

Nemec, David. *Major League Baseball Profiles: 1871–1900* (Lincoln: University of Nebraska Press, 2011), 2: 203.

New York Times, August 6, 1885.
Sporting Life, September 30, 1885.

October 15, 1885

Place: St. Louis
Leagues: World's Series between the National League and the American Association pennant winners
Field: Sportsman's Park I
Clubs: Chicago (NL) versus St. Louis (AA)
Umpire: Dave Sullivan

Although the first World's Series bringing together the pennant winners from the American Association and the National League had proved to be something of a fiasco the previous year when NL Providence dismantled the AA flag winning New York Mets in three straight games, a second such Series was scheduled in 1885. The postseason match this season was expanded to seven games, it was agreed to split the gate receipts 50/50 and each team put up $500, with the additional $1,000 kitty to go to the winner. The battle commenced on October 14 with a 5–5 tie that was preceded by throwing and base running contests among members of both contesting teams, the AA champion Browns and the NL champion Chicago White Stockings.

In St. Louis the following afternoon, Browns player-manager Charlie Comiskey pulled his club off the field when umpire Sullivan called a roller Chicago third baseman Ned Williamson tapped down the first-base line fair after it had started out foul, then hit either a pebble or a tuft of grass out-side the line and ricocheted back into fair territory subsequent to Sullivan's initial ruling that the ball was foul. (Since the start of the 1877 season, any batted ball that did not pass either first or third base while in fair territory was ruled foul.) After Williamson had beat Comiskey's belated throw to second baseman Sam Barkley covering first, Sullivan at first agreed with Comiskey that he had to stand by his original call of foul and ordered Williamson to return to the plate. "Then [Chicago player-manager Cap] Anson and [Mike "King"] Kelly came to the front and in a few minutes convinced the umpire that the ball was fair." By that time quite a large number of the crowd of some 3,000 had begun to gather on the field to join in the dispute and the game might not have been able to proceed even if Comiskey had kept his men on the field and let the action continue. As it was, Sullivan soon began to deny that he had ever called Williamson's ball foul, claiming Anson was the one who had shouted foul from the Chicago bench, and several hours later, safely ensconced by then in his hotel room, he forfeited the game to Chicago since St. Louis, trailing 5–4 at the time it left the field, had refused to continue.

Debate resounded for weeks afterward in *Sporting Life* and the sports pages of many other papers over whether Sullivan's forfeit ruling should stand. It was eventually mutually agreed upon by both teams that the contest should be called a draw, but that changed after the two clubs split the next four games and St. Louis won the seventh and seeming deciding game and claimed the "world championship" three games to two. Stunned by that turn of events because his club had been heavily favored prior to the Series, Chicago majority owner and president Al Spalding declared, that contrary to his manager Cap Anson's concession that the forfeited game should be considered a draw, he still viewed the forfeit as valid and considered the Series therefore a draw at three games apiece. In late November 1885, *Sporting Life* roused fury throughout the upstart American Association which was desperately seeking to establish that in just its fourth season of existence it was already the equal if not the superior of the National League when it declared the Series a tie at 3-all, with St. Louis the loser of the disputed forfeit game, and said all bets were therefore off "while the championship of the United States for 1885 remains in abeyance."

Notwithstanding *Sporting Life's* verdict that Game 2 of the 1885 World's Series was forfeited by St. Louis, authorities are still at odds over its status. For those in the forfeit camp, it remains the only one of its kind in postseason play.

Sources

Chicago Tribune, October 16, 1885.
Nemec, David, *The Beer and Whisky League* (New York: Lyons & Burford, 1994), 103–104.
Sporting Life, November 4, 1885, November 11, 1885, and November 18, 1885.

July 30, 1886

Place: Washington
League: National League
Field: Swampoodle Grounds (aka Capital Park)
Clubs: Washington versus Detroit
Umpire: Joe Ellick

Washington led 9–6 in the top of the seventh inning but throughout the game had been roiled by several calls made by umpire Ellick in favor of Detroit. The trouble peaked in the fifth inning when Detroit claimed its pitcher Charlie Getzien was too ill to continue. Washington refused to allow a substitute and summoned a doctor to examine Getzien. The doctor declared there was nothing wrong Getzien "except fright," apparently unsettling Ellick further and forcing Detroit to bring Hardy Richardson in from left field to trade positions with Getzien. After a purportedly rank umpiring decision at first base in the seventh inning, followed by Ellick refusing to call any of Nationals tosser George Keefe's pitches strikes, Washington began delaying the game, hoping Ellick would end the affair because of darkness. The exasperated Nationals finally made no attempt to put the Detroit team out, allowing the Wolverines to tally seven runs to make the count, 13–9. To thwart the Nationals, Ellick then started calling the Detroit batters out on every play, the last coming at the plate where Washington catcher Jackie Hayes caught left fielder Cliff Carroll's throw several feet in front of home plate and made no attempt to tag the runner coming home from third. When Nationals manager Mike Scanlon refused to send his club to bat in the bottom of the frame, the game was forfeited to Detroit.

To escape the hostile crowd, Ellick had to be whisked to safety by police. The opinion in Washington was the "secret of the matter" was that Ellick owed his appointment as umpire to the Detroit club, which may have been true, at least to some degree, as umpiring appointments in that era were often the result of having a particular team in a prospect's camp to act as a kind of godfather. Ellick resigned his NL umpiring post late the following month and never worked another game in the senior loop after the 1886 season. A former ML player, he nonetheless remained in the game as a minor league umpire and manager for a number of years thereafter.

Not until recent years was Richardson rightfully credited with a relief win in this game.

SOURCES

Brooklyn Daily Eagle, July 31, 1886.
Nemec, David. *Major League Baseball Profiles: 1871–1900* (Lincoln: University of Nebraska Press, 2011), 1: 168–169, 535.
Sporting Life, August 28, 1886.
Washington Post, July 31, 1886.

September 29, 1886

Place: Washington
League: National League
Field: Swampoodle Grounds
Clubs: Washington versus St. Louis
Umpire: Gracie Pierce

St. Louis, which had found fault with umpire Pierce's decisions ever since the second inning, contended prior to the start of the seventh inning in a 2–

2 game that it was too dark to continue play, but Pierce turned a deaf ear. With two out in the top of the seventh, he then proceeded to call St. Louis pitcher Jack Kirby out on strikes. Kirby did not question the call but argued in vain, along with the entire St. Louis nine which encircled Pierce, that he had been rung up on only two strikes. The Maroons also appealed to the official scorer who claimed the umpire was the sole judge of play. The majority of the Maroons refused to take the field including their captain, Jack Glasscock, and after waiting five minutes after calling for "play," Pierce then forfeited the game to Washington. Since the score was tied at the time, no pitching decisions were awarded; but as is the case now in all forfeited games that last five or more innings, all other statistics have been counted.

Pierce was hired by the NL in August 1886 as a replacement for of all people Joe Ellick, who was reviled in Washington by the time he resigned, and then was taken on as a regular umpire in 1887 against the better judgment of several team owners who knew him as a borderline alcoholic that had not always given his best during his playing days. He lasted only 33 games as an NL umpire in 1887 before Detroit manager Bill Watkins forced his ouster for alleged crooked umpiring. Upon hearing the news, a Chicago *Sporting Life* correspondent chortled: "Chicagoans are glad of Grace Pearce's retirement. His connection with the game did it no good."

SOURCES

National Republic, September 30, 1886.
Nemec, David. *Major League Baseball Profiles: 1871–1900* (Lincoln: University of Nebraska Press, 2011), 1: 370–371.
Sporting Life, August 28, 1886.
Washington Critic, September 30, 1886.
Washington Post, September 30, 1886.

October 7, 1886

Place: Washington
League: National League
Field: Swampoodle Grounds
Clubs: Washington versus Kansas City
Umpire: Joe Quest

John Gaffney, who had taken time off from umpiring to manage the Washington Club, sent a telegram to Kansas player-manager Dave Rowe on September 26th, asking, "Will you play three postponed games in the morning?" Rowe's response, received on the 28th, stated, "Yes: go ahead. All O.K." However, Rowe thought he was responding to Gaffney regarding the playing of a postponed game with St. Louis on September 27th and refused to play any morning games with Washington thereafter. The 7th place Cowboys consequently failed to put in an appearance in the morning game of a scheduled doubleheader on October 7, which was the first of three scheduled makeup games on consecutive days. Umpire Quest forfeited the contest to last place Washington and then stuck around to officiate the afternoon game, which the Nationals won on the field, 12–3. The game was noteworthy in that Kansas City brought so few men to its season-ending series in Washington that novice pitcher Silver King occupied right field for the Cowboys.

SOURCES

National Republic, October 8, 1886.
Washington Critic, October 8, 1886.
Washington Post, October 8, 1886.

October 8, 1886

Place: Washington
League: National League
Field: Swampoodle Grounds
Clubs: Washington versus Kansas City
Umpire: Joe Quest

When Kansas City again failed to show up for the morning game of a scheduled doubleheader, it grew apparent the Cowboys were simply refusing to play any of their three meaningless makeup games between the two tail enders and would agree only to play the originally scheduled three afternoon games in their season-ending series with the Nationals. After Quest again forfeited the early game to Washington, he umpired a 2–2 tie between Kansas City's King and Washington's Hank O'Day in the afternoon affair.

SOURCES

National Republic, October 9, 1886.
Washington Post, October 9, 1886.

October 9, 1886

Place: Washington
League: National League

Field: Swampoodle Grounds
Clubs: Washington versus Kansas City
Umpire: Joe Quest

When the Kansas City club was a no show for the third straight morning, Quest went through the motions of giving the game to Washington via forfeit. Meanwhile there were rumors that Washington intended to give the afternoon game away in a very different manner. Sometime that morning Washington manager John Gaffney, both a former and a future National League umpire, received a flurry of telegrams from St. Louis manager Gus Schmelz expressing his fear that there was a plot afoot to throw the season ending game to his Cowboys. Since no game could be rigged with confidence unless the pitcher for the paid-off team was involved, Gaffney held out his scheduled battery of Dupee Shaw and catcher Barney Gilligan as a precautionary measure. Their replacements, the rookie "Bones Battery" of string bean hurler Frank Gilmore and his catching counterpart Connie Mack, spearheaded Washington to a 3–0 win.

The five games the Nationals won in three days—only two of them on the field of play—were more than they won in most months during the 1886 season. What's more, Washington collected four home forfeit victories altogether in 1886, all in the space of a single month, to set a still extant season record not only for the most home forfeit wins but also for the highest percentage of a team's total wins via forfeit (14.3).

SOURCES

Washington Post, October 10, 1886.
National Republic, October 10, 1886.

April 30, 1887

Place: Louisville
League: American Association
Field: Eclipse Park I
Clubs: Louisville versus Cincinnati
Umpire: Ned Cuthbert

Cincinnati journeyed to Evansville, Indiana, on Friday to blast the local club 14–0 in a meaningless exhibition game and then was unable to get to Louisville in time for Saturday's match with the Colonels owing to a railroad accident. It has yet to be ascertained whether, in situations like this where it was known well in advance there would be no game, protocol demanded that the home team and the scheduled umpire had to come to the park in full regalia so that a forfeit could be formally declared in front of witnesses or whether a simple wire from the dilatory visitors stating the unfortunate circumstances sufficed.

SOURCES

Cincinnati Enquirer, May 11, 1887.
Sporting Life, May 11, 1887.

July 3, 1887

Place: Louisville
League: American Association
Field: Eclipse Park I
Clubs: Louisville versus St. Louis
Umpire: Ben Young

A swirling misty rain began falling in the second frame with Louisville ahead, 5–1. Umpire Young stopped play for 10 minutes, but when it continued to rain "so lightly that the uncovered seats were not vacated by the people," he ordered the game to resume. St. Louis player-manager Charlie Comiskey did so grudgingly, but after the Colonels posted two more runs in their half of the second, he wanted the game postponed because it "began to sprinkle again." Young denied his request, contending that the skies were doing little more than lightly dampening the field. Comiskey "refused to play, whereupon Young gave the game to Louisville." An excellent and innovative umpire according to most accounts, Young was drummed out of the AA almost immediately thereafter—the July 3 contest was his AA coda in fact—with Comiskey leading the movement to get rid of a man who would not buckle to his will, and never returned to the majors. He died in a railroad accident on September 1, 1890, while on his way to umpire a minor league game. During transport from the accident site to the nearest morgue, Young's corpse was robbed of all money and personal effects.

SOURCES

Nemec, David. *Major League Baseball Profiles: 1871–1900* (Lincoln: University of Nebraska Press, 2011), 2: 218–219.
St. Paul Daily Globe, July 4, 1887.
Sporting Life, July 13, 1887.

July 22, 1887

Place: Philadelphia
League: American Association
Field: Athletic Park
Clubs: Philadelphia versus Cleveland
Umpire: Mitchell (First name not known)

In the 6th inning of a game that ranks high among the most bizarre forfeits ever, Philadelphia had Harry Stovey on third base and Lou Bierbauer on first with Ted Larkin at bat. Bierbauer took a long lead off first to draw a pickoff throw from Blues pitcher Mike Morrison and then got into a run down between first and second, ostensibly to allow Stovey an opportunity to score. Spotting Stovey starting for home out of the corner of his eye, Cleveland second baseman Cub Stricker rifled the ball to his catcher Charlie Snyder in ample time to catch Stovey. But Larkin, seeing that Stovey would be an easy out, blocked Snyder from throwing, allowing Stovey to return to third. Umpire Mitchell (first name unknown) at first called Stovey out at third but then changed his mind and called Larkin out instead for interference. Cleveland, preferring to have the runner taken off third base, had scarcely started to argue its case when Mitchell "to the surprise of everyone gave the Athletics the game."

Since Cleveland was leading 6–4 at the time, no pitching decisions were assigned, sparing the A's novice hurler Chapman a likely loss in his lone ML game. Chapman for years was believed to be a 14-year-old named Fred Chapman and was credited with being the youngest player in big league history. Not long ago, however, researcher Richard Malatzy determined the game belonged to a minor leaguer named Frank Chapman, thereby solving a long-standing mystery since the Fred Chapman in question had already been discovered never to have been a ballplayer.

SOURCES

Nemec, David. *Major League Baseball Profiles: 1871–1900* (Lincoln: University of Nebraska Press, 2011), 2: 226.
New York Sun, July 23, 1887.
Sporting Life, July 27, 1887.
Washington Post, July 23, 1887.

August 12, 1887

Place: Staten Island, New York
League: American Association
Field: St. George Grounds
Clubs: New York versus Philadelphia
Umpire: Jerry Sullivan

Exactly three weeks after their eerie forfeit win over Cleveland, the A's were embroiled in another forfeited game that was even weirder in some respects. With his team trailing the New York Mets 9–7, in the bottom of the sixth inning, rookie A's pitcher Gus Weyhing hit a low liner that caromed off right fielder Eddie Hogan's foot and disappeared into the baroque "Fall of Babylon" scenery in deep right field. Weyhing made third base before the ball was found but was told to retreat to second by umpire Sullivan because the park rule entitled a batter only to two bases on a ball hit into Mets owner Erasmus Wiman's decorative brainchild. Weyhing was told by his captain, first baseman Harry Stovey, not to return to second. Sullivan called "wildly for a watch," which was delivered by director Walter Watrous and again demanded that Weyhing return to second. Stovey argued unsuccessfully that Hogan's intervening foot should make the hit a home run, if anything. When Stovey refused to return to the bench, Sullivan waved Watrous's watch menacingly and the Mets were soon in possession of their lone forfeit win in their five-year history as an AA franchise.

According to the *New York Tribune*, after the game was called Sullivan and managers Charlie Mason of Philadelphia and Opie Caylor of New York had an "animated conversation." Mason remarked, "I can't see why that idiot out west (meaning Wheeler Wikoff, president of the Association) can't appoint men as umpires instead of a lot of bums." Sullivan replied "indignantly" that he was not a bum and simply umpired for fun.

The issue appears never to have been resolved whether the ground rule still applied to a batted ball that made contact with a fielder before bounding into the Fall of Babylon. This point may not even have been considered when the park rules were written. The *New York Daily Tribune* reported, however, that "several of the Metropolitan players say that Sullivan was right and that each club had agreed that a hit in to the scenic Babylon should only count for two bases no matter whether a player made an error on it before the ball got there or not."

SOURCES

New York Daily Tribune, August 13, 1887.
The Sporting News, August 24, 1887.
Washington Post, August 13, 1887.

May 31, 1888

Place: New York
League: National
Field: Polo Grounds I
Clubs: New York versus Pittsburgh
Umpire: Stewart Decker

After playing a Decoration Day doubleheader against the Giants the day before, Pittsburgh did not appear at the Polo Grounds at 4 p.m. for the scheduled Thursday afternoon game and umpire Decker declared the Alleghenies the loser by forfeit after Stump Wiedman, one of the Giants' seldom used hurlers, threw three balls plateward around 4:15 in front of a sparse crowd of around 500. To please the few onlookers that cared to remain, a game was then played between a mix of members of the Giants' regular squad and their "colts" or practice team.

That evening Pittsburgh manager Horace Phillips broadcasted his intention to protest the forfeit, claiming he had called the Polo Grounds around 3 p.m. to see if there would be a game that day since it had rained heavily earlier in downtown Gotham where his team was staying and was told there would not be by someone who was never identified. Shortly thereafter he received a telegraph stating the game was on, but by that time it was too late to assemble his team and get to the uptown Harlem area, where the Giants' park was then situated and considerably less rain had fallen than in the downtown sector.

Phillips was disbelieved and his protest was disallowed, but it has at least a faint air of credibility. New York's twin aces, Tim Keefe and Mickey Welch, had each worked a full game in the previous day's doubleheader and its third starter, Cannonball Titcomb, had hurled on the 29th. Perhaps sensing an opportunity to rest a tired pitching staff, someone connected with the pennant-bound New York club just might have called Phillips on the morning of the 31st and concocted a plausible reason why the game that day had been postponed.

SOURCES

New York Times, June 1, 1888.
Sporting Life, June 6, 1888.
Washington Post, June 1, 1888.

July 14, 1888

Place: Kansas City
League: American Association
Field: Association Park
Clubs: Kansas City versus Brooklyn
Umpires: Bill Terry and Jim Donahue

In 1888 both major leagues experimented on occasion with a two-man umpiring crew for a game, but this was not planned to have been one of them. Permission was given in advance to use Brooklyn pitcher Bill Terry as the umpire because Fred Goldsmith (a former ML pitcher who is credited by some as the inventor of the curveball), the scheduled umpire, was unable to make the game. When Kansas City captain and second baseman, Sam Barkley, demanded that there be two umpires in the absence of Goldsmith and nominated his catcher, Jim Donahue, to monitor the bases, Brooklyn manager Bill McGunnigle grudgingly acceded to his request since there had been frequent disputes the previous day when Brooklyn outfielder Darby O'Brien worked the game alone and "had it not be [sic] for three questionable decisions, all of them against the home team, the score would have been 9 to 8 in favor of the Cowboys" rather than an 8–6 triumph by Brooklyn.

With one out in the bottom of the ninth inning Kansas City led 5 to 4. As the *Brooklyn Daily Eagle* reported, "and here the beauty of player umpires was displayed." Terry gave Brooklyn second sacker Bill McClellan a walk on pitches Kansas City hurler Red Ehert swore were strikes. Ehret then tried to pick McClellan off of first base and Donahue called McClellan out.

Bill Terry was called on to officiate in the absence of a regular umpire no less than 10 times during his playing career, an unusually high number. Called "The Adonis" by distaff fans, he seemed a natural to handle an indicator when his pitching days were over but lasted just 39 games in the rowdy 1900 season after National League president Nick Young appointed him to the circuit's umpiring staff.

Brooklyn captain Dave Foutz vigorously protested, the audience "hooted" and Terry refused to umpire any longer. Terry said he'd heard Barkley command Donahue to call McClellan out. Barkley huffily denied the accusation and claimed that "Donahue had the sole right to decide on field plays when the Brooklyns were at bat."

Foutz called his club off the field and they were met by president Charlie Byrne and manager Bill McGunnigle, both of whom approved of his actions. McGunnigle and Barkley then "had an exciting colloquy which was quite bitter at times." Barkley kept his club on the field for ten minutes and then Donahue forfeited the game to Kansas City, 9–0.

Brooklyn protested that Terry had the right to overrule Donahue's call because he was the plate umpire in charge of the game and Donahue could not declare a forfeit without Terry's agreement. Kansas City claimed that the local umpire had sole jurisdiction and that Terry had no right to intervene.

Byrne was asked by a *Brooklyn Daily Eagle* reporter if he would protest the game or not. "I certainly shall not," he said, "the score 9–0 means nothing. It will be called a draw game and may be played off at some future time, but I can hardly think we can find time to do so." He was asked, "On what grounds will it be called a draw?" "Under the rule that where there are two umpires and they cannot agree the game shall be called a draw," he replied.

But loop president Wheeler Wikoff dissented. Wikoff's logic for his decision, if it was ever recorded, has been lost.

This was the first of several forfeited games in the nineteenth century that pointed up the existing fuzziness in how disputed decisions were handled when the double-umpiring system was initially employed.

SOURCES

Brooklyn Daily Eagle, July 15, 1888.
Nemec, David. *Major League Baseball Profiles: 1871–1900* (Lincoln: University of Nebraska Press, 2011), 1: 76–77.
New York Sun, July 15, 1888.
Sporting Life, July 18, 1888, and July 25, 1888.
Washington Post, July 15, 1888.

September 12, 1888

Place: Chicago
League: National League
Field: West Side Park I
Clubs: Chicago versus New York
Umpires: Charlie Daniels and Phil Powers

At the end of the 5th inning, with Chicago ahead 9 to 2, New York catcher Buck Ewing claimed he injured his wrist on a ball that "bounded back from fair ground" and could not continue playing. The *Brooklyn Daily Eagle* had this to say about Ewing. "In his imitation of Anson's worst habit—That of needless kicking against umpires—Ewing has prejudiced every league umpire against him, and the result is that in every doubtful case they all give the doubt against him."

Ewing sent in Will Brown as his replacement. Cap Anson, the Chicago player-manager, rushed to home base umpire Daniels and said, "That won't do sir, that won't do. I can't stand that." When Daniels professed ignorance of what had prompted Anson's complaint, Anson assumed that base umpire

Powers had ruled that the substitution could be made and ran to his station behind first base screaming that his ruling was illegal. Powers declared he'd made no such ruling. Daniels, upon hearing this, ordered Ewing to return to the field. Ewing refused to catch and also refused to switch positions with left fielder Jim O'Rourke, using "very strong language" in his protest.

Anson was not averse to the position switch but was adamantly opposed to New York inserting a replacement player for Ewing. Anson was convinced that Ewing wasn't hurt and was just trying exit a one-sided game to save himself for the following day's contest with Chicago. His sense of the situation was no doubt correct, for Ewing throughout his career

Wheeler Wikoff fell heir to the American Association presidency almost by default after the AA's original president, Denny McKnight, was ousted for his role in the controversial Sam Barkley case. Barkley would later help present Wikoff with a thorny decision to deliver in the first forfeited major league game involving two umpires (collection of David Nemec).

was wont to leave games early and beg for days off at every opportunity, especially when he was due to catch, in an effort to spare himself injury. Daniels and Powers gave Ewing ten minutes to put on his gear and resume his position. When the time expired Powers said to the New York catcher, "Time is up, Ewing." Ewing shouted back, "All right, I'll take my men off the field." Powers tried to cool the crowd who voiced their disgust at the Giants for forfeiting. The verbal abuse grew harsher as the New Yorkers moved across the field into their omnibus. As the vehicle left the grounds, it was pelted with mud from the angry mob. New York not only lost the match, but their management was hit with a $500 fine.

It was later reported that prior to the game Ewing openly stated that Powers had pulled for a Chicago victory in the previous day's 5–3 Chicago win and that New York manager Jim Mutrie agreed.

The *Brooklyn Daily Eagle* reported, "The [New York] *Herald* this morning again charges the loss of yesterday's game at Chicago to the umpires, when the score shows that the New York team received the worst drubbing they have had since there 9 to 1 defeat in Washington in July last." Later in the report of the game the *Eagle* wrote, "The *Herald* fails to give the score of the game this morning in the effort to lay the defeat to the umpires."

Anson's on field protest was exactly correct as per the rules for the 1888 season. Rule 43 states: *"A substitute shall not be allowed to take the place of any player in a game, unless such player be disabled in the game then being played, by reason of illness or injury of the nature or extent of which the Umpire shall be the sole judge."*

Until fairly recently Chicago's Gus Krock was not credited with a win in this game, nor was New York's Tim Keefe with a loss.

SOURCES

Brooklyn Daily Eagle, September 13, 1888.
Chicago Tribune, September 13, 1888.
Nemec, David. *Major League Baseball Profiles: 1871–1900* (Lincoln: University of Nebraska Press, 2011), 1: 271 and 2: 204–205.
New York Herald, September 13, 1888.
New York Sun, September 13, 1888.
New York Times, September 13, 1888.
Spalding's Official Base Ball Guide, 1888.

October 13, 1888

Place: Philadelphia
League: National League
Field: Philadelphia Base Ball Grounds
Clubs: Philadelphia versus Chicago
Umpire: Charlie Daniels

A downpour, which conflicting reports said began at noon, raining "sharply" for half an hour and ending at 2 p.m. and also as beginning at 2:15 p.m. and ceasing well before the 3:30 p.m. scheduled start time, was the apparent cause for the forfeit. With the sun shining brightly, Philadelphia manager and baseball legend, Harry Wright, refused to open the gates to the estimated 2,500 spectators eager to see a game, until the Chicago club arrived. When it was evident that Chicago would not appear at the grounds the crowd called for an exhibition game but was denied. Chicago captain and first baseman, Cap Anson, who had cancelled transportation to the Philadelphia Base Ball Grounds, was questioned later that evening and replied, "I was fooled yesterday, when we could have played, and I didn't propose to take chances to-day. If we had gone out there, we wouldn't have played anyway." Anson claimed he had telephoned Philadelphia President Al Reach, at his sporting goods store, at 3 p.m. and asked if the game was still scheduled and Reach had replied he didn't know. Meanwhile, at the field, when queried by Wright umpire Daniels agreed that the grounds were playable. With Philadelphia ready to play, Wright pressured Daniels to forfeit the game to Philadelphia until at last he did so. Anson subsequently admitted that he didn't intend to take his men to the field once the rain began and didn't care if the game was forfeited. The forfeit win enabled Philadelphia to finish in 3rd place, one game ahead of Boston, and deepened the growing resentment among other league members toward Chicago and Anson, whose arrogant behaviorisms by the late 1880s had become legendary among his worshipers but insufferable not only to Chicago's opponents but also to many of his own teammates.

Beginning in 1887, the home team captain or manager was empowered with deciding if the condition of the field was suitable after rain. Daniels had no jurisdiction to forfeit the game to Philadelphia until Harry Wright had declared the field ready for play. The game could only have been cancelled by Wright.

"Rule 44. The choice of innings shall be,
(1.) Given to the Captain of the Home Club, who shall also be the sole judge of the fitness of the ground for beginning a game after rain, and no game shall begin later than two hours before sunset."

SOURCES

Brooklyn Daily Eagle, October 14, 1888.
Los Angeles Times, October 14, 1888.
Nemec, David. *The Great Encyclopedia of Nineteenth Century Baseball* (Tuscaloosa: University of Alabama Press, 2006), 445.
Spalding's Official Base Ball Guide, 1888.

May 5, 1889

Place: Brooklyn
League: American Association
Field: Ridgewood Park
Clubs: Brooklyn versus Philadelphia
Umpire: Jack Holland

With a reported throng of 12,614 spectators on hand for a 3 p.m. start and many of the overflow standing two- and three-deep in a semi-circle in front of the outfield fence, "the wall of humanity" made for largest crowd ever to witness a game at Ridgewood Park, Brooklyn's Sunday home field. The contest stood at just 1-all at the beginning of the 6th inning despite the fact that the some members of the crowd stood so close to the outfielders that even a routine fly ball could become a ground rule double if it fell into their midst. At the top of the frame the A's collected four tallies. As the Bridegrooms first baseman Dave Foutz stepped to the plate to lead off the home half of the 6th inning, the crowd began to surge forward and soon the entire outfield became a "sea of humanity." As the *Brooklyn Daily Eagle* wrote, pertaining to the police who attempted to push back the crowd, "...but a battalion of the finest could not have cleared the field after the crowd broke in on the diamond..." When not even Brooklyn president Charlie Byrne's and left fielder Darby O'Brien's pleas that the game would be forfeited unless the field were cleared could make the crowd budge, Holland threw up his hands and left the field after declaring the game a draw. A's captain Harry Stovey immediately stated his intention to claim the game under Rule 61, "which says in substance that the home club must have sufficient police arrangements to handle the crowds."

Brooklyn predictably later claimed that A's outfielders had incited the near riot. The *Brooklyn Daily Eagle* reported that Philadelphia left fielder Harry Stovey and center fielder Curt Welch told the crowd that "they could move in if they liked." Both players denied the charge. Philadelphia countered by saying the Bridegrooms had riled up the crowd in order to break up the game and avoid a defeat since a stoppage in play would have reverted the score back to the 1–1 tie after five innings of play. Byrne held back Philadelphia's share of the gate receipt at the conclusion of the game but later made good his debt after AA president Wheeler Wikoff sided with the A's and upheld Stovey's claim that his club was entitled to a win via forfeit.

As for Holland, who had abdicated his post in the face of fire from the crowd, the 1889 season was his last as a big league umpire.

The rule book for 1889 addressed instances covering such an event as this; however, it is not entirely clear-cut. *Rule 61. Every Club shall furnish sufficient police force upon its own grounds to preserve order, and in the event of a crowd entering the field during the progress of a game, and interfering with the play in any manner, the Visiting Club may refuse to play further until the field be cleared. If the ground be not cleared within fifteen minutes thereafter, the Visiting Club may claim, and shall be entitled to, the game by a score of nine runs to none (no matter what number of innings have been played).*

It would seem obvious that if the umpire could prove that the visiting club, in this match Philadelphia, provoked the crowd and in fact induced the stoppage of play, than the home club should be awarded the game. The rules, however, are not so specific. Wikoff was correct in his thinking that the game should have been forfeited to Philadelphia.

SOURCES

Los Angeles Times, May 6, 1889.
New York Sun, May 6, 1889.
Pittsburgh Dispatch, May 6, 1889.
Reach's Official Base Ball Guide, 1889.
Spalding's Official Base Ball Guide, 1889.
Sporting Life, May 15, 1889.

June 24, 1889

Place: Brooklyn
League: American Association
Field: Washington Park I
Clubs: Brooklyn versus Columbus
Umpire: Bill Paasch

When scheduled umpire Fred Goldsmith did not appear when scheduled, according to the *Brooklyn Daily Eagle*, nor did he send word about his absence, he found himself $15 poorer and forced Brooklyn to summon local semipro pitcher Paasch to serve in his stead. Columbus manager Al Buckenberger refused to allow Paasch, a member of the local Brooklyn Athletic Club, to substitute even though he was on the official Brooklyn substitute umpire list and the only one on the list at the game. (As per the 1889 AA Constitution, Rule 58, drafted on April 10th, each club was required to submit three names of possible umpires who were residents of the home club's city or preferably in the immediate neighborhood of the home club's playing grounds, for consideration in the event the scheduled umpire did not make an appearance. One of these men was to be chosen by the home club to umpire the game.)

Paasch, at the direction of Brooklyn president Charlie Byrne, took his position on the field and called "Play." After waiting more than the five minutes—seven according the *New York Sun*—prescribed in the rule book, he declared a forfeit win to the Brooklyn club by the score of 9 to 0.

Upon losing the contest via forfeit, Buckenberger testily agreed to "play off a postponed game of April 25" so as not to disappoint the 2,217 spectators even though Paasch would officiate that game. Buckenberger nonetheless initially held his club off the field when Paasch called "Play" but then had second thoughts about losing two games in one day.

The game began at 4:30 p.m. and Columbus won a raucous and shabbily played contest 13–7. The "festivities" erupted in the bottom of the fifth inning. Second baseman Bill Greenwood was called out at home base to end the fifth with Columbus leading 7-5. Greenwood had attempted to score on a wild pitch by Brooklyn's Tom Lovett. Said the *Eagle*, "[Doc] Bushong threw the ball to

Lovett, who, seeing Greenwood lying on the ground trying to get back to touch the base, touched him while off it." The feces hit the ventilator and "Greenwood acted like a crazy man: Captain [Dave] Orr lost his senses and a scene ensued which was simply a disgrace to the visiting club. Greenwood got up and looked and acted like a maniac, and nearly the whole of the visiting team surrounded the little umpire, gesticulating like Comanches, headed by Orr, who openly charged the umpire with dishonesty, thus setting the example to his men.... It was a scene such as one can witness any Saturday afternoon on the bare lots where the roughs congregate."

The already incendiary spectacle was heightened by Solons center fielder Jim McTamany's actions in the sixth inning. McTamany, once a member of the Brooklyns from 1885–1887, "was a quiet gentlemanly player; but from his conduct yesterday he appears to have sadly degenerated," said the *Eagle*. Paasch called McTamany out on strikes and, "he abused the umpire as if he were a pickpocket and threatened to strike him with the bat." The headline in the *Eagle* the following day above its description of the game screamed: THE COLUMBUS TEAM GIVES A DISGRACEFUL EXHIBITION.

An even more disgraceful exhibition that season by a visiting team in Brooklyn loomed some 10 weeks ahead.

SOURCES

Brooklyn Daily Eagle, June 25, 1889.
Nemec, David. *The Rank and File of 19th Century Major League Baseball* (Jefferson, NC: McFarland, 2012), 284.
New York Sun, June 25, 1889.
Reach's Official Base Ball Guide, 1889.

September 8, 1889

Place: Brooklyn
League: American Association
Field: Ridgewood Park
Clubs: Brooklyn versus St. Louis
Umpire: Fred Goldsmith

Umpire Goldsmith awarded Brooklyn a Sunday forfeit win that had been prearranged. Earlier that day St. Louis owner Chris Von der Ahe had wired Brooklyn president Charlie Byrne that he would not bring his players to the park because, with a huge Sunday crowd expected, he feared for their safety after the previous day's debacle had also resulted in a St. Louis forfeit loss that was later rescinded and went into the books as a 4–2 Browns win, the score at the time all of Washington Park (Brooklyn's weekday home) exploded into chaos over the exaggerated stalling antics the Browns had employed in an attempt to thwart a last-ditch home-team rally.

The *Brooklyn Daily Eagle* lambasted Von der Ahe for his team's actions the previous day and his refusal to appear for the game on the 8th. The headlines read: *The St. Louis Club Likely to be Expelled from the American Base Ball Association—Ferguson Demands an Investigation—The Browns Must Play Tomorrow's Game or Forfeit it—No Remission of the $1,500 Fine to be Permitted*

One of the most scathing indictments in the lengthy attack on Von der Ahe was: "Without referring to Von de Ahe's actions in past years, it is only necessary to mention his escapades of 1889, the most prominent of which is his charge of dishonesty against Latham, his open charge of collusion against Umpire Ferguson and the latest of his reckless statements made against the President of the Brooklyn Club." Latham was Arlie Latham, Von der Ahe's regular third baseman. Von der Ahe's remarks about president Charlie Byrne stemmed from his experience on September 7. The article continued: "Patience has ceased to be a virtue in the long endurance of Von der Ahe's conduct, and Mr. Byrne and Mr. Ferguson owe it to the welfare of the association, as well as to themselves individually, that the reckless charges of this man be subjected to a thorough official investigation, and it should be promptly made."

Brooklyn appeared on the grounds on the 8th. Byrne instituted free admission to those who wished to attend and promised at least an exhibition match if the schedule championship match did not occur. From all reports, he knew full well in advance that it would not. A five-inning exhibition match was played between nines captained by Brooklyn left fielder Darby O'Brien and the Bridegrooms' first baseman Dave Foutz. Foutz's side won, 7–5.

The perilous trouble in the game of September 7 had begun in the 9th inning at 6:18 p.m. when Browns player-manager Charlie Comiskey yanked his club off the field after protesting in vain to Goldsmith that it was too dark to continue play after Brooklyn catcher Bob Clark reached first base when St. Louis backstop Jack Milligan missed his third strike. While Milligan muttered to Goldsmith that he hadn't been able to see the pitch in time to catch it, Clark tried to swipe second. Comiskey contended that Milligan's throw beat Clark to the bag and Goldsmith's inability to see that obvious accomplishment was conclusive evidence that there was too little light left to finish the game. To underscore the conditions several of the Browns, including Von der Ahe, had previously lit candles that Von der Ahe had purchased from a nearby grocer and arranged them around the team's bench like footlights. Throughout the 9th inning members of the crowd gleefully threw beer steins at the candles, knocking them over like bowling pins and igniting a pile of papers near the grandstand. Frightened when the fire threatened to grow and the beer steins began shattering against the stack of bats piled beside their bench, the Browns gathered their belongings and fled. When the crowd of 15,000 saw the St. Louis players abandoning the field, they directed their beer steins at them, forcing them to cover their heads with their hands as they sprinted for the dressing room. But no sooner were they ensconced there behind barred doors than all the windows "were broken by beer glasses and stones ... and it required a large detachment of police to get them safely away from the grounds."

On Tuesday afternoon, for the scheduled finale of the series that played a pivotal role in eventually deciding the pennant in Brooklyn's favor and breaking St. Louis's four-year lock on the AA title, the Browns rode out to Washington Park with trepidation, still fearing another crowd assault, but were spared life and limb when a heavy rainstorm washed out the game.

Sources

Brooklyn Daily Eagle, September 9, 1889.
Sporting Life, September 18, 1889.
Washington Post, September 9, 1889.

April 20, 1890

Place: Louisville
League: American Association
Field: Eclipse Park I
Clubs: Louisville versus St. Louis
Umpire: Terry Connell

Prior to the game both teams agreed rather fecklessly that a ball hit to left field, which had an overflow Sunday crowd, would allow the batter to get as many bases as possible "except a hit along the foul line, which would go into foul ground" and be worth only two bases. With St. Louis ahead 3–0 in the third inning, the Browns first protested that Louisville right fielder Jimmy Wolf's ball hit up against the left field seats, which scored catcher Jack Ryan from first base, should be ruled an out because spectators had prevented Browns left fielder Tom Gettinger from snaring it. The Browns then softened their protest, willing to give Wolf two bases for a hit winding up in foul ground but only on the condition that Ryan be made to return to third base. Contending that the pregame agreement on balls entering foul ground applied only to the batter and not to base runners, Connell declined to send Ryan back to third and then gave the game to Louisville after St. Louis refused to desist in its argument. Since the "crowd was hard to handle, threatening to pour into the field and do the players violence, to keep them quiet" the teams then agreed to continue the game as an exhibition, which ended in a 13–13 tie.

Connell, who had already been involved in an inflammatory forfeited game in Washington six years earlier, had imprudently thought to return to the umpiring ranks on a full-time basis in 1890 but turned in his papers to AA officials after working only nine games.

SOURCES

Brooklyn Daily Eagle, April 21, 1890.
Sporting Life, April 26, 1890.
Washington Post, April 21, 1890.

April 24, 1890

Place: Boston
League: National
Field: South End Grounds
Clubs: Boston versus New York
Umpire: Sandy McDermott

Boston had just knotted the game at 2-all in the seventh inning when Beaneaters shortstop Herman Long, stationed on third, spotted Giants third baseman Jerry Denny playing "well ahead of the base" and dared to take a lengthy lead. New York catcher Pat Murphy "made a bluff" to throw to second, which was occupied by Patsy Donovan, and then threw instead to shortstop Jack Glasscock covering third. Long raced home ahead of Glasscock's return throw to Murphy. The Giants ranted at umpire McDermott that Murphy tagged Long before he slid across the plate. During the argument McDermott fined Glasscock, Denny and Giants hurler Mickey Welch $10 each for using foul and abusive language. Welch then ignored McDermott's warning to desist the argument and eventually threw the ball down and stalked off the field despite Glasscock's plea for him to resume pitching. Whereupon McDermott pulled out his watch and forfeited the game after a minute had passed. There are conflicting accounts of this denouement, some having it that Welch claimed he didn't continue because McDermott had fined him and ordered him out of the game, which McDermott denied and said that instead he'd told Welch to get back in the box. Others have it that the umpire ordered the game to resume, pulled out his watch and put Glasscock and New York on the clock. The *New York Sun* reported that after thirty seconds Glasscock "beckoned to [Jack] Sharrott to take Welch's place in the box. McDermott's back was turned and he did not see Glasscock's signal, neither did he see Sharrott approaching. Glasscock had not changed his position, so the umpire at the expiration of sixty seconds, closed his watch with a snap and gave the game to Boston."

The *Brooklyn Daily Eagle* printed a third explanation of the incident. Glasscock continued to "kick" at McDermott after the fining of Welch and was under the impression that he had five minutes to resume after McDermott called "Play." That would have been the case in 1889; however, the rules were changed at the annual meeting that winter and reduced the time to resume playing after the announcement from the umpire from five minutes to one minute. Glasscock also argued that he had ordered Sharrott to the box while chinning with McDermott.

No pitching decisions were credited in any event.

McDermott served parts of two seasons as an NL umpire with a seven-year hiatus between them. His first tour in 1890 ended in midseason after several managers complained that Chicago player-manager Cap Anson had him in his pocket, an accusation that many marginal NL umpires faced during Anson's long reign as Chicago's kingpin player-manager.

SOURCES

Boston Globe, April 25, 1890.
Brooklyn Daily Eagle, April 25, 1890.
Nemec, David. *The Rank and File of 19th Century Major League Baseball* (Jefferson, NC: McFarland, 2012), 283.
New York Sun, April 25, 1890.
New York Times, April 25, 1890.
Sporting Life, April 26, 1890.

July 2, 1890

Place: Toledo
League: American Association
Field: Speranza Park
Clubs: Toledo versus Philadelphia
Umpires: Fred Smith and Sadie McMahon

This game was a virtual repeat of an 1888 forfeit win by Kansas City of the AA in that it turned on whether one player acting as an umpire could declare his team a winner by forfeit when his fellow player-umpire from the opposing team disagreed. With scheduled umpire Bob Emslie unavailable, Toledo selected rookie pitcher Smith to officiate and Philadelphia chose its staff bulwark, McMahon. With his team trailing 5–3 in the 9th inning and two men out, Smith, working the plate, called his teammate, first baseman Perry Werden, safe at home on a wild pitch. When the A's clustered around Smith to argue the call, the plate was left unguarded long enough for George Tebeau to sneak in from third base and score the tying run since time had not been called. "The Athletics then refused to play and left the grounds, whereupon the game was given to Toledo—9–0." McMahon later claimed he had called time while the argument fomented, but no one apart from his own teammates believed him. Nonetheless, this game fortifies the conviction of many historians that Wheeler Wikoff, the AA president at the time, took the easy way out in deciding many debatable forfeits during his tenure, giving the verdict either to the home team or the one with the most clout. In any case, it is not known whether the Toledo club ever collected the $1,500 fine from the A's that the American Association imposed on any team that left the grounds before a game was played out.

Pitching for Toledo that day was Ed O'Neil. Since the game was tied at the time it was forfeited no pitching decisions were credited, unhappily for him. It was the only time his team won with him in the box; he finished his lone ML season with a 0–8 career record.

SOURCES

Brooklyn Daily Eagle, July 2, 1890.
Sporting Life, July 5, 1890.

July 27, 1890

Place: Brooklyn
League: American Association
Field: Polo Grounds II
Clubs: Brooklyn versus Columbus
Umpire: Jimmy Peoples

There is a lot of meat here for historians. Brooklyn Gladiators manager Jim Kennedy claimed on the evening of July 27, 1890, that the Columbus team's directors were instrumental in Peoples landing his umpiring job after he washed out as a player and he was "in duty bound to favor" his former teammates. He further attested that AA president Zach Phelps had pledged to "keep [Peoples] away from" umpiring games involving Columbus but then reneged on his agreement. Kennedy, a New York sportswriter and a highly resourceful sports promoter, was speaking from season long experience of having his team treated as a stepchild by the AA, which had granted it a last-minute franchise only for the lack of any other viable candidates to fill out the circuit to eight teams in 1890.

In the 5th inning of the very first game Peoples worked involving his former team, Columbus pitcher Hank Gastright was knocked out of the box and replaced by Elton Chamberlain, who was fined and sent to the bench in the 7th inning for refusing to pitch with a new ball. Contrary to the rules, Peoples then allowed Gastright to return to the game because Columbus had no other bona fide pitchers available. Rule 28, Section 2—new to the rule book in 1890—specifically addressed substitutions and should have been enforced here.

Two players, whose name shall be printed on the score card as extra players, may be substituted at any time, by either club, but no player so retired shall thereafter participate in the game. In addition, thereto a substitute may be allowed at any time in place of a player disabled in the game then being played, by reason of illness or injury, of the nature and extent of which the umpire shall be the sole judge.

With last-place Brooklyn ahead 13–8 in the 8th inning and having every expectation of achieving a rare victory in front of a fair-sized Sunday home crowd, Columbus right fielder Jack Sneed hit several foul balls into the stands with his captain, center fielder Jim McTamany, on first base. After the last foul hit, Peoples was tossed a playable ball from the Brooklyn bench but rejected it as well as the old ball when it was returned from the stands and supported McTamany when he insisted that Brooklyn provide a new ball. With no more new balls on hand, Kennedy argued that a new one was unnecessary since the last ball fouled into the crowd was perfectly good. According to one report, Peoples claimed the ball that had just been returned to the field was not the same ball that had gone into the stands and declared a forfeit. Other sources, most of them New York papers, contended that Peoples had his choice of several playable balls, including one that lay right near his feet, but rejected them all. Peoples himself allegedly recognized after the game that he may have acted hastily and sheepishly admitted that he did not expect the forfeit would stand.

The tawdry incident strengthened Kennedy's already compelling case that the American Association was against his ragtag team when Phelps subsequently backed Peoples's seemingly arbitrary decision not to continue the game with anything less than a brand new ball and also denied a protest from Brooklyn captain and second baseman Joe Gerhardt that Gastright should not have been permitted to re-enter the game. The patchwork Brooklyn club folded less than a month after this episode.

Except for courtesy runners and players that were temporarily removed for courtesy runners (a custom that ended in 1950), Gastright's reappearance in a game after being removed from it is the only one of its kind in ML history in as much as it was rightfully protested through proper channels but its illegality was ignored. Making the AA's decision to uphold the forfeit and deny Brooklyn's protest all the more unfathomable is that Kennedy later swore that on Tuesday, two days after the game, "he had received notice from one of the directors of the American Association that Columbus cannot possibly be credited with the game that Umpire Peoples forfeited in their favor, and he will have the board decide it in favor of Brooklyn as soon as possible." If all forfeited games in ML history were put to a vote, this would be our hands-down choice for the most wrongful. It not only was baseless but also embarrassed a struggling team in front of one of its largest home crowds of the season and robbed its fans of the opportunity to get their money's worth by seeing a complete game.

SOURCES

Brooklyn Daily Eagle, July 28, 1890.
Nemec, David. *Major League Baseball Profiles: 1871–1900* (Lincoln: University of Nebraska Press, 2011), 1: 269–270 and 2: 129–130.
New York Times, July 28, 1890.
Reach's Official Base Ball Guide, 1890.
Sporting Life, August 2, 1890.

August 3, 1890

Place: Syracuse
League: American Association
Field: Iron Pier Grounds
Clubs: Syracuse versus Louisville
Umpire: Unknown

Despite being told in no uncertain terms by Syracuse Chief of Police Wright that Sunday baseball was illegal within his jurisdiction and their scheduled game would be interrupted forthwith if an attempt was made to play it, the Stars nonetheless showed up at Iron Pier and manager George Frazier had his club on the field at 3:30 p.m. Louisville's Jack Chapman, the opposition manager, refused to appear with his team, however, and left for Louisville on a 5:25 p.m. train. Likewise, the scheduled umpire, Wes Curry, also didn't appear, fearing arrest, and a local umpire was drafted to go through the formalities of awarding the game to Syracuse.

Upon learning of the forfeit loss, Chapman said he hadn't willingly given up the game but was afraid of having his team arrested and detained in Syracuse for participating in a Sunday contest, causing it to miss its next scheduled contest against Brooklyn in Louisville on August 5. In a letter to *Sporting Life*, he stressed that Frazier had not guaranteed his team any money for keeping its scheduled August 3 date and said Louisville would simply have to take its chances on getting a share of the gate receipts if it showed up at the Iron Pier venue. Lastly, he argued that Frazier should have played the game at the location where it was originally scheduled, Three Rivers Park, since the two teams had played a Sunday contest there without interruption on May 25. Chapman's arguments all give the appearance of having been strong ones, yet the AA directors upheld Syracuse's claim to a forfeit win. It would have added insult to injury if Louisville had also been fined for its nonappearance.

That same day another American Association game between St. Louis and Rochester, played at a neutral site in Buffalo, was stopped in the third inning by the local police. Sabbatarians in 1890 wreaked havoc throughout the season in almost every AA city that embraced Sunday ball. It is fortunate that their staunch views on whether playing ball on Sunday should be permitted played no part in the AA pennant race.

SOURCES

New York Times, August 4, 1890.
Sporting Life, August 16, 1890.

August 5, 1890

Place: Toledo
League: American Association
Field: Speranza Park
Clubs: Toledo versus Rochester
Umpire: Jimmy Peoples

After scoring five runs in the bottom of the 6th inning to take a 7–3 lead, Toledo put two men on base with two out in the home half of the 7th with its top run producer, first baseman Perry Werden, due to bat. At that point Rochester second baseman Bill Greenwood "got to chinning the umpire and after being repeatedly ordered to play ball ... was finally fined $50 and ordered from the game." Greenwood refused to depart and Peoples pulled his watch. After the game was forfeited, "the spectators left disgust with Manager [Pat] Powers for permitting Greenwood's obstinacy to stop the game before it was concluded." Their disdain for both Powers and Greenwood was entirely justified since they had paid their good money to see a full nine-inning game. Yet it need be noted that this was the second forfeited game rookie umpire Peoples had perpetrated in little more than two weeks. He was canned by the AA less than a month later.

Because the affair had gone the necessary length to be official and Toledo was ahead, Black Pirates pitcher Ed Cushman drew a win and luckless Bob Barr took the loss. In his five-year ML career, almost all of it spent with rotten teams, Barr won only a third of his 137 decisions despite being a terror everywhere he went in the minors.

SOURCES

Brooklyn Daily Eagle, August 6, 1890.
Nemec, David. *Major League Baseball Profiles: 1871–1900* (Lincoln: University of Nebraska Press, 2011), 1: 11–12.
Sporting Life, August 9, 1890.

September 21, 1890

Place: St. Louis
League: American Association
Field: Sportsman's Park
Clubs: St. Louis versus Rochester
Umpire: Herm Doescher (aka Doscher)

With St. Louis up 10–3 in the 8th inning of the second game of a doubleheader, umpire Doescher ejected Rochester outfielder Sandy Griffin from the game and fined him $10 for excessive arguing. Griffin was at bat at the time and had just told Doescher, "You can see that all right," after a called strike, venomously implying that it was still light enough to continue play. Minutes earlier Rochester captain Jim Knowles had derided Doescher's contention that it was too dark to continue and the 8th inning would be the last. When Griffin refused to leave the batter's box, claiming he had done nothing to deserve ejection, let alone a fine, Doescher gave the game to St. Louis. In the interest of fair play after witnessing a number of questionable calls against Rochester, the home crowd by then was strongly on the visitors' side and actually had encouraged Griffin "to stick it out" and laughed when he was witnessed "shaking his fist at Doescher" as he "invited him outside of the lot, where he intimated he would whip him in less time than it took to forfeit the game."

Joe Neale received credit for a win that he almost certainly would have obtained anyway, and Cannonball Titcomb drew the loss for Rochester.

SOURCE

Sporting Life, September 27, 1890.

April 8, 1891

Place: St. Louis
League: American Association
Field: Sportsman's Park
Clubs: St. Louis versus Cincinnati
Umpire: Bill Gleason

Gleason had been the regular shortstop for St. Louis from 1882 through 1887 and was appointed as a full-time umpire by the American Association in 1891. This Opening Day game in front of some 2,500 spectators was his first ever ML officiating assignment. Cincinnati catcher-manager Mike "King" Kelly was ejected from the game by Gleason in the fifth inning and replaced behind the bat by Jerry Hurley, but continued surreptitiously to manage from the bench. In the 10th inning, with the scored tied at 7-all, Kelly claimed to the high heavens that it was too dark to continue and ordered his club to stall. As Gleason grew increasingly irritated, Cincinnati stalled all the more and Kelly began brazenly accusing the novice umpire of favoring his old club. Meanwhile St. Louis scored eight runs, bringing the score to 15–7, before Gleason finally forfeited the game to St. Louis and rapidly left the field having umpired his first and only major league game. Sources conflict as to whether he wired his resignation to AA headquarters that evening or was fired for incompetence. *Sporting Life* commented that "Gleason's umpiring was something weird, and even Von der Ahe and the St. Louis press couldn't stand it." The forfeiture was ruled a tie by acting AA president Lewis Kramer as soon as he learned of it, and the game was replayed on April 13. Gleason never umpired another major league game.

We are including this game because we feel something of an injustice was done to both Gleason and his old team in overturning his decision. While Gleason admittedly was not cut out to make a career of umpiring, he was probably no worse than several other ex-players who turned to officiating. It was his ill luck to draw both Kelly and his old team in his very first assignment. In all likelihood his forfeit declaration was summarily dismissed almost as quickly as it was made at least partially to placate Kelly whose support and morale needed to be constantly curried if he was to maintain the necessary enthusiasm to run the poorly stocked last-minute Cincinnati entry in the rapidly crumbling AA. As it was, he jumped to the National League anyway before the season was out and was instrumental in bringing about the demise of the AA as a strong rival major league to the NL that winter.

SOURCES

Nemec, David. *The Great Encyclopedia of Nineteenth Century Baseball*, 2d ed. (Tuscaloosa: University of Alabama Press, 2006), 573–574.
New York Times, April 9, 1891.
St. Louis Post-Dispatch, April 9, 1891.

September 12, 1891

Place: St. Louis
League: American Association
Field: Sportsman's Park
Clubs: St. Louis versus Boston
Umpire: Tom McLaughlin

With St. Louis ahead 4–1 in the 8th inning, Boston loaded the bases with one out against Browns novice pitcher George Rettger. Reds second baseman Cub Stricker sent a grounder to St. Louis shortstop Shorty Fuller, who opted to concede a run and go to first base rather than try for a force at home. The throw to first sacker Charlie Comiskey beat Stricker to the bag, but with the force no longer on, Reds pitcher Charlie Buffinton, who had been on first, found himself caught between first and second. During the ensuing rundown Boston's Hardy Richardson scored, but it was questionable if he had crossed the plate before Buffinton was tagged for the third out. Meanwhile Stricker circled the bases as if he had not heard McLaughlin call him out at first. He was joined in his argument by Boston captain Hugh Duffy. The pair quickly drew other Boston Reds players into the fray. When the brouhaha continued after McLaughlin ordered play to resume, he forfeited the game to St. Louis.

Boston did not take issue with Buffinton being called out, only Stricker. The protest was groundless in any case and doomed to fail. We think that this may have been one of numerous protests in the early days of ML ball that seemed designed mainly to test the mettle of a novice umpire. McLaughlin was working his first ML game on this day and may well have shocked the first-place Reds who were accustomed to having their way when he not only pulled his watch but stuck to his guns after their time for kicking expired. Rettger was credited with a win and Buffinton with a loss.

SOURCES

Boston Globe, September 13, 1891.
Sporting Life, September 23, 1891.

September 20, 1891

Place: Louisville
League: American Association
Field: Eclipse Park I
Clubs: Louisville versus Philadelphia
Umpire: Tom McLaughlin

During the second game of a doubleheader, Philadelphia led 3 to 0 in the first inning when umpire McLaughlin tossed Philadelphia first baseman Ted Larkin out of the game for cursing him after flying out with two strikes. Larkin had already argued that both strike calls came on high pitches that were balls. Player-manager George Wood refused to replace Larkin, so McLaughlin awarded the game to Louisville. Louisville was also the victor 7–2 in the first game. Wood later claimed he had no one on the bench to replace Larkin except pitcher Elton Chamberlain who had worked the first game and was exhausted. Louisville manager Jack Chapman countered by saying he would have protested the game had the Athletics won after all their gratuitous kicking.

Note that this was the second game McLaughlin forfeited in his first eight days as an AA umpire. He worked only 19 games altogether before the league cut all ties with him. McLaughlin's first name is believed to have been Thomas, but nothing concrete is known about him; there were several McLaughlins umpiring professionally in the early 1890s, and these 19 games may have belonged to almost any one of them.

SOURCE

Sporting Life, September 30, 1891.

September 25, 1891

Place: Chicago
League: National League
Field: West Side Park I
Clubs: Chicago versus Pittsburgh
Umpire: Jack McQuaid

After Chicago scored two runs to tie the game at 4-all with two out in the 8th inning, Pittsburgh catcher, Doggie Miller, took exception to the second run, which had been tallied by Chicago third baseman Tom Burns. The *Brooklyn Daily Eagle* described Burns's slide as one, "that will live in base ball history.

It was a headlong plunge through a cloud of dust." Miller first argued that Burns had missed the plate, and, when that argument failed, third baseman Charlie Reilly, along with the majority of the Pittsburgh club, joined him in claiming that Burns, en route to scoring, had cut across the diamond "and no portion of his figure had passed within ten feet of third base." During the discourse Miller launched a torrent of verbal abuse and was ejected by umpire McQuaid. He "turned sullenly and obeyed," but Pittsburg Manager Bill McGunnigle angrily refused to put in a replacement for him and sent him back out on the field. Again Miller obeyed. McQuaid borrowed Chicago pitcher Jack Luby's timepiece and put Miller on the clock. "I'll give you one minute to get out of the game," stated McQuaid. According to the *Eagle,* "Miller laughed and leered at McQuaid and made faces at the audience. "

The umpire's next words were, "The game is forfeited to Chicago!" The Chicagos rushed away from the field, followed by the Pittsburgh players. McGunnigle followed Anson and begged, "Let's finish the game. It's a good one." Anson retorted, "It's already ours."

McGunnigle later filed an unsuccessful protest on Rule 26 that McQuaid had not given him the maximum length of five minutes to put in a substitute before declaring a forfeit. McGunnigle was apparently unaware that since 1890 the umpire only had to wait one minute after calling "play" before forfeiting a match.

Sources

Brooklyn Daily Eagle, September 26, 1891.
Chicago Tribune, September 26, 1891.
Pittsburgh Dispatch, September 26, 1891.
Washington Post, September 26, 1891.

October 5, 1891

Place: Washington
League: American Association
Field: Boundary Field
Clubs: Washington versus Baltimore
Umpire: Jack Kerins

Holding a 6–1 lead after six innings, Baltimore wanted the game called on account of darkness. Umpire Kerins, a former ML catcher and first baseman, disagreed that the light was insufficient to continue play. After Washington scored five runs in the 7th inning, Baltimore started kicking and throwing the ball around aimlessly. Washington tallied 20 runs in the frame before purposely making the final out when a batter refused to run to first base after hitting the ball. Earlier Kerins had not called Washington's Sy Sutcliffe out for the same offense, but eventually both teams wore out his patience. Baltimore captain George Van Haltren again claimed it was too dark by then to see the fielders, not to mention the ball, and refused to send a batter to hit in its half of the 7th frame, forcing Kerins to forfeit the game. That evening Baltimore manager Billy Barnie wired a formal protest to Association offices, but it went nowhere although his report on the episode did lead to Kerins being fined $20 for using "indecent language on the field."

From all reports, Baltimore probably was correct in that it was too dark by the 7th inning to continue. The statistics for both sides in Washington's half of the 7th inning were dismissed in any case.

Sources

Sporting Life, October 31, 1891.
Washington Post, October 6, 1891.

April 20, 1892

Place: Baltimore
Leagues: National League and American Association of Professional Base Ball Clubs (NLAAPBBC)
Field: Union Park
Clubs: Baltimore versus New York
Umpire: Michael Mahoney

On a cold clammy day in front of a sparse crowd and with his club leading 6–5 after five and a half innings were completed, Baltimore player-manager George Van Haltren announced to umpire Mahoney that the Orioles had to quit so they could catch a 5:55 p.m. train to Boston. New York captain and catcher Buck Ewing professed dismay as did Giants manager Pat Powers, but Van Haltren cited the game's unusually early starting time, 3:30 p.m. as evidence that it was expected to end by the team's necessary 5 p.m. departure time from the park. Mahoney sided with Ewing and Powers and forfeited the game to the Giants even though it was true that early in the season games in Baltimore regularly started at 4 p.m.

Afterward Baltimore vice president Billy Waltz produced written evidence that he had informed Powers of the necessity to have his men at the park early and proof that Powers had acceded to his request and also to allowing the Orioles to depart before the game was completed if that became necessary. Waltz and Baltimore owner Harry Vonderhorst also attested that Mahoney had been brought into the loop in advance, but when the issue arose during the game the umpire "was excited and was influenced by the arguments ... of the New York club, not listening to anything the representatives of the Baltimore club said."

The decision to uphold the forfeit appears to have fixated on Section 52 of the 1892 rules which required that a game be started three and a half hours before the departure of the last train. Even though he had evidently agreed to the 3:30 p.m. starting time, Powers prevailed when he said the game should have been started at 2:20 p.m. Withal, it looks as though the Giants got a cheap win in every sense of the word.

SOURCES

Brooklyn Daily Eagle, April 21, 1892.
New York Times, April 21, 1892.
Sporting Life, April 30, 1892.
Washington Post, April 21, 1892.

April 23, 1892

Place: Chicago
Leagues: National League and American Association of Professional Base Ball Clubs
Field: West Side Park II
Clubs: Chicago versus Louisville
Umpire: Jack Sheridan

Prior to the game about 1,000 of the crowd of some 8,500 broke down the barrier separating the cheap 25¢ bleacher seats from the posh 50¢ and $1 grandstand seats, enabling spectators to enter the playing field and accounting for the riot that eventually halted the game. The contest started out in sunny warm weather, but by the 9th inning it was a raw cold day. With Chicago leading 4 to 2, a fierce fight with chair cushions broke out between the crowd in the stands and the crowd lining the outfield. "In less than a minute the stands were practically deserted, and the field was in possession of the mob," reported the *Brooklyn Daily Eagle.* Fearing a forfeit, Chicago player-manager Cap Anson tried to quell the disturbance single-handedly by taking a bat to the rowdies. Louisville players, knowing a gift win was in the offing, joined in the fray by throwing chair cushions also. Eventually Anson cleared the field with the help of police and umpire Sheridan, but Louisville captain and second baseman, Fred Pfeffer, a former Chicago star who had become Anson's bitter enemy by 1892, refused to play. The crowd then mutinied again and once again Anson and Sheridan helped clear the field. When Pfeffer still refused to play, claiming that the conditions were unsafe, the crowd poured back onto the field. Anson and Sheridan could not clear the field a third time and the umpire had no alternative but to award the game to Louisville.

This was the first forfeit in ML history that was a direct result of the not infrequent crowd class-war clashes in the game's early years between the well-to-do and the rabble. Ironically, prior to the game the recalcitrant Pfeffer had been presented with an elegant floral piece by his erstwhile adoring fans and also serenaded by an amateur band organized for the occasion.

SOURCES

Brooklyn Daily Eagle, April 24, 1892.
Chicago Tribune, April 24, 1892.
Sporting Life, April 30, 1892.

May 10, 1892

Place: Pittsburgh
League: National League and American Association of Professional Base Ball Clubs
Field: Exposition Park II
Clubs: Pittsburgh versus New York
Umpire: Jimmy Macullar

A heavy rain fell all morning and into the afternoon, and Pittsburgh was compelled to employ a gang of men to prepare the field for the advertised 4 p.m. start time. The field was made playable eventually in Pittsburgh's opinion, but a slight drizzle would not let up. Nevertheless umpire Macullar called, "Play" sometime after 4:00—sources conflict as to the exact time. Just so, New York manager Pat Powers removed his team from the field at 4:10 p.m. claiming "a right to do so under the rules, as the game was not called on the advertised time, 4 o'clock." Powers's actions may have been governed by his view that the field was still unfit for play, but Macullar was hamstrung by Rule 29 of the 1892 edition of the playing rules, which read: "The choice of innings shall be given to the Captain of the Home Club, who shall also be the sole judge of the fitness of the ground for beginning a game after rain." Since Pittsburgh wanted the game to proceed, albeit a few minutes late, Macullar had to declare a forfeit.

SOURCES

Brooklyn Daily Eagle, May 11, 1892.
New York Times, May 11, 1892.
Sporting Life, May 28, 1892.

August 16, 1892

Place: Pittsburgh
Leagues: National League and American Association of Professional Base Ball Clubs
Field: Exposition Park II
Clubs: Pittsburgh versus Washington
Umpire: Charlie Mitchell

With the score knotted at 2-all in the bottom of the 10th frame and Pittsburgh shortstop Frank Shugart perched on first base with one out, Pirates left fielder Doggie Miller was hit on the left arm below the elbow by a Jesse Duryea pitch. Washington claimed that Miller had purposely let the ball hit him, a common occurrence at that time. Miller put on a somber face and maintained, "with the air of a man arguing for his life that he had tried to get out of the way of the ball." Mitchell agreed with his plea and handed the game to Pittsburgh by forfeit when Washington continued to kick at his decision. According to *Sporting Life*, Washington never protested Mitchell's decision, nor did Pittsburgh follow through on its claim that it would request Washington be fined $1,000 for leaving the grounds before the game was completed.

Mitchell began the season as a substitute umpire but was assigned to a regular post in June when a regular umpire became ill. He quit a few days after this game and never umpired in the major leagues again.

Led by Curt Welch, so many batters deliberately allowed pitches to nick their hands and forearms after the hit batsman rule was universally installed in the game in 1887 that following the 1892 season Section 4 under Rule 46 was revised to deny a batsman his base if he was hit by a pitch in the hand or forearm. The revision to Section 4 was rescinded after a famous incident on May 2, 1896, that approached the height of absurdity when Brooklyn's Tom Daly suffered a broken wrist in a game against Louisville when he was struck by a pitch but had to convince the umpire the ball hit him on the shoulder to get his base.

SOURCES

Brooklyn Daily Eagle, August 17, 1892.
Nemec, David. *Major League Baseball Profiles: 1871–1900* (Lincoln: University of Nebraska Press, 2011), 1: 351.

Nemec, David. *The Rank and File of 19th Century Major League Baseball* (Jefferson, NC: McFarland, 2012), 284.
Spalding's Official Base Ball Guide, 1893.
Sporting Life, September 10, 1892.
Washington Post, August 17, 1892.

September 22, 1892

Place: Pittsburgh
Leagues: National League and American Association of Professional Base Ball Clubs
Field: Exposition Park II
Clubs: Pittsburgh versus Chicago
Umpire: John Gaffney

In the top of the 5th inning, with Pittsburgh leading 9 to 2 after scoring four runs, the Colts did their best not to retire Pittsburgh players, hoping that the threatening skies would open before the game became official. Their behavior was deplored by player-manager Cap Anson and umpire Gaffney alike. With two outs and Chicago clearly making no effort to get the third out, Gaffney gave the game to Pittsburgh. Authorities today remain in disagreement about whether this game was later thrown out, but there is evidence that its statistics at the very least were counted. The game, in any case, is of utmost importance to forfeit mavens because if it is counted then Pittsburgh was the beneficiary of four home forfeit wins in 1892, tying the record set by the 1886 Washington Nationals.

SOURCES

Brooklyn Daily Eagle, September 23, 1892.
Chicago Tribune, September 23, 1892.

October 12, 1892

Place: Pittsburgh
League: National League and American Association of Professional Base Ball Clubs
Field: Exposition Park II
Clubs: Pittsburgh versus Cleveland
Umpire: John Gaffney

The previous day's game between the two teams had ended in a 4–4 tie called by darkness after nine innings. Pittsburgh wanted to replay it on the afternoon of October 12 and according to the rules notified all concerned. Cleveland had a benefit game scheduled back in the Forest City on the 12th, however, and left Pittsburgh on an early train that morning. Gaffney thus declared on the afternoon of the 12th that Pittsburgh would receive a forfeit win for the game of the 11th. No pitching decisions were awarded. Cleveland was not happy upon being notified of the forfeit loss but did not protest it as vigorously as it surely would have if it had not already clinched first place in the second half of the only split season in ML history except for the 1981 strike year. What's more, the benefit game at Cleveland's League Park on October 12 between members of the Spiders and the Cleveland Athletic Club netted each Spiders player $100, not a trifling sum in the season following the merger or the NL and the AA when many lesser players were making under $1,000.

SOURCES

Sporting Life, October 15, 1892.
Washington Post, October 12, 1892.

September 16, 1893

Place: Cleveland
Leagues: National League and American Association of Professional Base Ball Clubs
Field: League Park I
Clubs: Cleveland versus Baltimore
Umpire: Tim Hurst

Once Cleveland had scored four runs in the top of the 8th inning to take a 15–11 lead in front of 500 chilled spectators, Baltimore catcher Wilbert Robinson decided it was too dark to continue play and refused to return the ball to his pitcher, Kirtley Baker, despite being ordered to do so by umpire Hurst three times. Hurst then forfeited the game to Cleveland. In addition to the dwindling light a gale force wind had blown through the park the entire game, and Baltimore had wanted the game halted as soon as Cleveland got two runners on base in the 8th frame. Cy Young was credited with a win in the game and Baker took the loss.

SOURCES

Boston Globe, September 17, 1893.
Brooklyn Daily Eagle, September 17, 1893.
Sporting Life, September 23, 1893.

May 1, 1894

Place: Washington
League: National League and American Association of Professional Base Ball Clubs
Field: Boundary Field
Clubs: Washington versus Brooklyn
Umpire: Billy Stage

Trailing 2–1 in the bottom of the 6th inning on Ladies Day at the park, Brooklyn filled the bases on an infield single by pitcher Jack Sharrott, a single to left field by second baseman Tom Daly, a sacrifice bunt by center fielder Mike Griffin and an intentional base on balls issued to left fielder George Treadway against the loud protests of many of the spectators calling for rarely used pitcher Ben Stephens to let Treadway hit the ball. Player-manager Dave Foutz then drilled "a hot one" to Kip Selbach, an outfielder filling in that day at shortstop. Selbach fielded the ball cleanly and stepped on second to force Treadway, the runner on first, and then threw to first baseman Ed Cartwright to complete the double play and seemingly end the Bridegrooms' threat. But Stage called Foutz safe, which allowed Sharrott to score from third and tie the game. While captain and third baseman Bill Joyce and the rest of Washington's infielders surrounded Stage and were arguing with him, they were joined by utility man Piggy Ward, who was not in the game that day. During the heated conference, since time had apparently not been called, Daly came around from second base to score the go-ahead run. According to the *Washington Post*, Stage forfeited the game "less than one minute after the argument started" and "did not, according to the rules, walk up to home plate and call on the team to play ball."

The Brooklyn Daily Eagle, in contrast, reported that as the argument began Stage calmly took out his watch and gave Joyce three minutes to return to the field. When Joyce continued to "kick," Stage gave the game to Brooklyn. Joyce, seeing that Stage was serious, attempted to re-take the field, but Stage would not reverse his decision. Meanwhile Brooklyn, also apparently expecting the umpire to change his mind, waited on its bench. The Brooklyn players had already had an eventful day. They were forced to evacuate their hotel at 5 a.m. due to a fire. During their visit to the Capital later that morning, they witnessed Coxey's army and the police in a vicious confrontation. This protest march by United States unemployed workers, initially led by Ohio business man Jacob Coxey, began in Ohio on March 25, 1894, with 100 men and gained followers as it moved toward Washington, D.C. By April 30, the "army" had 500 recruits and on May 1, with the Bridegrooms in attendance, Coxey and other leaders of the movement were arrested when they walked on the grass of the United States Capital.

Washington subsequently protested to no avail to the league that Stage's assertion that Joyce refused to continue to play was incorrect. Joyce, however, was ultimately successful in protesting the $1,000 fine the league levied against his team for refusing to play. There had previously been reports from Washington claiming that Stage had been uniformly against the Senators in all games he officiated involving them, and this incident evidently helped substantiate them. Stage was seldom scheduled to work games that involved Washington after that.

Stage first appeared as a NL umpire a few months after equaling the world record in the hundred-yard dash, but apart from his speed in racing around to make his calls, he seemingly lacked the essentials to make a satisfactory umpire and officiated less than 50 ML games. However, *Sporting Life* went out of its way to compliment him on "his firmness of purpose, which he showed so strikingly in that Washington forfeiture."

Never blessed with great luck, Stephens lost a chance to raise his career record to 2–7 in what proved to be his final ML appearance. Little more than two years later he died of consumption

Sources

Brooklyn Daily Eagle, May 21, 1894.
Nemec, David. *The Rank and File of 19th Century Major League Baseball* (Jefferson, NC: McFarland, 2012), 78.
New York Times, May 21, 1894.
Sporting Life, June 2, 1894.
Washington Post, May 2, 1894.

May 26, 1894

Place: Cleveland
Leagues: National League and American Association of Professional Base Ball Clubs
Field: League Park I
Clubs: Cleveland versus Pittsburgh
Umpire: Bob Emslie

With Cleveland trailing 12–3 and only one out to go before the Spiders were officially defeated, many in the near record Cleveland crowd of some 9,000 had already long since abandoned the park. Several boys in the bleachers, out of boredom as much as anything else, idly started heaving seat cushions at the Pirates' outfielders. Umpire Emslie waited 15 minutes for the police to get control of the hooligans. But by then several of them had streamed onto the playing field, putting the Pittsburgh fielders in harm's way, and he forfeited the game.

SOURCES

Brooklyn Daily Eagle, May 27, 1894.
Los Angeles Times, May 27, 1894.
Sporting Life, July 2, 1894.
Washington Post, May 27, 1894.

May 26, 1894

Place: Philadelphia
League: National League and American Association of Professional Base Ball Clubs
Field: Philadelphia Baseball Grounds
Clubs: Philadelphia versus Boston
Umpire: Dan Campbell

With rain already falling, the Phillies scored seven runs in the top of the 8th inning to take a commanding 8–2 lead. Boston at that point stopped trying to retire batters in an attempt to delay the action long enough for the rain to increase to a degree that umpire Campbell would have to cease play, in which case the score would have reverted to 2–1 Boston where it had stood after seven innings.

Campbell, who was subbing for ailing Billy Stage, watched four more Phillies traipse across the plate before taking matters into his own hands and calling Sam Thompson out for purposely missing second base on his return to first after rounding the bag on a long foul by Ed Delahanty. Boston captain and third baseman Billy Nash made a loud outcry that Campbell couldn't declare Thompson out since the Beaneaters had not called the missed base to his attention. "Finally, after his usual warning," Campbell forfeited the game to Philadelphia. To vent their disgust, the crowd then stormed the field and began slugging every Boston player that had not made his escape quickly enough. During the melee, Boston first baseman Tommy Tucker sustained a broken left cheekbone when he forgot his sweater and returned to bench to retrieve it. Two men were arrested after the riot, William Leonard and Lavis Sailor, but denied having any part in the assault. It eventually took 25 policemen and several Philadelphia players to escort the Boston players safely to their awaiting buggy.

Campbell's ruling was expeditious, especially under the circumstances, but eminently incorrect. While Thompson's act unquestionably violated the rules, he could not be called out for simply not re-touching second base. In order for Boston to put him out, one of its fielders, with the ball in hand would have needed to step on second base or touch Thompson with the ball, before he re-touched second base. If the Beaneaters had been able to mount any sort of plausible defense for their stalling tactics, they would have had a valid protest.

Even more so that 1884, when there were three major leagues, 1894 was the most fertile year in ML history for forfeits. May 26, 1894, and September 24, 1884, are the only two occasions when there were two forfeited games in the majors on the same day.

SOURCES

Boston Globe, May 27, 1894.
Brooklyn Daily Eagle, May 27, 1894.
Nemec, David. *The Rank and File of 19th Century Major League Baseball* (Jefferson, NC: McFarland, 2012), 281.
New York Times, May 27, 1894.
Spalding's Official Base Ball Guide, 1894.

August 3, 1894

Place: Louisville
Leagues: National League and American Association of Professional Base Ball Clubs
Field: Eclipse Park II
Clubs: Louisville versus Chicago
Umpire: Tom Lynch

When Chicago player-manager Cap Anson refused to play with the balls Louisville furnished, umpire Lynch forfeited the game to the home team. Anson had also protested the balls used the day before to league president Nick Young, claiming they were "punky," and one of his substitute catchers, Kit Kittridge, gave a leftover "lively" ball from the Players League to outfielder Walt Wilmot, who then somehow slipped it into play, bringing an official protest from Louisville manager Billy Barnie after the Colts tallied all four runs in the 5th inning of their 4–3 win before Lynch "took the ball out of the game." Barnie then managed to secure it as evidence, but his protest nonetheless was dismissed.

New balls had been sent several days earlier by the league office to both clubs, arriving in time for the game of August 3. Prior to the contest, Lynch took the balls furnished by Colonels captain Tom Brown out of the same package as Anson's allotment of the shipment, making it seem that Anson wrongly assumed his stature would sway Lynch to disallow the balls Brown proffered and perhaps let Chicago ring in another batch of "lively" balls. However, there had been complaints for some weeks from rival teams coming into Louisville that the balls the Colonels provided had about as much life as bean bags, so there may have been more to the incident than the slim amount of information we have thus far been able to unearth. We do know that Anson evidently felt the forfeiture was worth it, for *Sporting Life* remarked that "it is hard to see how Chicago will be able to avoid paying the $1,000 fine imposed for leaving the field."

SOURCES

Brooklyn Daily Eagle, August 4, 1894.
Chicago Tribune, August 3, 1894, and August 4, 1894.
Sporting Life, August 11, 1894.
Washington Post, August 4, 1894.

September 5, 1894

Place: Washington
Leagues: National League and American Association of Professional Base Ball Clubs
Field: Boundary Field
Clubs: Washington versus St. Louis
Umpire: Bill Betts

After Washington scored four runs in the top of the 9th inning to pull ahead 7–4, the Browns wanted the game stopped due to darkness so the score would revert to 4–3 in favor of the Browns after eight innings of play. When Betts refused St. Louis began stalling until he was finally driven to award the game to Washington by forfeit.

Even the partisan *Washington Post* felt Betts's decisions during the game that day went mostly against St. Louis to atone for his failure the previous day to call the game after five innings owing to darkness with Washington ahead. The game, according to the *Post*, was snail-paced from the outset with frequent delays attributable to St. Louis's stalling tactics, and Betts was scorched by the paper not only for allowing the game to continue long enough for St. Louis to score six runs in the 6th frame and pull ahead 10–7 but also for several bad calls.

A machinist by trade, that winter Betts, by no means an ineffectual umpire, invented a new indicator that was smaller and more reliable than the old model and distributed one to each NL staff member prior to the 1895 season.

S<small>OURCES</small>

Brooklyn Daily Eagle, September 6, 1894.
Nemec, David. *Major League Baseball Profiles: 1871–1900* (Lincoln: University of Nebraska Press, 2011), 2: 201.
Washington Post, August 4, 1894, September 5, 1894, and September 6, 1894.

May 23, 1895

Place: Louisville
Leagues: National League and American Association of Professional Base Ball Clubs
Field: Eclipse Park II
Clubs: Louisville versus Brooklyn
Umpire: Bill Betts

The Brooklyn Bridegrooms, after their previous series at Cleveland, discovered their practice baseballs were missing. When they arrived at Louisville's field, Brooklyn player-manager Dave Foutz asked Louisville manager John McCloskey for a couple of balls to practice with. Customarily the home club provided two practice baseballs for the visiting team at market rate or simply by common courtesy. If by the latter, the visiting team would reciprocate when the home team played on their grounds. McCloskey stated there were only five balls total on the Louisville grounds, two of them practice balls that his own club needed to use, and sent Foutz to see the officials in the park's office and inquire if more could be rousted up. At 2:55 p.m. Foutz was told that a messenger had been sent into the town to get "a new supply."

The game began at 3:30 p.m. with three new baseballs whereas ordinarily a dozen new balls would have been on hand. Two of the new balls were hit over the fence, one on a leadoff home run by Brooklyn captain and center fielder Mike Griffin, in the top of the first inning. The home run ball was never returned. The third new ball "was sent out of sight" in the bottom of the second inning by Louisville's pint-sized outfielder Dan Sweeney. Neither Brooklyn manager Foutz nor his captain, Griffin, asked for a new ball on this occasion, perhaps expecting at least one of the lost new balls would soon be returned. In the top of the third inning, with two men out, Brooklyn third baseman Billy Shindle hit a long foul over the leftfield fence. Since none of the new balls had as yet been returned, Griffin now called for a new ball to be put into play. Louisville was unable to produce one. Umpire Betts gave the Louisville team between eight and ten minutes to comply, and when they were unable to do so he awarded the game to Brooklyn via forfeit. Brooklyn was leading 3–1 at the time. Betts had barely declared the game forfeited when the

Louisville messenger arrived on the grounds with a full box of new baseballs, claiming that a trolley accident detained him. A five-inning exhibition match was played after the forfeit, which ended in a 2–2 tie. However, most of the crowd had already chosen to exit by then and receive tickets for a future game.

It would seem that since Louisville fielded a wretched team in 1895 Foutz could at the very least have tried to persuade Betts to rescind the forfeit and allow the game to resume for the sake of the crowd and to help a foundering fellow franchise if nothing else, especially since his team was leading at the time, but if he had it probably would have been a first. Teams, then as now, had little sympathy for the financial woes of their brethren.

SOURCES

Brooklyn Daily Eagle, May 24, 1895.
New York Times, May 24, 1895.

August 28, 1895

Place: Baltimore
Leagues: National League and American Association of Professional Base Ball Clubs
Field: Union Park
Clubs: Baltimore versus Pittsburgh
Umpires: Hank O'Day and Fred Jevne

Plate umpire O'Day declared the first game of a doubleheader forfeited to Baltimore when Pittsburgh had still not arrived at the park by the 2 p.m. starting time. The Pirates' train from Boston got them to the park in time for the second game which resulted in a 12–5 Orioles win, giving front-running Baltimore a sweep on the day. *Sporting Life* later said this forfeited game was thrown out; however, it was counted in the standings and remains so to this day.

SOURCES

New York Sun, August 29, 1895.
New York Times, August 29, 1895.
Sporting Life, August 30, 1895.

May 13, 1896

Place: Chicago
Leagues: National League and American Association of Professional Base Ball Clubs
Field: West Side Park II

Clubs: Chicago versus Boston
Umpires: Tim Keefe

The two clubs began the 11th inning tied at 4-all. After Boston pushed across four runs in the second extra frame, Chicago began stalling in the hope that umpire Keefe would call the game due to darkness. Intentional errors brought another Boston run, at which point Keefe gave the game to Boston to the wrath of every Chicagoan in attendance.

In the sixth inning, Keefe had refused to call interference on Boston first baseman Tommy Tucker when he "threw down" Chicago third baseman Bill Everitt as he rounded first on a ball hit to left field that would otherwise have been a sure double. The two started to fight and Everitt was tagged out. Chicago player-manager Cap Anson immediately notified Keefe that he was filling a protest. Keefe also refused to award the next batter, Chicago shortstop Bill Dahlen, a home run on a ball that was hit over the right field inner fence because it was retrieved before he could score. That hit, in which Dahlen was given a triple, would have tallied Everitt with the probable winning run. It appears to have been properly called by Keefe since the park rule then disallowed a batter an automatic home run on a ball hit into an enclosed area unoccupied by seats, giving him only the number of bases he could compile before a fielder retrieved it.

At the end of nine innings, Boston captain Hugh Duffy pleaded for the game to be stopped and called a tie so his club could catch a train to Pittsburgh. Chicago player-manager Cap Anson refused to support Duffy's request and demanded that the game continue. However, he changed his mind in the 11th inning and, in a rare action for a man who always played to win until the last out was recorded, opted to let his men play for a forfeit rather than to the game's completion so that he could then protest it to the league office. The protest was ignored by NL president Nick Young since it was based entirely on an umpire's decision. Reference works, in conflict for years on this game, now carry the score as 9–4 at the time of the forfeit and count all the statistics that were compiled prior to its declaration.

SOURCES

Brooklyn Daily Eagle, May 14, 1896.
Chicago Tribune, May 14, 1896.

July 24, 1896

Place: St. Louis
Leagues: National League and American Association of Professional Base Ball Clubs

Field: Sportsman's Park II
Clubs: St. Louis versus Baltimore
Umpire: Bob Emslie

In the top of the fourth extra frame, after Baltimore notched five runs to make the score 13–8, St. Louis began stalling at every opportunity and urging umpire Emslie to stop the onslaught owing to darkness. Emslie insisted it was still light enough for Baltimore to be retired and the Browns to get their final at-bats in the 13th inning. When the stalling continued he gave the game to the Orioles. Bill Hoffer was credited with a win since Baltimore led at the time and Red Donahue, then in his first full big league season, took the loss. The following year Donahue would lose a post–1892 record 35 games.

SOURCES

Brooklyn Daily Eagle, July 25, 1896.
Chicago Tribune, July 25, 1896.
Los Angeles Times, July 25, 1896.

May 3, 1897

Place: Washington
League: National League and American Association of Professional Base Ball Clubs
Field: Boundary Field
Clubs: Washington versus New York
Umpire: Tom Lynch

On a cold rainy afternoon in the Nation's Capital, the Giants led 9–0 in the bottom of the 4th inning with two out and were deliberately making outs as rapidly as they could so that they could retire Washington in the top of the 5th and make the game official before the downpour became too heavy. Washington, meanwhile, was stalling at every opportunity but in such a "clumsy manner" that umpire Lynch tired of the farce and gave the game to New York. Washington owner J. Earle Wagner registered an official protest that Lynch should have forfeited the game to his team instead when it became obvious the Giants were no longer trying to score, which, after all, was the entire purpose of the game. Unsurprisingly, Wagner's complaint was not taken very seriously by league president Nick Young.

SOURCES

Brooklyn Daily Eagle, May 4, 1897.
Los Angeles Times, May 4, 1897.

New York Times, May 4, 1897.
Sporting Life, May 8, 1897.
Washington Post, May 4, 1897.

June 1, 1897

Place: New York
League: National League and American Association of Professional Base Ball Clubs
Field: Polo Grounds III
Clubs: New York versus Pittsburgh
Umpire: Sandy McDermott

The Pirates led 7–0 going into the bottom of the 7th inning, but there had been continual carping at umpire McDermott from player-manager Patsy Donovan, the rare skipper who ran his team from his right field slot, and his pitcher Frank Killen. New York suddenly rallied and posted four runs on three singles and a double. Poor fielding by Pittsburgh aided the Giants' cause. After Ducky Holmes's ground ball was booted by Pittsburgh shortstop Bones Ely, allowing the third and fourth runs to score, Parke Wilson's easy bounder was bobbled by second baseman Dick Padden. Padden snatched up the ball in time to get Holmes who was racing past him to second base but missed the tag and then threw too late to first baseman Harry Davis in an attempt to put out Wilson. McDermott declared both men safe and the entire Pittsburgh team ran from their positions in the field and surrounded him, shouting that while Wilson might have been safe Holmes unquestionably had been tagged out. Violent language spewed forth along with threats and gestures at McDermott after he ejected Killen, Padden and Donovan and ordered the rest of the Pirates to resume their positions. The ejected trio refused to leave the field and McDermott awarded the game to New York. The home crowd then sprinted out on the field and all but carried McDermott from it, applauding him all the way for his brave stand against the rowdy Pirates.

Since Pittsburgh led 7–4 at the time the game was forfeited no pitching decisions were recorded.

SOURCES

Brooklyn Daily Eagle, June 2, 1897.
New York Times, June 2, 1897.
Sporting Life, June 12, 1897.

June 4, 1897

Place: Philadelphia
Leagues: National League and American Association of Professional Base Ball Clubs
Field: Philadelphia Baseball Grounds II
Clubs: Philadelphia versus Pittsburgh
Umpire: Jim McDonald

Three days after their calamitous forfeit loss in New York the Pirates found themselves in Philadelphia on an overcast afternoon trailing 4–0 in the 4th inning when Pirates catcher Joe Sugden lined a shot over the third base bag that umpire McDonald ruled foul. Led by player-manager Patsy Donovan, Pittsburgh mounted such a vicious protest that McDonald eventually fined Donovan and ejected him and also fined first baseman Harry Davis and pitcher Frank Killen. After Pittsburgh took the field for the 5th inning with Charlie Kuhns, an infielder by trade, in Donovan's outfield spot, during warm-ups with first baseman Davis while he waited for Sugden to put on his catching gear Killen threw a pitch over Davis's head and into the crowd, resulting in a stoppage while Davis awaited the ball's return. Philadelphia catcher Jack Boyle howled that Pittsburgh was purposely delaying the game in hopes it would rain, which was almost certainly true. In any event, McDonald awarded the game to Philadelphia. A few moments after play was stopped it began to pour.

Sources

New York Times, June 5, 1897.
Sporting Life, June 12, 1897.
Washington Post, June 5, 1897.

July 24, 1897

Place: Cleveland
League: National League and American Association of Professional Base Ball Clubs
Field: League Park I
Clubs: Cleveland versus Philadelphia
Umpires: Tom McGinty and Jack Boyle

Bob Emslie, one of the scheduled umpires, was sent to Cincinnati instead at the last minute, and Philadelphia catcher Jack Boyle, who otherwise had the day off, was drafted to assist novice umpire McGinty, working only his fourth ML game, on the bases. Prior to the game Phillies manager George

Stallings protested McGinty's presence and was assured by Cleveland player-manager Pat Tebeau that he was not only a regular substitute but "a thoroughly honest and competent young man." With Philadelphia leading 4–3 going into the 9th inning, McGinty allowed Cleveland catcher Chief Zimmer to take his base on balls. The next batter, first baseman Tebeau, received two called balls, and Philadelphia launched a lengthy protest that McGinty was squeezing its pitcher, Jack Fifield. Order was restored and the next three pitches brought the count to full when the third was also called a ball. Philadelphia again began to rag on McGinty for his faulty eyesight. "The epithets hurled" at him "could be heard plainly all over the ground." Play was nonetheless quickly resumed, but when McGinty called the next pitch a ball, giving Tebeau his base, Philadelphia refused to continue. McGinty waited three minutes for the Phillies to take the field and then awarded the game to Cleveland, which happened to be his lifelong home. It was the last ML game he ever umpired.

No pitching decisions were awarded since Philadelphia led at the time of the forfeit.

SOURCES

Boston Globe, July 25, 1897.
Sporting Life, July 31, 1897.

August 1, 1897

Place: St. Louis
League: National League
Field: Sportsman's Park II
Clubs: St. Louis versus Louisville
Umpires: Charlie Dexter and Red Donahue

The brother of ML players Dan and Alex McFarlan, Horace McFarlan worked the first game of a scheduled Sunday doubleheader at St. Louis, won 8–1 by Louisville. McFarlan had been one of the youngest men ever appointed a regular ML umpire when he was named to the job at age 22 on July 7, 1896, prior to a game at Louisville. He hailed from PeeWee Valley near Louisville and spent his first three weeks in the NL working games only in the Falls City. According to *The Sporting News,* "As soon as he was sent away from Louisville he was chased out of the game and resigned." But McFarlan then reconsidered and returned briefly to the NL officiating ranks in 1897; however, he had the ill luck to be assigned to the twinbill in St. Louis on one of the hottest days that summer in the Mound City. On the verge of passing out from heat prostration after the first game, he staggered from the park and never umpired another day in the majors.

With McFarlan unavailable for the second game, each team chose a player from its roster to carry on in his stead. Louisville selected utility man Charlie Dexter and St. Louis chose pitcher Red Donahue. The game moved along fairly smoothly until the bottom of the 9th inning. Louisville had tallied two runs in the top of the frame to take a 5–4 lead. Then "in the second half of the ninth inning when [Tuck] Turner went to bat, he knocked a foul fly and a new ball was given to [Louisville starter Bert] Cunningham. He rolled it in the dirt, when Donahue [working the plate] objected and handed him another new one. Five fresh balls in all were handed to Cunningham, and all treated alike." The exasperated Donahue at that pointed awarded the game to his St. Louis club by forfeit. The forfeit was later overruled by NL president Nick Young, though one must wonder why. If indeed five new balls were deliberately soiled by Cunningham, it would seem that anyone umpiring in that situation had ample provocation to stop play and declare a forfeit. Yet it is entirely possible that Cunningham simply resented having to work with a new ball when his team had batted in the top of the inning against an old one and was merely trying to even matters. One might wonder how St. Louis could even have a supply of five new balls on hand that late in the game when several contests not that much earlier in the 1890's had been forfeited because the home team no longer had any. But the doubleheader had drawn a Sunday crowd of around 10,000 and the "Done Browns," as they were known by then were evidently in an expansive mood on that day, even though they were not about to escape an abysmal cellar finish.

SOURCES

Boston Globe, August 2, 1897.
Nemec, David. The Rank and File of 19th Century Major League Baseball (Jefferson, NC: McFarland, 2012), 283–284.
Sporting Life, August 7, 1897.
The Sporting News, August 1, 1896.

August 4, 1897

Place: Louisville
Leagues: National League and American Association of Professional Base Ball Clubs
Field: Eclipse Park II
Clubs: Louisville versus Cleveland
Umpire: Jimmy Wolf

Tim Hurst had umpired the game in Louisville the previous day but was sent to work on August 4 in Cincinnati, where he ended the afternoon in jail for throwing a beer stein into the crowd there and skulling a spectator. Meanwhile his replacement in Louisville was former Colonels outfielder Jimmy Wolf, now working as an occasional umpiring sub. In the first game of a scheduled doubleheader Louisville led 3–2 in the 2nd inning with Cleveland left fielder Jesse Burkett at the plate. Burkett, in taking exception to one of Wolf's strike calls, referred to him by a vile name. Wolf ejected Burkett from the game, and when Cleveland player-manager Pat Tebeau refused to insert a substitute batter, Wolf waited five minutes and then awarded the game to Louisville.

But Wolf had not seen the last of Burkett that day, for players ejected in the first game of a twinbill were at that time allowed to return to the lineup in the nightcap. With Louisville comfortably ahead 7–4 in the 9th inning, Burkett again insulted Wolf and was ordered to leave the field, marking his second ejection of the day. Burkett refused to vacate his spot as a runner on first base. Wolf finally summoned two policemen who had to forcibly assist the Cleveland outfielder in leaving the grounds. Burkett's removal allowed the game to continue to its conclusion and the 11th place Colonels to bank a rare doubleheader sweep.

Sources

Louisville Courier-Journal, August 5, 1897.
New York Times, August 5, 1897.

September 8, 1897

Place: Washington
Leagues: National League and American Association of Professional Base Ball Clubs
Field: Boundary Field
Clubs: Washington versus Cleveland
Umpire: Bill Carpenter

During the second game of a doubleheader, with Washington leading 6–2 in the 5th inning, Cleveland had two on and two out with shortstop Ed McKean due up. While he was leaving the on deck circle on his way to the plate, player-manager Pat Tebeau, who was coaching third base, came part way down the third base line to tell him sotto voce to let a pitch by novice Washington hurler Roger Bresnahan hit him. But umpire Carpenter's sharp ears overheard Tebeau, and when McKean was hit on Bresnahan's second pitch, a slow curve, he was denied his base. Tebeau argued the point awhile and then refused to continue the game, giving Carpenter an easy decision to make—forfeit to Washington—that was no doubt made even easier by Carpenter's attitude toward Tebeau ever since he'd had to eject him in the first game of the twinbill for excessive kicking..

Because the game did not go five innings, Bresnahan was denied a probable win that would have enabled him to finish the season 5–0 instead of 4–0, which would have set a new record for the most wins in a season by a pitcher without a loss.

SOURCES

New York Times, September 9, 1897.
Sporting Life, September 18, 1897.
Washington Post, September 9, 1897.

September 10, 1897

Place: Baltimore
Leagues: National League and American Association of Professional Base Ball Clubs
Field: Union Park
Clubs: Baltimore versus Louisville
Umpire: "Honest" John Kelly

With the game tied at 5-all in the bottom of the 7th inning umpire Kelly called Orioles outfielder Willie Keeler safe at first on a bang-bang play, allowing Baltimore's Joe Quinn to score the go-ahead run. From the outset, the game had swiftly evolved into a long string of squabbles with Kelly, leaving Louisville convinced it was almost always getting the worst of them. Colonels outfielder Charlie Dexter had already been ejected, and player-manager Fred Clarke feared that he too was soon headed for an early shower. Rather than continue, he pulled his team from the field, and Kelly forfeited the game to the Orioles.

This was one of the last contests that the once-illustrious Kelly umpired. He had returned to officiating in 1897 after a nine-year hiatus, during which he ran a gambling establishment and also served as a boxing referee. By 1897 the rowdyism that had permeated the game made his nights in the ring seem tame in comparison. In the 39 games he worked that season before leaving the umpiring ranks forever he was forced to eject no less than 15 players and managers. In his lone forfeit game as an official, Kelly fined Clarke, Louisville's battery of pitcher Bill Magee and catcher Bill Wilson, and Baltimore's Joe Kelley $25 apiece in addition, a fairly hefty sum at the time.

"Honest" John Kelly is outranked only by John Gaffney as the nineteenth century's most influential umpire. Ostensibly nothing he did during his career in blue belied his nickname, but historians have noted that home teams won significantly more than their expected share of games that he officiated.

SOURCES

Brooklyn Daily Eagle, September 11, 1897.
New York Times, September 11, 1897.
Sporting Life, September 18, 1897.

July 25, 1898

Place: New York
Leagues: National League and American Association of Professional Base Ball Clubs
Field: Polo Grounds III

Clubs: New York versus Baltimore
Umpire: Tom Lynch

This game ranks high on everyone's list of infamous forfeits. In the fourth inning, with the score tied at one apiece, Baltimore left fielder Ducky Holmes was fanned by New York pitcher Jouett Meekin. While he was returning to the bench a spectator flung a derogatory comment at him about his hitting ability. Holmes bristled as he faced the crowd and said loudly, "Well, I may be a lobster, but I'm f******g glad that I don't work for a Sheeny anymore." New York Owner Andrew Freedman heard the remark while seated in the upper grandstand. He instantly sent a representative to tell Baltimore manager Ned Hanlon to remove Holmes from the game. Hanlon directed Freedman's man to speak to umpire Lynch, who said he hadn't heard the remark. When Baltimore took the field, Freedman entered the diamond area and sent a police officer to remove Holmes from left field. Lynch stated to Freedman that there were no grounds for Holmes's removal from the game and that if action wasn't allowed to continue with Holmes still on the field, he'd award the game to Baltimore. After Freedman instructed player-manager Bill Joyce not to send a man to bat unless Holmes was removed, Lynch made Baltimore the victor by forfeit.

Immediately upon learning the game had been stopped spectators near Freedman demanded their money back and he eventually announced that all who paid to attend (about 2,500) would receive a refund if they wanted it. He later stated that he would report Holmes to the Board of Discipline and that Baltimore would not receive its share of the gate money since no game was played. Baltimore owner Harry Vonderhorst angrily said he would appeal to the National League for his club's allotment of the gate money. As per the Constitution of the NLAAPBBC, New York was socked with a $1,000 fine for forfeiting a game, and Freedman incurred a $1,500 fine in addition. Freedman also demanded that Holmes be suspended for the remainder of the season. Never known for his brave stances when confronted by a thorny situation, league president Nick Young compromised by fining Freedman and suspended Holmes indefinitely. Freedman traveled to Europe and while he was on "holiday," Young quietly rescinded his fine and reinstated Holmes.

Freedman formally protested each game in which Holmes appeared for the rest of the 1898 season, but no one paid him any mind. Holmes played 136 games in 1898 and was a Baltimore regular again the following year when he enjoyed his best season, hitting a solid .320. But Freedman then appears to have gotten a measure of comeuppance, for Holmes was left without a team in the NLAAPBBC when the league downsized from 12 clubs to eight after the 1899 season.

SOURCES

Brooklyn Daily Eagle, July 26, 1898.
Nemec, David. *Major League Baseball Profiles: 1871–1900* (Lincoln: University of Nebraska Press, 2011), 1: 558–559 and 2: 164–165.
New York Times, July 26, 1898.

September 16, 1898

Place: Philadelphia
Leagues: National League and American Association of Professional Base Ball Clubs
Field: Philadelphia Base Ball Grounds II
Clubs: Philadelphia versus Chicago
Umpire: John Gaffney

With Chicago leading 2 to 1 in the 5th inning of the first game of a doubleheader on a wet day, Philadelphia catcher Ed McFarland stumbled past the plate on a throw home by Chicago outfielder Bill Lange and fell in the mud on the other side of it. While McFarland lay there mustering himself, Chicago catcher Tim Donahue patiently straddled the plate waiting to tag him. In the judgment of umpire Gaffney, however, McFarland managed to elude the tag on his dive back to the plate and scored the tying run. Acting Chicago captain Sam Mertes argued that while McFarland might have dodged Donahue's tag, he had gone out of the baseline in his initial plunge, but he kicked too long and Gaffney eventually ejected him. When Mertes refused to leave the game, Gaffney declared it forfeited to Philadelphia.

When Chicago rebounded to win the second game handily, 10–5, it seemingly achieved a split on the day, but over the years this game, for unknown reasons, was determined not to be a regulation contest, although it is still counted as such in several reference works.

SOURCES

Brooklyn Daily Eagle, September 17, 1898.
New York Times, September 17, 1898.

May 19, 1899

Place: St. Louis
Leagues: National League and American Association of Professional Base Ball Clubs
Field: Sportsman's Park II
Clubs: St. Louis versus New York
Umpires: Tommy Burns and Billy Smith

With New York up 10 -3 going into the bottom of the 6th inning, Giants pitcher Jouett Meekin encountered a sudden wild streak, giving up five walks along with three singles, leading to six runs. Southpaw Ed Doheny was summoned from the bench to relieve Meekin. While Doheny was warming up, New York captain and second baseman Kid Gleason used the interlude to question plate umpire Burns's decisions on balls and strikes. Gleason's opinions of Burns's judgment grew increasingly heated. When they showed no signs of abating after Doheny completed his warm-up tosses, Burns ejected Gleason for interference and indecent language. Meanwhile Giants manager John Day, who was not in uniform and thus not allowed to come on the field, could only plead with his captain to desist from his spot on the bench.

When Gleason refused to leave the field, "after waiting four minutes" the former Brooklyn and New York outfielder Burns declared a forfeit win for St. Louis. Earlier in the game Burns had ejected St. Louis player-manager Pat Tebeau, who left without an argument. The *Brooklyn Daily Eagle* seized on the incident to pontificate on the hatred against the Giants' owner Andrew Freedman. "It is open secret that the majority of the owners are only waiting a breach of the rules to take summary revenge on Freedman for his policy of ruin, and it is confidently believed yesterday's forfeit by the Giants is the last straw. The case is a duplicate of the Holmes incident on the Polo Grounds last year, and it is believed that New York will be treated as summarily as in the former instance. The maximum penalty for forfeiting a game is $1,000, and so intense is the feeling against Freedmanism that New York is likely to be fined the full amount."

Since the Browns were trailing 10–9 at the time, no pitching decisions were given out in this game.

SOURCES

Brooklyn Daily Eagle, May 20, 1899.
New York Evening Telegraph, May 20, 1899.
New York Times, May 20, 1899.

June 16, 1899

Place: New York
League: National League and American Association of Professional Base Ball Clubs
Field: Polo Grounds III
Clubs: New York versus Brooklyn
Umpire: Tommy Burns

In the top of the 1st inning Burns ruled Brooklyn third basemen Doc Casey was safe at home on a close play. The entire New York club surrounded Burns and argued the call until the crowd turned on the home team and cried for it to stop whining and continue the game. Once it resumed, however, the crowd turned on Burns and hurled increasingly malicious barbs at him when his decisions continued to cause confrontations with New York. Burns must have marveled at how short memories in the Gotham were. Earlier in the decade he had been one of the most popular players in New York while serving stints with both Brooklyn and the Giants. Now, according to the *New York Times,* he "has had trouble in every city in which he officiated, and less than a month ago declared a game forfeited by New York in St. Louis..." Prior to June 16, Brooklyn president Charlie Ebbets had sent a missive to the League president, Nick Young, requesting Burns not be assigned to umpire the series between the two New York clubs as it generated a great deal of emotions.

Brooklyn ended its half of the inning up 5–0. When New York batted Brooklyn pitcher Jack Dunn found fault with several of Burns's ball calls but was warned by his teammates to keep his mouth shut since the home team had already alienated the umpire. After New York scored a single run, Casey led off the Brooklyn half of the 2nd frame and watched a pitch from lefty Cy Seymour cut the heart of the plate, only to be called a ball by Burns. The New York fans roared their disapproval while Seymour and catcher Jack Warner argued with Burns until he ejected Seymour. When other New York players continued to shower their frustration on Burns, he also ordered Warner, captain and second baseman Kid Gleason and shortstop George Davis out of the game.

After the remaining New York players had further abused Burns for ten minutes, the few sane voices in the crowd shouted for play to resume. Parke Wilson went into catch in place of Warner, Pop Foster was called off the bench to replace Davis at short and pitcher Tom Colcolough took second base in Gleason's place. In the confusion before order was restored, Burns became so flummoxed that he evidently forgot he'd ejected Seymour, and the lefty, still on the mound, delivered a high fast ball to Brooklyn's Willie Keeler, which Wilson adroitly dodged, allowing the ball to nearly strike Burns full in the chest. Wilson's gambit was instantly seen for what it was by Burns and he was promptly ejected, leaving New York manager John Day with no other healthy catchers available, as Mike Grady was out with an injury. While Day scouted around for someone with catching experience Gleason and Warner resumed their verbal assault on Burns from the bench. When they were told by him to leave the field and he felt they didn't depart quickly enough, he awarded the game to Brooklyn by forfeit. Three policemen immediately rushed on the field to protect him, but no further threats were made toward him as he sped to the dressing room.

Once the game was declared a forfeit, the crowd angrily descended on the box office and was not quelled until it was announced that rain checks would be issued for the next game at the Polo Grounds.

The forfeit cost the New York club $1, 000, which went to its opponent, Brooklyn, and Kid Gleason, the captain, was fined $100.

SOURCES

New York Evening Telegraph, June, 17, 1899.
New York Times, June 17, 1899.
Sporting Life, June 24, 1899.

October 14, 1899

Place: Brooklyn
League: National League and American Association of Professional Base Ball Clubs
Field: Washington Park II
Clubs: Brooklyn versus Baltimore
Umpire: John Hunt

Baltimore right fielder Jimmy Sheckard shoved umpire Hunt after being called out in an attempt to steal second base in the 2nd inning. Sheckard was promptly ejected by Hunt but refused to leave the field. Hunt appealed to the Baltimore field captain, catcher Aleck Smith, and then to player-manager John McGraw, but neither would comply with his order to remove Sheckard from the field. Hunt next appealed to Brooklyn manager Ned Hanlon, who was in an awkward position in as much as the two clubs were under syndicate ownership and he was also the Baltimore club's president. Hanlon assured Hunt he'd support any action taken by him and Brooklyn was awarded the game. Baltimore, as per a league rule, was required to pay a $500 fine to the opposing team because it forfeited the game. Since both teams were owned by the same parties it was both literally and figuratively a case of a club paying money to itself.

To placate the angry spectators who felt a full refund was due them because it was the last day of the regular season in Brooklyn, the clubs then played off a previously postponed game, which was won by Brooklyn 8 to 3 in five innings. It was reported that Baltimore employed stalling tactics in order to not allow the postponed game to reach the necessary five full innings before darkness fell.

Note that the league later voted not to count the 15 games infielder Sailor Wrigley played for Brooklyn, which included this forfeit game. Wrigley had been designated an ineligible player at the time while his controversial contract situation was under investigation. But the records committee set up for the 1969 Macmillan encyclopedia opted to reinstate the discounted games.

SOURCES

Nemec, David. *The Great Encyclopedia of Nineteenth Century Baseball*, 2d ed. (Tuscaloosa: University of Alabama Press, 2006), 803.
New York Evening Telegraph, October 15, 1899.
New York Times, October 15, 1899.
Sporting Life, October 28, 1899.

June 22, 1900

Place: Philadelphia
Leagues: National League and American Association of Professional Base Ball Clubs
Field: Philadelphia Base Ball Grounds II
Clubs: Philadelphia versus Brooklyn
Umpire: Hank O'Day

Brooklyn scored three runs in the top of the 11th inning to take a 16–13 lead with just one out. At that point the Phillies, under orders from captain Ed Delahanty, began stalling by walking batters and refusing to tag out runners, hoping to entice O'Day into calling the game on account of darkness. When the score reached 20–13, he forfeited it instead to Brooklyn and "was nearly mobbed afterwards" by angry Phillies fans. Superbas ace Joe McGinnity garnered the win and Bill Bernhard was credited with a loss. All the statistics up until the point the game was stopped were counted.

SOURCES

New York Times, June 23, 1900.
Sporting Life, June 30, 1900.

July 15, 1900

Place: Stillwell, Michigan (now a part of Detroit)
League: American League (AL)
Field: Burns Park
Clubs: Detroit versus Cleveland
Umpire: Joe Cantillon

Even though the American League was still a minor circuit in 1900 we are including its most prominent forfeit that year, if only because it was but one of many ugly incidents which belied Ban Johnson's pledge that his fledgling loop would be free of the rowdyism that had long plagued the National League and American Association of Professional Base Ball Clubs and impaired its quality of umpiring, because too many officials either feared asserting their authority lest a player take physical action against them or chose not to work in the lone major loop at all. The forfeit in addition foreshadowed the numerous on-field skirmishes between players and umpires that haunted the AL's first season as a major circuit the following year.

On July 15, prior to a Sunday game with Cleveland at Burns Park (named after Detroit's owner at the time, James D. Burns) in Stillwell, Michigan— also the Tigers' Sunday home field in 1901–02—the management of the Detroit club, then still known as the Wolverines, barred scheduled umpire Joe Cantillon, a former minor league outfielder and Walter Johnson's first major league manager, from the grounds after an altercation involving him and Detroit shortstop Kid Elberfeld in Detroit's 4–2 loss to Chicago the previous

Norman Arthur Elberfeld (center), better known as "The Tobasco Kid," is pictured during his stint with Washington. The scourge of umpires throughout his career, he played a pivotal role in the first forfeited game in American League history. It came in 1900, the year before Ban Johnson's newly named loop declared its intention to fight the National League for major league status. Elberfeld is shown here with teammates including second baseman Red Killefer (right front).

day. Cantillon declared the game forfeited to Cleveland even though Detroit won, 6–1, Joe Yeager topping Charlie Chech, and Cleveland manager Jimmy McAleer allegedly agreed to play the contest with Wolverines utility man Sport McAllister serving as the umpire.

Contrary to league president Johnson's initial decree that the forfeited game would be counted in the 1900 AL standings, he himself agreed to throw it "out of the record" by the end of July 1900. To further cleanse the record, Johnson also threw out an earlier forfeited game at Milwaukee on June 29 that umpire Jim McDonald gave to the Brewers after he called Minneapolis outfielder Dan Lally out for interference on a play at home plate and Millers player-manager Walt Wilmot continued to deride his decision after he was ejected and refused to allow his club continue play.

SOURCE

Sporting Life, May 12, 1900, July 21, 1900, and July 28, 1900.

September 19, 1900

Place: Brooklyn
Leagues: National League and American Association of Professional Base Ball Clubs
Field: Washington Park II
Clubs: Brooklyn versus St. Louis
Umpire: John Gaffney

The last forfeited game in the nineteenth century exemplified in the extreme the rowdyism that corroded the game during the decade of the 1890s. In the 3rd inning, with Brooklyn's Duke Farrell on third base, Superbas outfielder Fielder Jones hit a grounder to St. Louis shortstop Bobby Wallace. Wallace attempted to nail Farrell at home, but his throw was wide and Farrell slid under St. Louis catcher Wilbert Robinson's tag. Umpire Gaffney called Farrell safe, prompting Robinson to throw the ball at him and then punch him in the chest. Gaffney retaliated by swinging his mask at Robinson and grazing his nose. He then fined Robinson $5 and summarily ejected him, a radical departure from his earlier style of umpiring. In the 10 games Gaffney worked in 1900 he issued four ejections, nearly half of his documented career total of nine.

When St. Louis captain John McGraw protested that his club had no healthy catchers to replace Robinson, Gaffney first approached Brooklyn captain Joe Kelley and asked him if he would agree to let Robinson return to the game even though it would have been an egregious violation of the substitution

John Gaffney, perhaps the first great umpire. An innovator throughout the 1880s, he had been turned by drink into a caricature of his former self by the late 1890s and left the game with his once sterling reputation irreparably tarnished (collection of David Nemec).

rules. After Kelley refused to give his consent, Lou Criger, who had a broken rib, started to put on his catching gear. But before he finished his preparations, Gaffney forfeited the game to Brooklyn when Robinson refused to leave the field and St. Louis captain John McGraw refused to force him to leave. "Part of the 800 spectators received rain checks, and those who requested it received their money back."

This farcical affair was the final major league game that Gaffney, once considered the finest and most innovative umpire in the game, ever worked. Afterward the gate receipts owed to St. Louis from the game were "attached" by Deputy Sheriff O'Donnell at the request of Supreme Court Justice D. Cady Herrick on behalf of former St. Louis pitcher Gus Weyhing who claimed St. Louis owed him $100 "for the ten days after his release."

SOURCES

Nemec, David. *Major League Baseball Profiles: 1871–1900* (Lincoln: University of Nebraska Press, 2011), 2: 205–209.
New York Times, September 20, 1900.
Sporting Life, September 29, 1900.

May 2, 1901

Place: Chicago
League: American League
Field: South Side Park
Clubs: Chicago versus Detroit
Umpire: Tommy Connolly

Following a wild throw to first sacker Frank Isbell by White Sox third baseman Fred Hartman that could have ended the game with Chicago victorious, 5–2, Detroit rang up four runs on the scoreboard to take a 6–5 lead. Chicago pitcher Clarke Griffith at that point began stalling in hopes that the game would be called due to darkness and rain and the score reverted to the previous inning. Umpire Connolly refused to end the game and issued repeated warnings to play ball. Griffith only continued stalling. He purposely walked Tigers second baseman Kid Gleason and attempted to do the same with right fielder Ducky Holmes, but Holmes doubled, plating Gleason and giving Detroit a 7–5 lead. Holmes then ran from second en route to home as the Chicago nine watched and refused to tag him. Connolly had enough and forfeited the game to Detroit before Holmes scored. This was the first upheld forfeit in American League history. The skies opened up immediately afterward and it began to pour, but that did not stop the crowd, some 5,000, from rushing the field, attempting to get at Connolly. One fan reportedly took a swing at him, missing, before the umpire could escape to a dugout. Chicago president and former player, Charlie Comiskey, hurried down to the field from his grandstand box and was able to scatter the crowd.

Because Detroit had taken the lead before the forfeit was declared the

Tigers' Emil Frisk received credit for a win and player-manager Clark Griffith, who was as responsible as anyone for his team's stalling tactics, took the loss. After the series between the two teams, which was clogged with kicking and bickering, *Sporting Life* observed, "Connolly will have to get up more nerve if he expects to succeed in the American League."

Kid Gleason would later be the manager of Chicago during the 1919–20 Black Sox scandal.

SOURCES

Chicago Tribune, May 3, 1901.
New York Tribune, May 3 1901.
Sporting Life, May 11, 1901
Washington Times, May 3, 1901.

May 13, 1901

Place: New York
League: National League
Field: Polo Grounds IV
Clubs: New York versus Brooklyn
Umpire: Hank O'Day

Brooklyn came to bat in the 9th inning trailing 7–6. With the bases loaded and two out, shortstop Bill Dahlen singled to left field, apparently scoring two runners. But Tom Daly, endeavoring to go from first to third, was thrown out by left fielder Kip Selbach for the third out in umpire O'Day's judgment before Willie Keeler, the trailing runner, crossed the plate. Brooklyn manager Ned Hanlon's Superbas took the field thinking they were ahead 8–7, but upon being informed by O'Day that the game was tied 7–7 "the Brooklyn team surrounded him, gesticulating and throwing their gloves down" in protest. Brooklyn first baseman and captain Joe Kelley was ejected, but when this failed to smooth matters, O'Day gave up trying to restore peace and pulled out his watch. When the Brooklyn players had still not returned to their positions after three minutes, he forfeited the game to New York.

SOURCES

New York Sun, May 14, 1901.
New York Times, May 14, 1901.
New York Tribune, May 14, 1901.
Sporting Life, May 18, 1901.
Washington Times May 14, 1901.

May 31, 1901

Place: Detroit
League: American League
Field: Bennett Park
Clubs: Detroit versus Baltimore
Umpire: Jack Sheridan

Detroit was trailing by a narrow 5–4 margin in the bottom of the 9th inning with one out when Tigers right fielder Ducky Holmes swatted a long drive to deep center. Baltimore center fielder Jim Jackson chased the ball down and gunned it home to catcher Wilbert Robinson, but umpire Sheridan ruled that Robinson's tag on Holmes was too late, enabling him to score the tying run on an inside-the-park homer. After Orioles player-manager John McGraw and pitcher Harry Howell were ejected for arguing, practically the entire Baltimore team charged Sheridan and Mike Donlin threw a bat at him from behind, fortunately missing his target. When Baltimore refused to take the field and resume play in the prescribed time, Sheridan forfeited the game to Detroit.

No pitching decisions were awarded since the game at been knotted at 5-all before Sheridan pulled out his watch.

SOURCES

Boston Globe, June 1, 1901.
Sporting Life, June 8, 1901.

June 9, 1901

Place: Cincinnati
League: National League
Field: Palace of the Fans (formerly League Park II and later Crosley Field)
Clubs: Cincinnati versus New York
Umpire: Bob Emslie

Sections of the overflow crowd of some 17,000 thronged the corner outfield positions before play began. Throughout the game the standees kept pushing closer and closer to the diamond. Many routine flies landed in the encroaching crowd and became ground rule doubles. In the bottom of the 9th inning, with New York leading 25–13 in a protracted and messily played game, some members of the crowd had reached portions of the infield by the time

Cincinnati was down to its final out. Realizing that the surging tide of people could no longer be stemmed without risking bodily harm to the New York fielders, Emslie forfeited the game to the Giants. New York's Bill Phyle was awarded a win and Bill Phillips a loss since the Giants were leading when the game was halted.

Sources

New York Sun, June 10, 1901.
New York Times, June 10, 1901.
New York Tribune, June 10, 1901.
Washington Post, June 10, 1901.

August 21, 1901

Place: Baltimore
League: American League
Field: Oriole Park IV
Clubs: Baltimore versus Detroit
Umpire: Tommy Connolly

There had been bad blood between the two teams all season. Magnifying the prospects for trouble on this day was a groundswell of public opinion in Baltimore on the regrettable subject of umpire Connolly. His work in Lobstertown for the past week reportedly had been so wretched that Orioles officials advised him in no uncertain terms to stay away from the park on August 21 and arrange for a substitute. His job already in peril because AL president Ban Johnson thought him somewhat callow, Connolly refused to vacate his post. The arrival of Connolly at the field on August 21 prompted the Baltimore club to request that the Baltimore Police Department send 50 men to Oriole Park as quickly as possible.

Trouble for Connolly began in the first inning when Detroit third baseman Doc Casey skied a high fly ball to right field. Cy Seymour raced to get the ball but pulled up short when he saw he couldn't get to it and it would alight in foul territory, a full foot outside the foul ball line. Connolly called the ball fair and Casey, running from the start, ended up on third base. The crowd went wild. Seymour ran in from the outfield to confront Connolly and begged to show him the place the ball initially hit, which left a small hole in the soft ground, but Connolly refused the invitation and called for the game to proceed.

In the 4th inning, with Detroit leading 7–4, Baltimore third baseman

Jack Dunn hit a hot shot to Detroit first baseman Pop Dillon, who could not initially corral the ball. Both men then raced for the bag. Connolly called Dunn out, although it appeared that Dunn got there first. The Baltimore players surround Connolly and began arguing the call. Amid the usual exchange of expletives Orioles pitcher Joe McGinnity stomped his spiked shoe on Connolly's right foot. Connolly immediately forfeited the game and the festivities began in earnest. Baltimore pitcher Harry Howell grabbed Connolly. Detroit shortstop Kid Elberfield tried to pull Connolly away and the two came to blows.

The police swarmed onto the field followed by the spectators. Connolly was hustled into the ticket office, but not before being assaulted. He stayed there "for an hour before the angry mob could be induced to leave." One of his assailants, a spectator named Frank Allen, was arrested and "fined $20 and costs." Connolly also had earlier fined both Howell and McGinnity. Meanwhile Elberfeld had already been placed under arrest by "a plain clothes man" and dragged off the field in handcuffs and Howell was also arrested. Both were later acquitted.

It was the second time in four days that Connolly required a police escort to escape a crowd at the same ball park. That night "a request was made [by Baltimore officials] upon the police commissioners to bar Connolly from the grounds on the ground of inciting a riot." When Connolly was not barred, the Baltimore PD notified the Orioles management on August 22 that he would not receive any protection in the future.

That same day in Washington, Chicago shortstop Frank Shugart slugged umpire Jack Haskell from behind, casting further doubt on the trustworthiness of Johnson's boast when he launched his fledgling major league that it would be free of the rampant rowdyism that had tarnished his NL counterpart for years. The following morning Johnson banned Shugart "for all time." One paper lectured: "It was a case of a player with a big weight of meanness in him, whose only control was a worn thread of decency that easily broke." But other members of the press chided that equally heinous incidents of rowdyism that season involving such luminaries as Hugh Duffy and Joe McGinnity had not been nearly so severely punished, and, after weeks under similar fire, Johnson was persuaded to reinstate Shugart in time to finish the season and join in the first pennant celebration by an AL club after the loop went major.

SOURCES

Chicago Tribune, August 22, 1901.
New York Sun, August 22, 1901.
New York Tribune, August 22, 1901.

Washington Post, August 22, 1901.
Washington Times, August 22, 1901.

June 16, 1902

Place: Boston
League: National League
Field: South End Grounds II
Clubs: Boston versus Pittsburgh
Umpire: Joe Cantillon

With two out in the top of the 5th inning and the Pirates leading 4–0, threatening skies encouraged the Bostons to begin to stall, hoping the heavens would break into some serious rain before they completed their turn at bat in the bottom half of the frame and the game became official. Boston shortstop and Captain Herman Long asked that the game be stopped when rain actually began to fall. When umpire Cantillon refused Boston embellished its stalling tactics. After two singles plated a run, the crowd had enough and overtook the field. Many from the cheap seats began invading the grandstand. Cantillon forfeited the game to Pittsburgh and later claimed in his defense that he was "master of the field and proposed to exercise his authority at all times." The rain then ceased altogether within 10 minutes.

The Pirates were speedily leaving the grounds with their share of the gate receipts even as the 3,000 or so fans rushed the box office thinking they could cash in their rain checks since the game had been halted before it became official. The penurious Boston management at first refused to issue refunds, complaining that "they could not really distinguish between those who were entitled to pavilion checks and those who were not" and also that Cantillon had not waited long enough before stopping the game. "The crowd was angry and gathered around where the money was being counted in the ticket office behind closed doors. It was an hour before the grounds were cleared." So said *Sporting Life,* but we are left to assume that the Boston club eventually complied with league regulations and either given fans another ticket or their money back.

SOURCES

Boston Globe, June 17, 1902.
Chicago Daily Tribune, June 17, 1902.
New York Tribune, June 17, 1902.
Sporting Life, June 21, 1902.

June 28, 1902

Place: Baltimore
League: American League
Field: Oriole Park IV
Clubs: Baltimore versus Boston
Umpire: Tommy Connolly

Boston led 9–4 in the bottom of the 8th inning with one out when Orioles catcher Roger Bresnahan hit a chopper to Boston player-manager Jimmy Collins at third base with runners on second and third. Dan McGann, the man on third, started home and was caught in a rundown. He eventually escaped and returned safely to third, but meanwhile Cy Seymour, the runner on second, had reached third and taken a step toward home. He quickly darted back to second when he saw his teammate would have to return to third. Boston short-stop Freddy Parent called for the ball once play stopped and tagged Seymour on second, claiming he had not touched third as per the rule on the way back to his point of origin. Umpire Connolly saw it the same way, but player-manager John McGraw and his foul tongue strongly dissented. When he was ejected by Con-nolly and refused to leave the field, the umpire gave the game to Boston. The Baltimore papers chastised Connolly for booting McGraw from the game without sufficient provocation and implied that he was far from impartial since he had "merely reprimanded a visitor [Boston player] who threw his hat and glove in the air and generally acted in an insulting way which would have justified removal from the grounds" earlier in the game. Cy Young was with credited with a win since his club led at the time and Jack Cronin took the loss for Baltimore.

Many readers will have observed by now that Connolly, who retired from the game in 1953 with an unimpeachable reputation as an official and was among the first umpires elected to the Hall of Fame, seemed to have far more than his share of trouble keeping order in a game during his early years in blue, especially when he was working alone. Indeed, Connolly, who had begun his ML career in 1898 when the National League first adopted the double-umpire system, had resigned his post in that loop 17 games into the 1900 season when league officials temporarily abandoned the two-umpire experiment because he feared he lacked the strength to handle players like McGraw on his own. He had no better luck in the American League until the two-umpire system was reinstated in both loops.

SOURCES

Boston Globe, June 29, 1902.
Sporting Life, July 5, 1902.

July 17, 1902

Place: Baltimore
League: American
Field: Oriole Park IV
Clubs: Baltimore versus St. Louis
Umpires: Jim Johnstone and Bob Caruthers

Through not particularly subtle machinations Andrew Freedman and John T. Brush, the majority owners of the New York Giants, abetted by Baltimore player-manager John McGraw, gained controlling interest in the Baltimore club. After a 6–5 home loss to St. Louis on July 16, most of the Orioles' better players including McGraw, catchers Wilbur Robinson and Roger Bresnahan, pitcher Joe McGinnity, outfielder Cy Seymour and first baseman Joe Kelley were transferred to the NL New York Giants and Cincinnati, where Brush also held controlling interests. By the morning of July 17, Baltimore no longer had enough manpower to field a team and had to forfeit not only the game but also its franchise. AL president Ban Johnson put the franchise under league control and enabled it to finish the season before shifting it to New York by calling on several other AL teams to supplement the Orioles' threadbare roster with some of their bench warmers. Consequently a whopping total of 36 players wore a Baltimore uniform during the course of the season, many of them for only a day or two.

Johnstone and Caruthers had officiated the July 16 game; it is not known if either was on hand to formally forfeit the game of August 17.

SOURCES

New York Times, July 18, 1902.
Washington Post, July 17, 1902, and July 18, 1902.

August 8, 1903

Place: Cleveland
League: American League
Field: League Park I
Clubs: Cleveland versus Detroit
Umpire: Tommy Connolly

Detroit took a 6–5 lead in the top of the 11th inning. During the bottom half of the frame, with one out Detroit catcher Fritz Buelow snuck "an old black ball into play" but was caught at it by Cleveland player-manager Nap

Lajoie. Lajoie protested the age old ploy to umpire Connolly after stopping the action to disgustedly show him the ball. Connolly, who disliked Lajoie, maintained it was still serviceable, whereupon Lajoie seized the ball and "threw it over the grand stand." Connolly promptly forfeited the game to Detroit. Part of the crowd of 6,265—large for Cleveland at that time—surged around him as he was leaving the park "but no violence was offered."

Lajoie likewise had little use for Connolly by the time of this incident. The two had already had a titanic clash during a game on May 12 between Cleveland and Boston, and Lajoie had been suspended indefinitely by AL president Ban Johnson when he refused to leave the game after Connolly ejected him. Johnson again belied his boast that his junior loop would support its umpires at all costs by lifting the suspension after only three days when even the Boston players testified that it was "uncalled for."

SOURCES

New York Tribune, August 8, 1902.
Sporting Life, May 23, 1903.
Washington Post, August 8, 1903.

October 4, 1904

Place: New York
League: National League
Field: Polo Grounds IV
Clubs: New York versus St. Louis
Umpire: Jim Johnstone

New York had long since clinched the NL pennant prior to playing a meaningless season-ending doubleheader and brought only a skeleton crew to the park. After dropping the first game, 7–3, the Giants trailed 2–1 heading into the 4th inning of the nightcap when the trouble first began. Jack Dunn seemingly bagged a lucky homer in the top of the frame after his fly ball bounced over right fielder Jack Dunleavy's head into the stands. (Any ball that reached the stands by whatever means was a home run until 1931.) Umpire Johnstone, on appeal, ruled that Dunn was out for missing first base, however, triggering an argument that culminated in the ejection of base coach Doc Marshall, one of the Giants' subs. In the bottom half of the frame Johnstone called the Cardinals' Danny Shay safe at second base on a steal attempt. Another argument brought the ejection of New York's shortstop Bill Dahlen and second baseman Billy Gilbert, leaving the Giants short of men. Several spectators attempted to get onto the field at that juncture to attack Johnstone but were dispatched back into the stands the police. After a long delay, when it grew apparent that New York would not replace the ejected players or discontinue arguing, Johnstone forfeited the game. On his way to the dressing room, Johnstone was slugged by a boy. His assailant was not arrested and Johnstone declined to press charges.

Sporting Life observed that NL president Harry Pulliam, seated in Giants owner John T. Brush's box, had attended the debacle and said "the umpire's action was perfectly proper and the game would stand forfeited." Nonetheless, Johnstone had even more trouble with McGraw and the Giants the following year. (**SEE: Forfeited game of August 7, 1906.**)

SOURCES

New York Times, October 5, 1904.
New York Tribune, October 5, 1904.
Sporting Life, October 15, 1904.

August 5, 1905

Place: Pittsburgh
League: National League
Field: Exposition Park III
Clubs: Pittsburgh versus New York
Umpires: Bob Emslie and George Bausewine

In front of over 18,000 fans, their largest crowd of the season, the Pirates gave up four runs in the 7th inning, creating a 5–5 tie. The game was still deadlocked when Pittsburgh second baseman Claude Ritchey led off the bottom of the 9th inning with a double off Giants ace, Christy Mathewson. Pirates catcher George Gibson dropped down a bunt as expected to try to sacrifice Ritchey to third base. Mathewson fielded the ball quickly and flipped it to Giants third baseman Art Devlin, who spun around to tag Ritchey. But Ritchey appeared to slide around him and was believed by the Giants to have been declared safe by base umpire Bausewine, a former ML pitcher, albeit for just one game. The Giants appealed to plate umpire Emslie, asking him to overrule his partner. But Emslie demurred since Bausewine had had the better view of the play in his estimation.

In actuality it emerged later that neither umpire had ever rendered a decision on whether Ritchey was out or safe at third, but this was lost on Giants manager John McGraw, although he later claimed he had refused to let his men continue play until a definite decision was made. When "Bausewine pulled his watch" on the Giants, McGraw "shook his fist in Bausewine's face while [Christy] Mathewson tried to knock the umpire's watch from his hand. The moment the hands of the watch showed the minute was up, Bausewine held up his hands, shouting" Pittsburgh was the winner by forfeit, "and the New York players started for Bausewine pell mell."

Bausewine was saved from assault largely because "about 10,000 of the 18,000 spectators in the field and stands started for McGraw and his men." Quickly "scores of police seemed to rise out of the ground, and the bloodthirsty crowd was hammered back with clubs." Pittsburgh player-manager Fred Clarke and some of his charges came to the aid of the visitors and helped "beat back" a group of angry spectators who gathered at the New York bench. As the Giants made their way to their carriages, they had stones thrown at them, many finding their mark. When the players arrived at the carriages they found "the yellow blankets bearing the inscription 'New York Champions' [from 1904] torn from the horses of McGraw's carriage." The entire club was stoned as it hastened down Robinson Street. It was reported that McGraw intended to protest the forfeit, but if so it came to naught.

All statistics from the game counted, but no pitching wins and losses were assigned since the game was tied when play ceased.

After his pitching days ended, Bausewine served on the Philadelphia police force for 29 years with the exception of 1905 when he took leave to umpire in the National League but quit before the season ended. In 1930 he was appointed chief of police in Norristown, New Jersey, and remained in the position until 1944 when he was forced to resign after being convicted in bribery charges in a slot machine conspiracy. Although the conviction was later overturned, Bausewine's reputation was ruined.

SOURCES

Nemec, David. *The Rank and File of 19th Century Major League Baseball* (Jefferson, NC: McFarland, 2012), 11–12.
New York Sun, August 12, 1905.
New York Times, August 6, 1905.
St. Louis Republic, August 6, 1905.
Sporting Life, August 12, 1905.

August 22, 1905

Place: Detroit
League: American League

Field: Bennett Field
Clubs: Detroit versus Washington
Umpire: Jack Sheridan

In a taut pitchers' duel between Washington's Casey Patten and Detroit's George Mullin, the game was deadlocked 1–1 through 10 innings. In the top of the 11th frame, with two out, the Senators' Hunter Hill blooped a single to right field and Charlie Hickman singled him to third. With a three-and-one count on the next batter, John Anderson, Mullin went into a full windup and Hill streaked for home. Detroit catcher Jack Warner brushed aside Anderson to grab Mullin's delivery and tag out Hill on his steal attempt for the third out, but Sheridan cited Warner for catcher's interference and gave Washington the go-ahead run and Anderson a base on balls. "Then bedlam broke loose. The Detroits stood in nonchalant attitudes while Capt. [Bill] Coughlin, Mullin and Warner delivered impassioned addresses." When their arguments showed no signs of abating, "Sheridan calmly drew his watch, listened to the debaters for the requisite two minutes, and declared the game forfeited to Washington." The angry crowd then followed the umpire to the clubhouse, and even though he was protected by a police escort, he felt in danger again the following day when Washington won the second game of the series 5–4 in 11 innings.

The statistics through the 10 full innings of play on August 22 all counted, but one of Hill's rare hits (He batted just .209 in 1905, his final ML season.) and his daring steal of home were erased because the 11th inning was not completed.

According to *Sporting Life*, after the final game of the series between the Tigers and Senators on August 24 "Sheridan announced his final appearance on local grounds." But it was a vow AL president Ban Johnson would not allow him to keep if he wanted to remain an official in Johnson's circuit. Sheridan continued to be a member of the AL umpiring staff until his sudden death from heart trouble shortly after the close of the 1914 season.

SOURCES

Nemec, David. *Major League Baseball Profiles: 1871–1900* (Lincoln: University of Nebraska Press, 2011), 2: 215.
New York Sun, August 23, 1905.
Sporting Life, September 2, 1905.
Washington Post, August 23, 1905.

June 9, 1906

Place: Philadelphia
League: National League

Bill Klem, generally considered to have been the top umpire in the first half of the twentieth century and, by many authorities, to have been the best ever. A chart listing the number of forfeited and successfully protested games each umpire throughout history was involved in might pose a problem for his supporters since he is at or near the top of the list in each department.

Field: Baker Bowl
Clubs: Philadelphia versus Pittsburgh
Umpire: Bill Klem

On the strength of outfielder Sherry Magee's run in the 3rd inning, Phils hurler Togie Pittenger carried a 1–0 shutout through six innings. The Phils, who had been having issues with Klem's officiating all day, thought the game should be halted at that point because the skies were threatening and there were occasional lightning flashes. Klem refused their request. The Pirates then proceeded to score seven runs in the top of the 7th frame, helped by several intentional Phillies misplays including center fielder Roy Thomas standing still as a statue while an easy fly ball fell safely and then rushing in to tell Klem he couldn't see it.

The denouement came shortly after Pittenger plunked his mound opponent, Pittsburgh's Vic Willis, in the slats and then took umbrage and refused to pitch anymore when he was accused of doing so purposely. After he was ejected for stalling, his replacement, John McCloskey, "took his time walking in from the clubhouse and when he finally got in the box to warm up he fired the ball high to [catcher Jerry] Donovan, who helped the bluff along by pretending not to see it." McCloskey "continued these tactics" for two more pitches until he too was ejected. Meanwhile "the heavy banks of clouds that had been overhanging the grounds passed over, and the light became better and better." But after John Lush was sent in to replace McCloskey, who had been bounced before he threw so much as a single pitch to a batter, he "repeated McCloskey's tactics although warned by the umpire." Abandoning hope of making the Phillies speed up play, Klem forfeited the game to the Pirates. "As Klem started for the gate, a few poor sportsmen ... started to throw cushions and tonic bottles, one of which hit the umpire, and there was a very hostile demonstration." Moments later "a heavy storm broke and this probably prevented further violence toward the umpire."

In Brooklyn on the same day in a game between Chicago and Brooklyn, umpire Jim Johnstone was assaulted by the spectators after he ruled that a potential three-run home run belted by Whitey Alperman in the bottom of the ninth inning had been foul when it left the park. A fair ball call would have given Brooklyn a 3–2 win. Johnstone was struck a number of times by the angry spectators and was escorted from the filed by the police before he suffered any lasting injuries.

SOURCES

Boston Globe, June 10, 1906
Chicago Tribune, June 10, 1906.
Sporting Life, June 16, 1906.
Washington Times, June 10, 1906.

July 2, 1906

Place: Philadelphia
League: American League
Field: Columbia Park
Clubs: Philadelphia versus New York
Umpires: Tim Hurst and Silk O'Loughlin

After losing the opening game of a twinbill, 5–4, New York won the nightcap by forfeit. Leading 5–1 in the bottom of the 9th inning, Yankees hurler Al Orth had retired the first two batters and had just delivered a strike to A's second baseman Danny Murphy when the home crowd suddenly surged onto the field "for the purpose of making a hasty exit" in *Sporting Life's* estimation after a wearying five-hour day in the ball park. Other papers speculated that a few had mistaken the number of outs and thought the game was over as they vaulted out of the stands, and others in the crowd had simply followed. Hurst and O'Loughlin swiftly decided that it was pointless to try to restore order so that the final out could be recorded, but the Philadelphia-based *Sporting Life* chastised Hurst, the umpire-in-chief for blemishing the A's by calling for a forfeit and offered the inane suggestion that he could easily have obviated the embarrassment by having Orth throw two quick pitches and ordering Murphy to swing at them.

Orth was credited with a win since his team led when play was terminated, and Andy Coakley took the loss for the A's.

SOURCES

Sporting Life, July 14, 1906.
Washington Post, July 3, 1906.

August 7, 1906

Place: New York
League: National
Field: Polo Grounds IV
Clubs: New York versus Chicago
Umpires: Jim Johnstone and Bob Emslie

Umpire Johnstone had a long history of disagreements with manager John McGraw and the rest of his Giants, as did many NL umpires in the early part of the twentieth century. Cubs third baseman Harry Steinfeldt testified in a letter to NL president Harry Pulliam that on August 4, 1906, he had heard McGraw call Johnstone "a damn dirty cock eating bastard, and a low-lifed son-of-a-bitch of a yellow cur hound, and that if he had anything to do with it, Johnstone would never come into the Polo Grounds." This letter reached Pulliam's desk on August 6. That same afternoon Johnstone had booted McGraw and Giants third baseman Art Devlin from a game for excessively arguing after he called Devlin out in a play at the plate in the Giants' 3–1 loss to Chicago. Johnstone then had needed a police escort to escape the field safely.

When Johnstone arrived at the Polo Grounds on August 7, half an hour before game time, he was denied entry by Giants officials. He then immediately called the game forfeited to the Cubs. His fellow umpire Emslie entered the grounds soon thereafter but quickly left once he sized up the situation. The Giants had wanted Emslie to work the game alone, but by NL rules he could not since his partner for the day had been fit to officiate but denied the right to do so by the home club.

Feigning ignorance of the state of affairs, McGraw sent his troops out on the field at game time, 4 p.m. and designated one of his subs, Sammy Strang to umpire in lieu of the absent officials, citing the custom to have a player umpire when no regular umpires were available. Chicago declined to take the field under these circumstances and bolted for the clubhouse, at which point McGraw and Strang announced to the crowd that the game had been forfeited to New York.

As if on cue, a representative of the New York club, Joe Humphreys, then sprang from the grandstand and in a loud and commanding voice made the following announcement to the crowd over the shouts of the angry spectators: "Johnstone was barred from these grounds today by Police Inspector Sweeney who feared that the presence of Johnstone after yesterday's tumult might incite a riot. Johnstone has declared the game forfeited by New York to Chicago 9 to 0."

Some of the crowd began to leave but many were lingering in the stands and on the infield and outfield when a second announcement was made by Humphreys, soon to become the most famous boxing ring announcer of his time after Tex Rickard took over Madison Square Garden.

"I am instructed by Manager McGraw to-day that he, having sent Strang out as an umpire and, the Chicago team having ignored his calling on them to "play ball," the game under the rules was forfeited by Strang to New York 9 to 0, and the New York Club will protest the claim of the visiting club."

Rain checks were issued prior to the game and were good for another match that season. Inspector Sweeney later stated, "As to the umpire being barred, I knew nothing." He claimed he had taken no measures to prevent Johnstone from entering the grounds and had acted as he did at the request of the New York club.

The New York Tribune printed lengthy statements from New York president John T. Brush, Chicago president Charles W. Murphy and NL president Harry Pulliam regarding this event.

New York later claimed it had refused Johnstone entry to the Polo Grounds solely because a riot was feared if he officiated, but the police refuted this. Pulliam ruled that both umpires Johnstone and Emslie had acted properly and upheld the forfeit. Pulliam was acutely aware that denying a vilified umpire entry to their park had long been a Giants tactic and one that his predecessor, Nick Young, had never been able to suppress. His actions on this occasion were designed to bring an end to New York's tyrannical shenanigans in an effort to manipulate the NL's umpiring schedule, but events would prove them only partially successful.

On the morning of the day the forfeit occurred the Giants were still very much in the pennant chase, trailing the first-place Cubs by only 5½ games. But soon after the forfeit the race broke wide open, and the Cubs went on to win a NL-record 116 games.

That same day in Boston's South End Grounds more aggression on the field occurred between Boston player-manager Fred Tenney and umpire Bill Klem. After his last-place team lost 7–5 to Pittsburgh, the frustrated Tenney claimed that Klem would not turn over the baseballs used in the game as they were property of the home club. While Tenney forcibly attempted to search Klem's pockets, the two came to blows. Klem skulled Tenney with a ball and both bore marks of the scuffle once separated.

Sources

Anderson, David W. *You Can't Beat the Hours* (North Charleston, SC: CreateSpace, 2013), 116–117.
New York Sun, August 8, 1906.
New York Times, August 8, 1906.
New York Tribune, August 8, 1906.
Washington Times, August 8, 1906.

September 3, 1906

Place: New York
League: American League
Field: Hilltop Park
Clubs: New York versus Philadelphia
Umpire: Silk O'Loughlin

After winning 4–3 squeaker in the first game of a doubleheader in front of 17,000 despite losing volatile shortstop Kid Elberfeld to an ejection at a key juncture in the 9th inning, New York was behind 3–1 in the 9th inning of the second game with Willie Keeler on second and Wid Conroy on third and no one out. At that point New York second baseman Jimmy Williams hit a high bouncer to Philadelphia third baseman Jack Knight. As Knight took a step backward to field the ball, he collided with Keeler, who was attempting to advance from second. Keeler lay sprawled in the dirt while the ball rolled unmolested into left field but then quickly picked himself up and followed Conroy home to score the tying run.

KEELER, N. Y. AMER.

Willie Keeler's bat was far more than half his height of 5'4½", but his small stature served him particularly well at times. A larger man might have been adjudged guilty of runner's interference with a fielder rather than the victim of a fielder's interference in a base path collision that led umpire Silk O'Loughlin to award him a critical run that triggered a forfeited game in 1906.

Athletics players swarmed around O'Loughlin demanding that he call Keeler out for runner's interference and send Conroy back to third. The most vociferous of the yowling group, first baseman Harry Davis and left fielder Topsy Hartsel, ignored O'Loughlin's warning to cease their argument. O'Loughlin soon despaired of regaining peace on the field and forfeited the game to the New Yorkers allowing them to take over the lead in the AL, two percentage points ahead of the eventual winner, Chicago. After the game O'Loughlin insisted to newspapermen that he had been right in his call and Knight had been the party guilty of interference, not Keeler. Though who of us was there to witness it, Knight's obstruction of Keeler was probably eerily similar to Boston third baseman Will Middlebrooks's violation of present-day rule 7.06 that brought a controversial end to Game 3 of the 2013 World Series when he was cited for obstructing Cards' runner Allen Craig.

SOURCES

New York Times, September 4, 1906.
New York Tribune, September 4, 1906.
Sporting Life, September 15, 1906.

April 11, 1907

Place: New York
League: National League
Field: Polo Grounds IV

Clubs: New York versus Philadelphia
Umpire: Bill Klem

On Opening Day in both major leagues the Giants were down 3–0 to the Phillies in the top of the 9th inning in front of a sellout crowd of over 17,000. The previous inning umpire Klem, with great difficulty, had cleared the outfield "of the first of the departing throng who attempted to avoid the crush by cutting across the field." As the Giants took field at the start of the 9th frame, however, suddenly realizing there were no policemen on the grounds to stop them, "the great crowd [of at least 1,000 men) with one rush overran the field and put a stop to further play" by circling around Giants right fielder George Browne. Klem and some of the Giants players tried to order them back behind the outfield ropes, "but instead of the situation improving hundreds joined the recalcitrants and laughed at the plea of players and officials alike. It was the work of another minute before hundreds of others surrounded the home plate, where Klem stood awaiting the possibility of renewing the game, and these laughingly threatened the umpire if he forfeited the game, as he was bound to under the rules. Another minute sufficed to start the kindred spirits in the grandstand throwing cushions into the mass and in an instant there was a whirlwind of cushions flying back and forth.... By this time it was evident that there was absolutely no chance for the game to proceed." Both teams had already threaded their way through the mob to the Polo Grounds clubhouse in deep center field when Klem "awarded the game to Philadelphia as forfeited."

Boredom and displeasure with the home side were no doubt a factor in the spectacle; through eight innings the Giants had collected only one hit off Philadelphia's Frank Corriden, a single by Cy Seymour. The *New York Times* even said: "The big crowd went to the ground with plenty of enthusiasm, expecting a home victory, but had little chance to display it." A second and much graver factor in the crowd's gradual deterioration was "the refusal of Commissioner Bingham to permit the police to serve to keep the crowd in check." Early that morning he had issued a statement that he "proposed to enforce the law which forbids the policing of private grounds with the city force" and informed the Giants they would have to provide their own source of protection for their season opener. "Whether the [Giants] officials determined to make a test case of the matter or not is not known [but] there was within the enclosure when the crowd finally settled down exactly two policemen, and these were attached to the police ambulance, which stood in the outfield in case illness or accident required their services."

Only when the riot within the Polo Grounds reached near epic proportions, wrote the *Times* with tongue in cheek, would Bingham consent to send in an "imposing force of four men" but order them to do no more than march in front of the grandstand and take no other action. Finally two of them broke ranks and arrested a pair of cushion throwers who were charged with disorderly conduct. Otherwise the police on this day might as well have been invisible in the Polo Grounds.

It was a landmark event in several respects. Not only was it the first Opening Day forfeit that was unequivocally upheld, but it also put an end to Bingham's militant attitude when Giants officials called on him in the future to provide support on occasions when possible trouble was anticipated. On a lighter note, Giants catcher Roger "Bresnahan created somewhat of a sensation when he appeared behind the bat for the start of play, by donning cricket leg guards. As he displayed himself, togged in mask, protector and guards, he presented no vulnerable surface for a wild ball to strike. The white shields were rather picturesque, in spite of their clumsiness, and the spectators rather fancied the innovation. They howled with delight when a foul tip in the fifth inning rapped the protectors sharply."

All but lost in the flurry of infiltrations and novelties was the absence of Giants manager John McGraw. The instigator of probably a record number of forfeited and protested games during his career was not present on this day because he "was confined to his bed by an ill-timed illness." And completely unnoticed was that the forfeit in the final frame deprived poor Frank Corriden of what might otherwise have become his career highpoint: hurling an Opening Day shutout against the vaunted Giants on their home grounds.

SOURCES

Boston Globe, April 12, 1907.
New York Times, April 12, 1907.
Sporting Life, April 20, 1907.

October 5, 1907

Place: St. Louis
League: National League
Field: Robison Field (formerly Sportsman's Park II)
Clubs: St. Louis versus Chicago
Umpire: Cy Rigler

On the closing Saturday of the season Chicago, which had already clinched the NL flag, lost a doubleheader to the lowly Cardinals. In the first game the Cubs carped at umpire Rigler all during the early innings for his

John McGraw may have been the first non-playing manager to don his team's uniform for every game. It allowed him to storm onto the field to browbeat umpires on every call that displeased him—and there were many. Ironically he was absent the afternoon his New York Giants were the victims of the only Opening Day forfeit in major league history that was not subsequently overturned.

calls. Matters reached a boiling point when Cubs second baseman Johnny Evers, with his team ahead 2–0, was called out at third base in the top of the 4th inning. Even after Evers's kicking earned his ejection, the Cubs continued to berate Rigler. When it grew evident they would not stop he forfeited the contest to St. Louis. Chicago then lost the second game as well, 4–3 to Stoney McGlynn.

Afterward Cubs player-manager, first baseman Frank Chance, swore that Rigler had caught him totally unawares when he forfeited the first contest. According to Chance: "Rigler said I did not have a full team on the field [after Evers's ejection]. He said he would give me half a minute to get the men and continue the game. Almost instantly he pulled his watch out of his pocket and walked off the ground, giving the game to St. Louis." Though Chance may have been exaggerating his case somewhat to spare a fine, it had grown abundantly clear by then that NL umpires were not uniform in the time they allotted a manager or field captain to cease arguing and continue play or face a forfeit. With the NL pennant already locked up, Chance otherwise couldn't have cared less about the forfeit—or his club's loss in the second game of the twinbill for that matter. According to *Sporting Life*, as soon as Rigler had declared the opening game forfeited to St. Louis, Chance had gathered two of his top pitchers, Jack Pfiester and Orval Overall, and the three had then gone to nearby Sportsman's Park to catch the rest of the game between the St. Louis Browns and Detroit.

A further point of interest: Though the forfeit abbreviated the game to less than five innings, it was included in the final statistics. Moreover, St. Louis starter Ed Karger, who hadn't even as yet worked four innings when the game was stopped, was credited with a win and Cubs starter Orville Overall drew a loss.

Sources

Chicago Tribune, October 6, 1907.
Sporting Life, October 12, 1907.

October 4, 1909

Place: New York
League: National League
Field: Polo Grounds IV
Clubs: New York versus Philadelphia
Umpire: John Mullin

With the score tied 1–1 in the bottom of the 4th inning of the second game of a doubleheader and the final regular season game for both teams, Phils pitcher Lew Moren objected to one of his pitches to New York's Art Wilson that was called a ball. The umpire was John Mullin, a late-season acquisition from the Western League who had been hired only two days earlier and was working the game alone. While he and Moren were jawing, they were joined by Phillies catcher Red Dooin and second baseman Otto Knabe. In his first opportunity to flex his authority at the ML level, Mullin made a clean sweep, ejecting all three of his tormentors. Probably they were testing the new recruit and were caught by surprise when he tossed them so precipitously. When they refused to leave the field, he forfeited the game to New York after waiting the required one minute.

Mullin was dropped by the NL after the season ended. Two years later he suffered the same fate after putting in a full campaign in the AL. He later umpired in the Federal League.

This game was included in the 1909 statistics even though it was later determined not to have been a regulation game. That decision in all likelihood spared the Phils from paying the then standard $1,000 fine for intentionally forfeiting a game. *Sporting Life* even recommended that if such came to pass the club should "mulct the offending players that much."

SOURCES

New York Times, October 5, 1909
New York Tribune, October 5, 1909.
Sporting Life, October 9, 1909.

July 6, 1913

Place: Chicago
League: National League
Field: West Side Grounds
Clubs: Chicago versus St. Louis
Umpires: Mal Eason and Bill Brennan

After Cubs southpaw George Pierce blanked St. Louis 5–0 in the first game of a doubleheader, "it was agreed to call the second game at 5 o'clock so the Cardinals could catch an early train for Boston." The second contest began at 3:45 p.m. Chicago player-manager Johnny Evers started Orval Overall who had been idled for over a month by a bad back. In the opening frame the Cardinals scored three runs off the rusty hurler "after exhausting fifteen minutes or more of the time."

With less than an hour left before the game was due to be called, Evers decided to have his men stall so that the game would not last long enough to become official. Overall came to bat in the second inning, took a strike and then was removed for pinch hitter Roger Bresnahan. He "was down in the corner of center field and the bat boy was sent out to get him." It took over five minutes for Bresnahan to step up to the plate and then he left the batter's box while Cards hurler Slim Sallee was in the middle of his delivery and whipped out his handkerchief to wipe something out of his eye. Plate umpire Eason, a former ML pitcher, ignored the delay and called the pitch a strike. The next inning, after the new Cubs pitcher, Ed Reulbach, took his time warming up, the Cards' Mike Mowrey singled and then, on the following pitch to Ed Konetchy, set out in a leisurely fashion to second base, begging to be caught stealing in an effort to speed up the action. But no one covered the bag on Cubs catcher Jimmy Archer's throw, so Mowrey then loped toward third, forcing the Cubs to throw him out there. Recognizing that his intentions could no longer be thwarted, the Cubs put him out. Konetchy then hit a lazy fly that was allowed to roll all the way to the fence with no one in pursuit, giving him time to circle the bases backward if he had wished to collect an inside-the-park home run. Later in the inning a fight broke out among spectators behind the Cubs' dugout, creating a further delay when some of the Cubs clambered over the roof of the dugout to join the fracas.

The climactic moment came at the start of the 4th inning with St. Louis now ahead 5–1 and about twenty minutes still left before the clock struck 5 p.m. Cards catcher Ivey Wingo deliberately tapped a pitch of Reulbach's right back to him and had no choice but to run it out when Reulbach fumbled the ball and then threw it over first baseman Vic Saier's head. "Wingo just kept running slowly" and by the time Evers, from his position at second base, had wandered over to retrieve the wild heave, he was just reaching second. Instead of throwing the ball, Evers "just walked into the diamond carrying it while Wingo strolled to third." At that point Eason threw off his mask and, after consulting with Brennan, forfeited the game to St. Louis. Altogether it had taken almost an hour to play just three innings. The game was included in the official statistics for the season even though Eason and Brennan curtailed it to well short of five innings and its statistics are still contained in most current reference works.

Sources

Boston Globe, July 6, 1913.
Chicago Tribune, July 6, 1913.

June 26, 1914

Place: Philadelphia
League: American League
Field: Shibe Park
Clubs: Philadelphia versus Washington
Umpires: Ollie Chill and Jack Sheridan

In the first game of a doubleheader there had been complaints by the Athletics from the outset that Washington right-hander Joe Engle's foot was not in contact with the pitching rubber when he released his deliveries. Finally, in the 4th inning, after the latest complaint from A's player-coach Ira Thomas, plate umpire Chill began calling balls on pitches to A's outfielder Rube Oldring that looked like obvious strikes in an effort to force Engle not to step off the rubber before he delivered the ball. The bases were loaded at the time, which meant a walk would bring home the runner on third and put the A's ahead 3–

0. Player-manager Clark Griffith protested when he realized what was afoot and refused to continue play. After waiting three minutes, Chill forfeited the game to Philadelphia.

The *Washington Post* tried to make something of Oldring's admission that Engle's pitches to him were strikes, but according to the pitching rules it made no difference since Chill considered Engle's pitches illegal, as did Sheridan, his partner that day on the bases. The forfeit angered A's manager Connie Mack, coming as it did in front of one of the A's largest crowds of the season. Mack declared that "Griffith had no real place in the league and should be run out of it." Griffith, while later admitting that he had mistakenly thought Chill was bluffing when he threatened a forfeit, made it a point to reply to Mack's charge by calling him "the cheapest skate in base ball."

The squabbling continued in the second game, this time involving both Chill and Sheridan, as the A's won 5–4 in 10 innings. The *Washington Post* made it seem the two umpires' work had been so deficient that their jobs would be in jeopardy, but that was never the case that season, although Sheridan died that November and Chill lost his post some eight years later owing to a botched call at first base in a crucial early-season game between the Yankees and the St. Louis Browns that created a 20-minute delay before he agreed to correct his call.

Sources

Nemec, David. *The Official Rules of Baseball Illustrated,* 3d ed. (Guilford, CT: Lyons Press, 2006), 152.
Sporting Life, July 4, 1914.
Washington Post, June 27, 1914.

July 18, 1916

Place: Chicago
League: National League
Field: Weeghman Field (later Cubs Park and now Wrigley Field)
Clubs: Chicago versus Brooklyn
Umpires: Bill "Lord" Byron and Ernie Quigley

With the score tied 4–4 in the 10th inning, Brooklyn put runners on second and third with none out. Brooklyn infielder Ollie O'Mara had run the count to two balls and two strikes when Cubs pitcher Hippo Vaughn "took an unusually long time on the slab" until O'Mara stepped out of the box to protest the delay. Since it was growing dark, there was naturally suspicion that Vaughn was under orders from manager Joe Tinker to stall in the hope the game would be stopped in time "to stave off an apparent defeat." After umpire Byron ordered Vaughn to hurry it up and pitch, Cubs third base-man Heinie Zimmerman told Byron to "empire the game," a play on the word umpire that emphasized Byron's lordly manner that at times bordered on arrogance while he officiated; Byron was known in addition as "the sing-ing umpire" for sometimes jollying the crowd by singing out his calls. "As Vaughn still deliberated on the mound, Byron called a ball," running the count to full.

Cubs manager Joe Tinker raced out to protest, claiming that Vaughn wasn't stalling but trying to silently communicate to catcher Bill Fischer that Brooklyn was stealing their signs. Not buying Tinker's explanation, Byron told him to leave the field and said he would call for a police escort if necessary. Realizing their manager was getting the worst of it, a few spectators began bombarding Byron with seat cushions and "other things." When Tinker refused to let a policeman escort him to the dugout, Byron forfeited the game to Brooklyn, known at the time as the Robins in honor of their manager, Wilbert Robinson. Chicago was also socked with the standard $1,000 league fine for forfeiting a game.

In calling a ball even though there had been no delivery by Vaughn, Byron was in compliance with Rule 33 in the 1916 rule book which stated: "The umpire shall call a ball on the pitcher each time he delays the game by failing to deliver the ball to the batsman for a period longer than twenty sec-onds."

Sources

Chicago Tribune, July 19, 1916.
New York Sun, July, 19, 1916.
Sporting Life, July 29, 1916.
Washington Herald, July 19, 1916.

September 9, 1917

Place: Chicago
League: American
Field: Comiskey Park I
Clubs: Chicago versus Cleveland
Umpires: Brick Owens and Billy Evans

In the top of the 10th inning of a 3–3 tie that had been played the entire way in a chilling rain, Cleveland loaded the bases with two out. Manager Lee Fohl sent substitute infielder Bill Wambsganss up to pinch hit for third baseman Joe Evans. Tribe outfielder Jack Graney, occupying third base, took a long lead, and seemed destined to be picked off when White Sox catcher Ray Schalk fired the ball to third baseman Fred McMullin. But the ball eluded McMullin and rolled toward the grandstand. Graney became entangled with McMullin, preventing McMullin from chasing the ball. By the time McMullin shook himself loose, Tribe shortstop Ray Chapman, who had been on second, also had reached third and he and Graney both scored before McMullin could retrieve the errant throw and make a play at the plate. Plate umpire Owens, who evidently had a better view of the play than base umpire Evans, called Graney out for interference and the game was delayed 20 minutes while Tribe captain, center fielder Tris Speaker, and

Fritz Coumbe, one of the first hurlers to build a solid major league career—eight seasons—largely as a reliever. His brilliant relief effort for the Indians on September 9, 1917, was wasted when his teammates' antics caused a game he might have won to be forfeited to the White Sox.

Fohl chinned with Owens and Cleveland players lazily took the field, where they tossed their gloves in the air and rolled in the dirt until Speaker and Fohl had their full say.

When the game finally resumed, pitcher Dave Danforth led off the Chicago half of the frame by fanning. Catcher Steve O'Neill threw the ball toward third as if to start the custom of sending the ball "around the horn" after a strikeout, but Ivan Howard, who had replaced Evans at third, let the ball sail past him. When Graney, stationed in left field, lagged in chasing after it, "Owens tore off his mask and awarded the game to Chicago by forfeit. The Indians had gone too far." Whether Speaker and Fohl thought the umpires had gone too

fast in forfeiting the game is the question. If not, they either lacked control of
their men on this day or else of their own tempers. The umpires were not about
to stop the game since the rain showed no signs of increasing, and Cleveland lefty Fritz Coumbe, who had come on in relief in the 1st inning, had
allowed the Sox only six hits and seemed to be gaining strength, if anything. Cleveland at the time of the forfeit still had every chance of winning
the game.

SOURCES

Chicago Tribune, September 10, 1917.
New York Tribune, September 10, 1917.
Washington Herald, September 10, 1917.
Washington Post, September 10, 1917.

July 20, 1918

Place: Philadelphia
League: American League
Field: Shibe Park
Clubs: Philadelphia versus Cleveland
Umpires: Dick Nallin and Bill Dinneen

After suffering an embarrassing 10–4 setback at the hands of the apathetic
last-place Athletics in the lidlifter of a doubleheader, the Indians led the A's
9–1 as the A's were due up in the bottom of the 9th inning. When a barrage
of seat cushions began flying from the hands of restive fans in the upper deck,
fans in the lower deck surged onto the field to escape being crowned. No police
were present to help quell the budding riot, perhaps because by that time most
of the crowd had left in disgust at the A's shoddy performance—the Indians
had made their nine runs on only nine hits while the A's had piled up 12 hits
in scoring but once. Nallin, working the plate in the second game, called for
a forfeit when the few Mackmen employees on hand made only a token effort
to clear the field.

The *Washington Times* reported humorously on the afternoon's denou-
ment. "John Shibe's stage cops did their best to shove the fans off the field,
but they failed. Cushions filled the air and one or two cops were upset and
lost their helmets. Here and there a brawny fan took a punch at a cop only to
get one in return. A merry time was had by one and all."

The forfeit deprived Johnny Enzman of a win and saved Bill Pierson,

Left to right: Ernie Quigley, Tommy Connolly, Hank O'Day and Bill Dinneen posed for posterity prior to a 1916 World Series game. Then as now, being chosen to work postseason contests was a badge of honor for an umpire. The quartet worked a total of 32 Series among them and both Connolly and O'Day are in the Hall of Fame. There is ample evidence, however, that the most deserving of the four was Dinneen. After a lustrous pitching career highlighted by his three wins in the first post–1900 World Series in 1903, he officiated more than 4,200 games with never a black mark against him and was not only selected to work eight World Series but was also behind the plate in the first All Star Game in 1933.

who had walked five batters and hit one before being removed in the 2nd inning, from a loss.

SOURCES

Boston Globe , July 21, 1918.
Jordan, David M. *The Athletics of Philadelphia* (Jefferson, NC: McFarland, 1999), 78.
New York Times, July 21, 1918.
Washington Post, July 21, 1918.
Washington Times, July 21, 1918.

September 2, 1918

Place: St. Louis
League: American League
Field: Sportsman's Park III
Clubs: St. Louis versus Cleveland
Umpire: Grover Lowdermilk

The day following the completion of its series in Chicago, Cleveland was scheduled to finish the war-abbreviated 1918 campaign with a Labor Day doubleheader in St. Louis. Cleveland notified the Browns business manager Bob Quinn as early as Saturday that it would almost certainly not appear in St. Louis. The Tribe by that point had nothing at stake; after their Sunday win at Chicago they still trailed first-place Boston by 2½ games and could not possibly catch the Red Sox even if they swept both contests in St. Louis and the Sox lost both games of their season-ending doubleheader with the Yankees on September 2 (the Sox split the pair). Despite the advance warning that Cleveland would not appear in St. Louis on September 2, Browns manager Jimmy Burke sent his starting nine out on the field at 1:45 p.m. and claimed both games by forfeit. Two pitchers threw five pitches each from the mound in compliance with the rules. There was a 10-minute break between their tosses. The umpire who officially declared both contests forfeited was Browns hurler Grover Lowdermilk and the results were sent afterward to AL president Ban Johnson.

Cleveland's two forfeit losses were reflected in the standings in the guides the following spring, but it appears that someone at a later point, perhaps Johnson, weighed the matter anew and decided to erase the defeats. The most likely reasons were that the games were meaningless and the argument was strong that Cleveland on the closing day of the season had the longest jump of the four AL road teams and therefore the most expensive, an important consideration in view of the travel restrictions that were imposed on other businesses to help defray unnecessary costs that could hinder the war effort. In any other season almost unquestionably the forfeits would have stood for time immemorial and Cleveland would probably have been heavily fined and perhaps suffered even further penalties. Witness what occurred in 1876 when the New York and Philadelphia NL clubs, both well out of contention, highhandedly refused to make their last western road swings of the season. Neither city was permitted to install a franchise in the NL again until 1883.

SOURCES

Cleveland Plain Dealer, September 3, 1918.
New York Times, September 3, 1918.

August 20, 1920

Place: Philadelphia
League: American League
Field: Shibe Park
Clubs: Philadelphia versus Chicago
Umpires: Ollie Chill and Brick Owens

Two years to the day since the last forfeit game—the longest stretch without a forfeit to that point in ML history—Shibe Park, the scene of the 1918 forfeit, again hosted the second game of a doubleheader that was halted by an unruly crowd. With his club behind 5–2 and two out in the bottom of the 9th inning A's skipper Connie Mack called on Lena Styles to pinch hit for hurler Scott Perry. Styles hit a slow roller down the first-base line that was grabbed by Chicago southpaw Dickie Kerr. Kerr tagged Styles as he was racing down the line to first base, and the crowd in the distant outfield bleachers immediately started to swarm on the field and race for the exits. But just before Kerr had snared the ball it had rolled foul according to base umpire Owens. The fans, unable to see Owens's signal, kept coming unawares that the game was not over, and when the A's were unable to clear the field, plate umpire Chill declared Chicago the winner by forfeit.

With the benefit of hindsight, it seems remarkable to us that neither major league as yet had put in a ground rule to stop the crowd from entering the field at the conclusion of a game, usually to use it as a short cut to their exit of choice. Had they done so a number of senseless forfeited games in the first half century or so of major league play might have been avoided.

SOURCES

Charles Mears Base Ball Scrapbook, vol. II, 1920, Part III.
Chicago Tribune, August 21, 1920.
New York Herald, August 12, 1920.
New York Times, August 21, 1920.

June 13, 1924

Place: Detroit
League: American
Field: Navin Field (later Briggs Stadium and Tiger Stadium)
Clubs: Detroit versus New York
Umpires: Billy Evans and Red Ormsby

With his club securely ahead 10–4, Babe Ruth led off for the Yankees in the top of the 9th inning. A young Tigers lefty, Bert Cole, was on the mound. He had been blasted for four runs in the 7th inning and in the 8th had already begun "showing his temper." In addition, he had been further piqued when he received a straight arm blow to the chest from Ruth in a 7th inning play at first base. Ruth had to duck out of the way of two pitches near his head before

fouling out to the Detroit first baseman Lu Blue. The next batter, left fielder Bob Meusel, "received a pitch in the ribs." He flung his bat aside, charged the mound and took a wild swing at Cole but missed. The two umpires grabbed Meusel and "dragged him away" but not before Ruth bolted from the Yankees' dugout flailing his fists and claiming that Cole was deliberately trying to "bean" Yankees batters on orders from Tigers player-manager Ty Cobb (which Cobb later "vehemently denied"). Players poured onto the field from both dugouts and a riotous melee ensued.

When both Evans and Ormsby maintained their cool, peace seemed to be restored after a few minutes. But while the Detroit players were returning to

Bob Meusel, the instigator of an on-field brawl in 1924 that ended in his team, the Yankees, winning a game by forfeit. Given Meusel's behavior throughout the event, were the same incident to happen today the result probably would be the reverse.

their positions—with the exception of Cole who had been banished from the game along with Meusel—and the other Yankees were heading back to their dugout, Meusel and Ruth did an about face after taking a few steps toward their dugout and stalked instead to the Tigers' dugout where they resumed fighting with any Tigers within reach of their fists. Angry Tigers fans lost all control at that point and streamed onto the field. Police quickly surrounded both dugouts and escorted the players to safety in their mutual locker rooms. They had little luck in subduing the fans on the field, however, and fights broke out every which way—between fans and police, fans and each other, fans and park employees. Only a heroic effort by Evans and Ormsby prevented Ruth and Cobb from coming to blows. "I rushed at him like a football player," Ruth was quoted afterward as saying. It took over a half hour to clear the field, but by then plate umpire Evans had long since awarded the game to New York. AL president Ban Johnson later fined Ruth $50 for his participation in the day's events, but Meusel, as much the instigator, was spared.

The following day the *Chicago Tribune* observed: "No such disorder as that which prevented completion of the Yankees'-Tigers' game is recorded in modern baseball history." It appears to us that if the Yankees had not had such a prohibitive lead at the time the game was stopped, Evans and Ormsby might have taken a somewhat different stance and the Tigers might have had a valid protest if the pair had not. Ruth and Meusel reignited the flames when they entered the Tigers' dugout area, and Meusel was particularly far out of line in lingering on the field and eventually resuming his assault on the opposition rather than leaving the grounds as soon as he was ejected.

SOURCES

Browning, Reed. *Baseball's Greatest Season, 1924* (Amherst: University of Massachusetts Press 2003), 48.
Chicago Tribune, June 14, 1924.
New York Times, June 14, 1924.

April 26, 1925

Place: Chicago
League: American League
Field: Comiskey Park I
Clubs: Chicago versus Cleveland
Umpires: Pants Rowland, Billy Evans and George Hildebrand

With some 44,000 on hand, the largest crowd in Comiskey Park history to that point, fans were permitted to stand behind roped off areas in left and right fields, shortening the unusually lengthy distance of 362 feet down the lines to the outfield walls. Cleveland led 7–2 with two out in the bottom of the 9th inning when White Sox third baseman Willie Kamm tapped a soft two-hopper to shortstop Joe Sewell who made a perfect peg to first baseman Ray Knode. Knode, an infrequently used sub, took the ball two feet in front of first base and then fumbled around behind him "hunting for the bag" with his foot. Before he found it, base umpire Evans ruled that Kamm had crossed the bag. As in other similar previous forfeits, the fans standing on the field were too far away to see Evans give the safe sign and rushed onto the main part of the field in the belief the game was over. Indeed, many of them had already begun to enter the field as soon as Sewell fielded the ball. The *Chicago Tribune* stated: "It was absolutely impossible to continue play. It would have taken a thousand bluecoats to clear that field and then they probably couldn't have accomplished the task in time. There was only one thing to do—forfeit the game to the visiting team by a score of 9 to 0." And forfeit it umpire-in-chief Pants Rowland, who was working the plate that day, was forced to do much to his chagrin. Rowland had been the White Sox manager in 1917, the last time they won a World Championship prior to 2005.

Sherry Smith earned a win since the Tribe was ahead when the forfeit occurred and Sloppy Thurston took the loss. Knode was charged with an error on the play that caused all the trouble.

This forfeit was the first in history that took place under the auspices of the relatively new three-umpire system. All three of the officials involved wore several different hats during their lengthy careers in the game, and each was unique. Hildebrand played briefly in the majors with the 1902 Brooklyn Superbas and is credited by some historians with discovering the spitball earlier that season while with Providence of the Eastern League and teaching it to teammate Elmer Stricklett, who first used it in a ML game in 1904. At age 22, Evans was the youngest full-time umpire in American League history. He was selected to the Hall of Fame in 1973 mainly for his officiating contributions but added to his thick dossier after leaving the AL umpiring ranks by serving as the general manager of the Cleveland Indians and later the Detroit Tigers. In between his front office stints with the two major league clubs, he was the general manager of the NFL Cleveland Rams. Evans had also worked as a sports writer while he was umpiring, but, with all that, he is best remembered for two on-field incidents that occurred during his officiating career. In 1907 he suffered a near-fatal fractured skull in the midst of a doubleheader between the St. Louis Browns and the Tigers when he was struck by a pop bottle hurled by an angry spectator. Some fourteen years later almost to the day he was embroiled in a bloody post-game fistfight with Tigers star Ty Cobb beneath the stands while players from both teams stood watch, most of them rooting for Evans. Both men had agreed before the fight not to report it to league officials, but AL president Ban Johnson learned of it anyway and said only that he was sorry he'd missed it.

Rowland's career in the game was even more checkered than Evans's. After washing out as a minor league player, he turned to managing and scouting and was a surprise hire when Charlie Comiskey handed him the White Sox reins after the 1914 season. Frequent quarrels with Comiskey over how to run the club got him fired only a year after he took the Sox to the World Championship in 1917 and spared him from the scandal that destroyed the team in the aftermath of the 1919 World Series. After seven years as an AL umpire, he returned to scouting for a while and then became president of the Los Angeles Angels of the Pacific Coast League. But it was as president of the PCL after World War II that he achieved his greatest fame. Rowland for a time seemed on the brink of establishing the PCL as a third major league but ultimately was blocked by both Commissioner Happy Chandler and ML owners like Brooklyn's Walter O'Malley who saw the PCL's largest cities as the lucrative future homes for their clubs as well as for expansion franchises.

SOURCES

Chicago Daily Tribune, April 27, 1925.
New York Times, April 27, 1925.

June 6, 1937

Place: Philadelphia
League: National League
Field: Baker Bowl
Clubs: Philadelphia versus St. Louis
Umpires: Ziggy Sears, Bill Klem and Lee Ballanfant

After a lengthy gap of a dozen years since the last ML forfeit, the streak was broken by a local law that is now archaic. The first game of a twin-bill was delayed 88 minutes by rain before the Cardinals prevailed, 7–2.

The second game as a result did not start until past 5 p.m. and had to be completed by 7 p.m. as per a Philadelphia Blue Law that impacted on all Sunday games in that city. By the 3rd inning the Cardinals had raced to an 8–2 advantage. The Phillies then began stalling with the intent to slow the action enough that the curfew would go into effect before five full innings had been played. After Phils manager Jimmie Wilson had already made a plethora of pitching changes, he summoned reliever Syl Johnson into the game. Johnson promptly threw a wild pitch to the Cards' leadoff hitter, center fielder Pepper Martin, that allowed shortstop Leo Durocher to all but walk home from third base when Phils catcher Bill Atwood merely ambled after the ball. Incensed, longtime NL umpire Klem, who was working the bases that day along with Ballanfant, "rushed to the plate, and after a few moments' conference, Sears [the umpire in chief that day] declared the game forfeited."

All statistics were eradicated since the game failed to go five innings. As a result, Cards slugger Joe Medwick lost a home run that would have been his 10th of the season. Medwick still eventually won the Triple Crown in 1937 but tied the Giants' Mel Ott for the home run title with 31.

Phils manager Wilson was later fined $100 for his stalling tactics by NL president Ford Frick. Generally the club could be expected to pick up this sort of fine, but the Phils by 1937 were running such a scruffy operation under owner Gerry Nugent that Wilson may have had to dip into his own pocket for the money. Nugent, a leather goods and shoe salesman, had the club fall into his lap when he married longtime Phillies secretary Mae Mallen in 1925. After Phillies owner William Baker died in 1930, leaving half of his estate to Mallen and half to his wife, with the support of Baker's widow, Nugent became team president. Baker's widow died in 1932, leaving Nugent in full control until 1942 when he was so broke that the National League had to loan him the money to take the Phillies to spring training. By that fall he was driven to turn over the club to the National League, which sold it to William Cox, a flashy 33-year-old lumber baron and former president of the rebel American Football League before it folded in 1942 prior to the beginning of its third season. A hands-on owner, in July 1943 Cox had the Phillies well on their way to their first season out of the basement in five years when he fired manager Bucky Harris, ostensibly for insubordination, at a press conference without bothering to first inform him. Harris retaliated by producing evidence that Cox had been placing bets on his own team. When the charges were proven Commissioner Judge Landis made Cox the last owner to date to be banned for life from baseball.

SOURCES

Chicago Tribune, June 7, 1937.
New York Times, June 7, 1937.

September 3, 1939

Place: Boston
League: American League
Field: Fenway Park
Clubs: Boston versus New York
Umpires: Eddie Rommel, Lou Kolls and Cal Hubbard

After sustaining their sixth straight loss in the 1939 season to the Red Sox, 12–11 in the opening game of a doubleheader that took what was then an interminable two hours and twenty-eight minutes to complete, the Yankees found themselves leading 7–5 in the 8th inning of the nightcap as the 6:30 p.m. Sunday curfew in Boston loomed. Since the game had been tied 5–5 after seven frames, the inning needed to be completed by the witching hour or the game would go into the books as a tie. Feeling their two-run lead was sufficient, "the Yanks sought to hustle things by deliberately running into two put-outs at the plate while the Red Sox endeavored to prolong matters by issuing an intentional pass."

Immediately following the second put-out at the plate, Boston skipper Joe Cronin rushed up to plate umpire Hubbard to protest the Yankees' lack of effort to score, "which consumed more time, and the crowd of 27,000 added to the confusion by showering the field with straw hats and pop bottles." Since in his judgment it was impossible to clear the field before the curfew would end the affair, Hubbard, after conferring with Kolls and Rommel, awarded the game to the Yankees by forfeit.

The Sox subsequently protested to AL president Will Harridge that the Yankees and not they had sparked the activities that led to the forfeit. Much to New York's dismay, Harridge agreed and declared the game a 5–5 tie, thus canceling all the statistics that occurred in the raucous top of the 8th inning. He fined the Yankees in addition, apparently for making outs on purpose. Taken out of context, Harridge's decision seems odd and against the grain since many teams throughout the game's history up until then had deliberately made outs without penalty in their haste to make a contest official either before darkness fell, a downpour began or a curfew took effect. By 1939, however, the Yankees had won three straight World Championships and would go on to win their fourth that fall when they swept the

Reds in the World Series. Harridge's decision to call the game a draw there-fore was a popular one with fans in the other seven AL cities who loathed seeing the Yankees win yet again, let alone by forfeit. It also preserved their losing streak against the Red Sox but only for three days. On September 6th Bombers southpaw Lefty Gomez beat Boston's Lefty Grove 2–1 in the opening game of a three-game series at Yankee Stadium that the Yankees went on to sweep.

The overruled forfeited game was slated to be made up on September 26 but was rained out that day and not rescheduled because it had no bear-ing on the final standings. The Yankees won their then AL-record fourth straight flag and fourth straight World Series with ease with what some authorities consider to have been their strongest team ever and amplified the piteous cry heard throughout the rest of the major leagues: "Break Up the Yankees."

SOURCES

Boston Globe, September 4, 1939.
New York Times, September 4, 1939, and August 22, 1949.

August 15, 1941

Place: Washington
League: American
Field: Griffith Stadium
Clubs: Washington versus Boston
Umpires: George Pipgras, Eddie Rommel and Harry Geisel

In *The Official Rules of Baseball Illustrated*, David Nemec wrote: "Officially control of groundskeeping crews was first given to the umpire-in-chief in 1906 for the purpose of making a playing field fit to resume action after a rain delay, but groundskeeping crews at that time were small and often swiftly overwhelmed if a sudden rainstorm hit. The umpire conse-quently was unlikely to make an issue out of it if the crew was slow in pro-tecting the field. But the middle of the twentieth century, however, most teams had a sizable staff of groundskeepers, and expectations had risen accord-ingly."

On August 15, 1941, with Washington leading Boston 6–3 and the Red Sox at bat in the top of the eighth inning, a sudden thunderstorm struck the area around the Senators' Griffith Stadium and caused a 40-minute rain delay. When the squall showed some signs of abating, Pipgras, the umpire-in-chief, "stuck a timid toe into the wet baselines, noted that the rain was still falling, and called it off officially. At the time the Red Sox had one man on base and none out."

Boston player-manager Joe Cronin immediately lodged a protest, arguing that the game could have continued if the Washington ground crew had not been laggard in covering the field. Washington skipper "Bucky Harris pooh-poohed the protest. He pointed out that if the tarpaulin was not ordered on the field, it was no fault of the Washington club in as much as the umpires are in complete authority once the game starts. It is the umpire-in-chief's province to order the canvas on the field, Harris declared."

After hearing from all parties, AL president Will Harridge sided with Cronin's contention that the Senators' ground crew went about covering the Washington field in a lackadaisical manner and awarded the game to Boston via forfeit. The Cleveland Indians then protested Harridge's decision arguing that it was unfair to them since both they and Boston were in strong contention for the AL pennant at the time, but their protest was to no avail.

SOURCES

Nemec, David. *The Official Rules of Baseball Illustrated*, 3d ed. (Guilford, CT: Lyons Press, 2006), 44.
New York Times, August 28, 1941.
Washington Post, August 16, 1941.

September 26, 1942

Place: New York
League: National League
Field: Polo Grounds V
Clubs: New York versus Boston
Umpires: Ziggy Sears and Tom Dunn

To help promote the war effort the Giants allowed all children in for free that lugged chunks of scrap metal to the park with them, presumably with the aid of their parents, and then piled it outside the park in a massive heap prior to an otherwise unappealing Saturday doubleheader with the lowly Boston Braves. Reportedly 11,205 children flocked into the park while the paid attendance was only 2,916; if the figures are genuine, nearly four children accompanied every adult who bought a ticket. The Giants won the first game 4–2 behind their aging ace, Carl Hubbell, and were leading 5–2 when the trouble began after the Braves recorded their final out in the top of the 8th inning. "When, casting aside all adult restraint, the youngsters came tumbling out of the stands, engulfing all before them, including the Braves, who sought to take their places in the field, and the Giants, who struggled to get to their bench."

Umpires Sears and Dunn were also "swallowed in the maelstrom—a hopeless, tangled, confused mass running helter-skelter all over the field." At great length Sears fought his way to the Giants' dugout, where he "took quiet counsel." He finally ordered the game forfeited if the field could not be cleared. His pronouncement "could not be heard above the din. With city police, special cops, ushers and ground crew unable to make faint impression against the mass swirling on the field, this was impossible." Giants owner Horace Stoneham merely threw up his hands when Sears rendered his forfeit verdict but promised that when a similar promotion was staged the following day, a season-closing Sunday doubleheader, the youngsters would be marshaled in special restricted sections of the park, widely separated from one another rather than packed into one area as they had been on Saturday, but the Sunday games were washed out.

No pitching wins or losses were given as per the revised rules at that time; the old rule was restored in 1963 to grant credit for both a win and a loss if the leading team after five or more innings had been played won via forfeit. The rule cost Braves rookie Warren Spahn what might otherwise have been his first ML win.

SOURCES

New York Times, September 27, 1942.
Washington Post, September 27, 1942.

August 21, 1949

Place: Philadelphia
League: National League
Field: Shibe Park
Clubs: Philadelphia versus New York
Umpires: Al Barlick, George Barr and Lee Ballanfant

After suffering a 4–0 whitewash at the hands of Phils lefty Ken Heintzelman in the first game of a Sunday doubleheader, the Giants seemed headed for a second shutout defeat that day when Schoolboy Rowe blanked them through six innings and Philadelphia meanwhile had clubbed two solo homers off New York righty Larry Jansen, whose career-long bane had always been surrendering gopher balls at key moments—he led all major league pitchers in homers allowed in 1949 with 36. In the 7th frame, however, New York pushed across two runs, helped by Phils third sacker Willie Jones's error on what should have been an inning-ending double-play ball. The Giants added another run in the 8th inning and led 3–2 in the top of the 9th when umpire Barr ruled that Phils center fielder Richie Ashburn had trapped the ball in a valiant effort to make a diving catch of Joe Lafata's sinking liner, which thereby scored Willard Marshall with the fourth New York run.

Spearheaded by rookie manager Eddie Sawyer, Phillies players immediately surrounded Barr and demanded that he ask his two fellow officials whether they saw the play differently. When Barr remained adamant that his decision was correct, empty pop bottles and fruit began to fly out of the stands and "Barlick, after warning manager Eddie Sawyer and ordering the Phils back to their places in the field, with a sweep of his right hand indicated the game was forfeited, the first such decision in the major leagues in many years [actually only seven]." Prior to Barlick's coda signal, he had been hit in the leg with a ripe tomato and Ballanfant's neck had been grazed by a pop bottle. Given the precariousness of the situation facing him and his fellow crew members, Barlick, the umpire- in-chief that day, had been extraordinarily patient. He had waited a full 15 minutes after the first of several pleas over the loud speaker system for the fans to cease their bombardment before stopping the game. Barlick, in our estimation, was among the best umpires in the game during his 30+ year tenure and played a key role in the permanent transition from the three-umpire to the four-umpire system. During his lengthy career he ran his piece of the game so commandingly that he ejected only 81 players, coaches and managers, fewer than three for every year he worked. He umpired seven World Series and seven All Star Games and was elected to the Hall of Fame in 1989.

Under the revised rules regarding forfeit games that were still in effect Jansen was deprived of a victory and Rowe was spared a defeat. All other statistics from the game counted.

SOURCES

New York Times, August 21, 1949.
Washington Post, August 21, 1949.

August 18, 1954

Place: St. Louis
League: National League

Field: Sportsman's Park III
Clubs: St. Louis versus Philadelphia.
Umpires: Bill Stewart, Babe Pinelli, Dusty Boggess and Bill Engeln

On a torrid Sunday in St. Louis, with temperatures during the afternoon approaching 110 degrees, the Phillies won the first game of a doubleheader 11–10 in 10 innings on Bobby Morgan's RBI single. Since the game took three hours and thirty-eight minutes to complete owing in part to a 78 minute rain delay, there was some question even before the second game commenced whether it could be completed before darkness fell. The rule at that juncture did not permit the lights to be turned on during a game unless it had been billed in advance as part of a twi-night doubleheader.

By the top of the 5th inning of the second contest the Phils had raced to a seemingly prohibitive 8–1 lead and had a runner on and two out. With darkness nearing and the game not yet official Stanky had already brought in three new pitchers during the frame—Royce Lint, Ralph Beard and Cot Deal—and was about to drag in a fourth, Tom Poholsky, when a donnybrook suddenly developed as Cards catcher Sal Yvars and Phils first baseman Earl Torgeson began tussling after they exchanged insults with Torgeson at bat. Quickly "players from both teams swarm[ed] onto the field swinging, punching and wrestling in one of the worst riots here since the old St. Louis Browns left town.... Rival managers Terry Moore and Eddie Stanky, at odds ever since Moore's ouster as a Cardinals coach [by Stanky two years earlier when he took over the Cardinals' helm] were in the thick of the free-for-all..." When Moore grabbed Yvars to drag him off Torgeson, "Stanky, in turn, sent Moore to the ground in an old-fashioned football tackle."

By the time a semblance of order was restored, both Yvars and Torgeson had been ejected and plate umpire Pinelli had forfeited the game to Philadelphia. "After the game Moore said he had made no protest to the umpires about the delaying tactics. Terry's face was dirty and his neck scratched. 'I left that strictly up to the umpires,' he said." Stanky, for his part, "had a mouse under his right eye and a scratch on the back of his neck." He "denied he had employed delaying tactics to halt the game before the 4½ inning official mark. 'My pitchers have been wild and ineffective all season, not only during this game,' Eddie said."

This forfeited game marked the end of an era in several ways. Not only was it the last that was generated to a large degree by an on-field brawl, but it signaled the end of teams stalling in an effort to prevent a game from becoming official before darkness intervened. Nowadays a team is allowed to turn on the lights in its home park even if the game was begun as a day game. In the event the lights fail or a local ordinance precludes them from being turned on the game is suspended at the point darkness halts it. The August 14, 1954, fiasco was also a first in as much as never before had a forfeit occurred under the current four-umpire system. Since the game was not official no statistics were counted and St, Louis outfielder Joe Frazier, who had accounted for the Cards' lone run to that point, lost a pinch homer. Many of the Phils lost hits and RBI, and rookie Bob Greenwood was denied a victory in his first major league start.

SOURCES

Nemec, David. *The Official Rules of Baseball Illustrated*, 3d ed. (Guilford, CT: Lyons Press, 2006), 63.
New York Times, August 19, 1954.
Washington Post, August 19, 1954.

September 30, 1971

Place: Washington
League: American League
Field: RFK Stadium
Clubs: Washington versus New York
Umpires: Jim Odom, Jake O'Donnell, Jim Honochick and Lou DiMuro

The current Texas Rangers' franchise was about to conclude its last game as the Washington Senators and the last game by a Washington club as a member of the American League, a night contest at RFK Stadium. The game meant nothing in the standings to Washington, which was buried deep in 5th place in the AL East Division, but the Yankees came into the contest at 81–80, needing a win to finish above .500.

The Senators were leading 7–5 in the top of the 9th inning with two out and the bases empty and their fourth pitcher of the night, southpaw Joe Grzenda, on the mound when the Yankees were the recipients of an unexpected gift as New York second baseman Horace Clarke strolled to the plate hoping to keep the inning alive. A number of fans had trickled onto the field while the Yankees' previous batter, Bobby Murcer, had been at the plate but had been successfully driven back to their seats, and there also had been a brief delay in the 8th inning when the crowd threatened to become unruly. Before the switch-hitting Clarke could assume his stance in the right side batter's box, however, the stadium began to come totally unraveled. Some of the crowd entered the field on the first base side, but the police moved them back to the stands. No sooner had that invasion been quelled than a number of fans scaled the wall in left field. That bunch was also escorted back into the stands but under greater duress. An announcement over the PA system sternly warned the crowd that encroaching on the playing field would result in the Senators forfeiting the game.

With action set to resume, a fan hopped the rail, eluded security and began removing first base. That was the spark that lit the fire that had been simmering ever since the first pitch was thrown. Outraged at owner Bob Short's decision a few days earlier to transfer the club to the Dallas-Fort Worth area, the bulk of the crowd of 14,460 stormed onto the field and began ripping up home plate, the bases and the pitching rubber, some to gain souvenirs but the majority simply vent their anger at losing their team. Realizing the chances of park policemen repelling the onslaught so the game could be completed were nil, umpire-in-chief Odom forfeited the game to the Yankees, thereby assuring them of a winning season. The result cost reliever Orlando Pina a win and saved Yankees reliever Jack Aker from taking the loss. All other statistics counted, including Frank Howard's solo 6th inning blast, the last home run hit in an AL game played in RFK Stadium.

SOURCES

Epstein, Dan. *Big Hair and Plastic Grass* (New York: Thomas Dunne Books, 2010), 41–42.
Nemec, David. *The Official Rules of Baseball Illustrated*, 3d ed. (Guilford, CT: Lyons Press, 2006), 49.
New York Times, October 1, 1971.
Washington Post, October 1, 1971.

June 4, 1974

Place: Cleveland
League: American League
Field: Cleveland Municipal Stadium
Clubs: Cleveland versus Texas
Umpires: Larry McCoy, Joe Brinkman, Nick Bremigan and Nestor Chylak

To bolster sagging attendance in a city riddled by inflation, rampant unemployment and a long string of poor baseball teams, the Indians designated the night of June 24 a special 10¢ beer night. The affair brought in a crowd of 25,134 but at a high cost when it proved to be perhaps the most embarrassingly inept promotional scheme in ML history. Cleveland failed to add extra security for the contest despite the fact that the same two clubs had a brawl on the field in Arlington the week before. There is no record of the number of cups of beer that were sold—one estimate was between 60,000 and 65,000

10-ounce cups of Strohs, that night at a dime apiece—but it was probably astronomical and, in any event, was instrumental in the sale of beer and other alcoholic beverages at major league parks now being prohibited after the 7th inning.

All during the game there were disruptions from fans darting (many of them streaking) onto the field to throw lighted firecrackers into the Rangers' dugout. A tipsy young blonde ran onto the field and attempted to kiss home plate umpire Nestor Chylak. However, in each instance park security had stifled the commotion before any harm was done. The crowd was remarkably subdued considering all the beer that was consumed and the amount of pot that was being lit up. "The marijuana smoke was so thick in out there in right field, I think I was higher than the fans," said Rangers outfielder Jeff Burroughs afterward.

In the seventh inning, as the home club trailed 5–3, the storm began to build. The Ranger's bullpen came under siege. Garbage, tennis balls, batteries, rocks, and firecrackers rained down on the Texas relief pitchers. Ranger's skipper Billy Martin removed the relief crew to the dugout for safety. The trouble nonetheless followed them, but the game moved forward.

Finally, however, with the score knotted 5–5 in the bottom of the 9th inning, as Indians second baseman Jack Brohamer stepped into the batter's box just moments after the Tribe's John Lowenstein's sacrifice fly off Rangers reliever Steve Foucault had brought Ed Crosby home with the tying run, male fans in varying stages of inebriation poured out of the right field stands. Two ran towards Burroughs and attempted to take his hat and glove. Burroughs fought back initially, but as more and more fans surrounded him, players from both teams rushed to his aid, many armed with bats. Order was eventually restored but not before Rangers players had been dowsed with beer by fans standing on the roof of their dugout, and at that the peace was short-lived. After umpire Chylak sustained a badly lacerated hand when a fan heaved a chair at him to start a fresh melee and all of the bases had been stolen, he declared the game forfeited to Texas. Remarkably the injuries to the players were minimal. Burroughs only jammed his thumb, Texas pitcher Steve Foucault obtained a black eye and Indians reliever, Tom Hilgendorf, came away with minor bruises and bumps even though he was hit in the head by a thrown metal chair. According to Dan Epstein, *Newsweek* wrote it was "one of the ugliest incidents in the 105-year history of the game." Nine fans were arrested after the riot; seven more were hospitalized; and Rangers skipper Billy Martin summed up the evening, declaring, "That's probably the closest we'll ever come to seeing someone get killed in the game of baseball."

All statistics amassed during the game counted since it was tied at the time of the forfeit. In the ensuing two nights the Indians and Rangers played two games to complete their three-game series without any further incidents but in front of sparse crowds—8,101 and 6,116 respectively.

SOURCES

Cleveland Plain Dealer, June 5, 1974.

Epstein, Dan. Big *Hair and Plastic Grass* (New York: Thomas Dunne Books, 2010), 133, 235–236.

Nemec, David. *The Official Rules of Baseball Illustrate,* 3d ed. (Guilford, CT: Lyons Press, 2006), 48–49.

September 15, 1977

Place: Toronto
League: American
Field: Exhibition Stadium
Clubs: Toronto versus Baltimore
Umpires: Marty Springstead, Vic Voltaggio, Larry Barnett and Jim Evans

With his club behind 4–0 in the bottom of the 5th inning, Orioles pilot Earl Weaver asked crew chief Springstead to order the Toronto ground crew to remove the tarps covering the mounds in the Blue Jays' bull pen area. A light rain was falling, making the tarps' protection necessary in case Toronto had to warm up a reliever, but Weaver claimed they posed a risk to his left fielder's footing in the event he had to chase after a fly ball or one that rolled into the tarped area. Springstead compromised and removed the tarp from mound closest to fair territory but contended that the risk the other tarp posed was minimal and Weaver could play the game under protest if he liked. Weaver then exploded at having his judgment questioned and argued with Springstead for close to 20 minutes in front of the restive 14,675 fans in attendance before pulling his team off the field. Springstead, as per the rules, gave Weaver five minutes to ready his team to continue the game. When Weaver stubbornly stood his ground and the Orioles still showed no signs by disobeying their commander, he then forfeited the contest to Toronto.

The Blue Jays, in their very first year of existence, thus became the first post–1960 expansion team to win a game via forfeit. Since the Orioles had completed their raps in the top of the 5th, the game had gone the necessary distance to become official and all statistics counted, Jim Clancy getting the win and Ross Grimsley the loss. Due to this loss the Orioles and Red Sox tied for second place, which meant that there was less money to be dispersed within the Baltimore club.

This forfeit is the only one thus far in ML history that resulted from a manager's protest of a standard piece of equipment being allowed to remain on or near the playing field.

SOURCES

New York Times, September 16, 1977.
Toronto Star, September 16, 1977.
Washington Post, September 16, 1977.

July 12, 1979

Place: Chicago
League: American League
Field: Comiskey Park II
Clubs: Chicago versus Detroit
Umpires: Dave Phillips, Dan Morrison, Dallas Parks and Durwood Merrill

This event was essentially Bill Veeck's unfortunate swan song in a game that he had once inspired to unparalleled new heights. In his first venture as a club owner with Cleveland in the late 1940s almost every gimmick Veeck mustered from his fertile imagination to bolster attendance and perk civic enthusiasm for his team had met with astonishing success, but he is best remembered today, particularly in Chicago, for staging inarguably the most dangerous promotion in ML history in his second stint as a White Sox owner.

Spurred by the backlash from rock and roll aficionados against the disco craze that swept the nation in the late 1970s, Veeck, in conjunction with his son Mike, the promotions director of the White Sox in 1979, hit upon the notion of engaging Chicago shock jock and anti-disco campaigner Steve Dahl during a lackluster White Sox season to help the team's brass treat fans to a gala extravaganza between games of a twi-night double header made necessary by the rain out of a scheduled game between the Sox and Detroit on May 2. Dahl had been fired from Chicago radio station WDAI on Christmas Eve in 1978 when the station caved in to the disco craze and dropped its rock format to feature all disco music. The 24-year-old DJ was hired soon thereafter by arch rival album-rock station WLUP, "the Loop."

Already scheduled for the evening of July 12 was a promotion allowing teenagers to purchase tickets at half the regular price. In keeping with his philosophy that "you can draw more people with a losing team plus bread and circuses than with a losing team and a long, still silence," Veeck sweetened the promotion by having Dahl announce in the weeks prior to the event that all spectators, adults and teenagers alike, would pay only 98¢ if they brought a disco record they wanted to see blown up between the first and second games to the park with them. The disc jockey stepped up the hype with each passing day for fear that the promotion would fail to draw enough people and he and WLUP would be humiliated. His concerns appeared to be realized when the attendance for the game of July 11, the previous night, was only 15,520. Mike Veeck also was not optimistic the event would be a success but nevertheless thought he'd bought more than ample protection by hiring enough security for a crowd of 35,000.

Veeck's father had a premonition, however, that the evening might turn into a disaster and checked himself out of the hospital, where he had been undergoing tests. Bill Veeck's worries heightened when he saw people streaming toward Comiskey Park late that afternoon—the first game was slated to start at 6 p.m.—lugging anti-disco signs. Long before starting time the doubleheader not only had sold out, but a huge crowd was left standing in frustration outside the park. Many of them eluded security and leaped over turnstiles, climbed fences and squirmed through open windows. The attendance was officially announced as 47,795, exceeding the park's capacity of 44,492, but neutral observers believed the crowd actually numbered somewhere between 60,000 and 90,000 by the time the first game of the twinbill concluded with Detroit winning 4–1. Those who failed after trying all means to get into the stadium hung out in the parking lot and partied. Meanwhile the plan to gather all the disco records fans brought to the park in a large box went awry when the collection box was filled quickly to the brim, forcing many people to take their hated disco disks to their seats.

Umpire Durwood Merrill said of the event, "I knew we didn't have your typical baseball crowd because instead of families and kids, I saw a bunch of hard rockers with long hair and spacey-looking eyes. I could smell the marijuana from the moment I walked on to the field."

During the first contest the game had to be stopped several times when disgruntled fans sailed their uncollected LPs and singles from the stands like Frisbees. The records sliced through the air and landed stuck in the ground in such vast numbers that players on both sides began wearing batting helmets in the field. Some in the crowd also threw lit firecrackers and empty liquor bottles onto the field. Detroit's reliever Aurelio Lopez had garbage thrown at him as he warmed up in the 8th inning and Tigers right fielder Ron LeFlore escaped being skulled by a golf ball. Others contented themselves with hanging signs bearing such legends as "Disco Sucks" from the park's railings. All the while an odor of marijuana permeated the stands and reached the press box, where both Harry Caray and his broadcast partner, former ML outfielder Jimmy Piersall, commented over the air on the unprecedented turn of events at a ballgame. Mike Veeck later said, in summing up the catastrophic evening, "This is the Woodstock they [the teenage fans who had been mere children in 1968] never had."

Wiser heads would almost certainly have cancelled the between-games record demolition on the playing field, but the Veecks worried that the consequences might be even direr if they pulled the plug on their ill-fated venture with the crowd already in a crazed state. Accordingly, Dahl blew up the overflowing box of collected records as promised shortly after the first game of the doubleheader ended. He then took a victory lap around the field while standing on the back of the jeep with a stadium security guard and a photographer on the hood of the vehicle. While the debris from the explosion was being cleared, White Sox pitcher Ken Kravec went to the mound to warm up for the start of the second game and fans began to trickle onto the field. Two young men ran from left centerfield and slid into second base. More fans began to spill onto the field from all angles. Kravec abruptly pulled the cord on warm-ups and sped to Chicago's dugout on the third base side of the field. Soon the field resembled the goings on at Woodstock which occurred ten years earlier, almost to the day. Amid the chaos, some fans climbed the foul poles, ran around the field, ripped up the grass and threw it at each other, destroyed a batting cage and lit small fires, many starting with the "Disco Sucks" signs. They were eventually dispersed by riot police. By then so much time had elapsed since the first game had had concluded that the second contest was postponed by crew chief Phillips and the fans sent on their way in moods ranging from satisfaction at witnessing the destruction of thousands of disco records to displeasure among the small minority that had come to the park expecting to see two ball games. Remarkably only 39 people were arrested and six were taken to the hospital; however, the field was left in unspeakably unplayable condition. The following day, by order of AL president Lee MacPhail, the status of the second game was changed from postponed to forfeited to the Tigers.

SOURCES

Chicago Tribune, July 13, 1979.
Epstein, Dan. *Big Hair and Plastic Grass* (New York: Thomas Dunne Books, 2010), 241–244.
New York Times, July 13, 1979.

Washington Post, July 13, 1979.
www.youtube.com.

August 10, 1995

Place: Los Angeles
League: National League
Field: Dodger Stadium
Clubs: Los Angeles versus St. Louis
Umpires: Jim Quick, Bob Davidson, Bill Hohn and Larry Poncino

Forty-one years after the last previously forfeited game in the NL a crowd of 53,361 packed Dodger Stadium for a special Ball Night Promotion that featured as an added attraction the ballyhooed rookie Japanese pitcher Hideo Nomo facing the Cardinals, one of the Dodgers' longest-standing NL rivals. The game was briefly delayed in the bottom of the 7th inning when several fans started indiscriminately throwing their souvenir balls on the field, but tension did not really begin to mount until the bottom of the following frame. With the Cards ahead 2–1, the Dodgers had two on and two out with slugging first sacker Eric Karros at the plate. Karros was rung up on strikes. When he argued the called third strike too vigorously in plate umpire Quick's estimation, Quick lived up to his name and swiftly ejected him. Fans then began winging balls on the field in protest. Pleas over the public address to cease fire were successful on this occasion.

After the Cardinals were retired in their half of the ninth inning, Dodgers right fielder Raul Mondesi led off the bottom of the frame against St. Louis closer Tom Henke. With a count of 3-and-0, Mondesi looked at a Henke fastball that he thought was ball four. As he started to jog toward fire base, however, Quick (belatedly in the crowd's estimation) called it a strike. It was the closest pitch to being a strike in the sequence. Mondesi returned unwillingly to the batter's box and Henke's next pitch was far outside, but Quick called it strike two. Mondesi again started toward first but then turned around in disbelief after the strike call and yelped his disgust at Quick. With the count now full, Mondesi swung wildly and missed the next pitch, barked his rage at Quick and was immediately thrown out of the game. He continued to argue and Dodgers pilot Tommy LaSorda rushed onto the field in support of his player. As the heated conference took place, the fans sporadically heaved their ill-advised souvenirs onto the field. In short time LaSorda was also ejected after verbally jousting with Quick. Upon seeing Quick give their manager the heave-ho, Dodgers fans let loose a fresh torrent of baseballs from the stands. The umpires hurriedly brought the Cardinals in from the field and waited in the security of the Dodgers' dugout until the grounds crew had cleared the field. But no sooner had play resumed than the still angry fans unleashed another hailstorm of baseballs. Quick stopped play and forfeited the game to St. Louis.

First base umpire Davidson afterward called the decision to forfeit the game "100 percent correct" and criticized Lasorda. "This whole thing was Tom Lasorda's fault," Davidson told the *Associated Press*. "He instigated the crowd, waving his arms. He has himself to blame, absolutely. He knows he's to blame."

Lasorda countered: "How did I instigate it? I was talking to Jim Quick. All I was asking was why he threw my players out. We didn't throw the balls."

Cardinals players felt they were in danger not only from baseballs. "I wasn't too worried until a bottle of Southern Comfort flew out of the stands and hit me," Cardinals right fielder John Mabry told columnist Bob Nightengale of *The Sporting News*. "I got hit by a rum bottle too." St. Louis center fielder Brian Jordan said: "I'm not going to stand out there and get busted in the head with a ball. The umpires made a good decision." Hall of Fame pitcher Bob Gibson, then a Cardinals coach, told Nightengale that "Dodger fans used to be among the best in baseball. I'm afraid you can't say that anymore."

The gift win meant nothing to the Cardinals who were mired well below .500 for most of the season, but it nearly cost the Dodgers dearly. The strike-abbreviated 144-game season concluded with Los Angeles a mere one game ahead of the Colorado Rockies in the NL West Division standings.

SOURCES

Los Angeles Times, August 11, 1995.
The Sporting News, August 14, 1995.
www.youtube.com.

Successfully Protested Games

Protested games over the course of major league history have usually but not always been initiated by the captain or manager or a high ranking official of the team that believes it was the victim of a wrongdoing. Some have been initiated for a variety of reasons (not all of which are discernible at our distance from them) by a team not involved in the game in question. The vast majority of protests of games are not upheld. There are numerous reasons for this with the most frequent two being:

1. The protest had an incorrect basis, most commonly a disagreement with an umpire's judgment, which cannot be protested. A prime example of this occurred in the 2012 National League Wild Card game at Atlanta's Turner Field between the Braves and the St. Louis Cardinals. Trailing 6–3 in the eighth inning, the Braves appeared to catch a break when Andrelton Simmons's fly ball to short left field dropped between St. Louis shortstop Pete Kozma and left fielder Matt Holliday after the two miscommunicated over which of them had the best shot at catching it. But just before the ball dropped safely, left-field umpire Sam Holbrook signaled an automatic out because of the infield fly rule even though it had become clear by that point that the ball would be caught in the outfield—if it was caught at all. Instead of the Braves having the bases loaded with one out, they had runners on second and third with two out. The fans instantaneously started angrily hurling cups and trash, strewing the field. The Cards went on to win the game and eventually the World Series after Major League Baseball denied the Braves' protest, maintaining it was an umpire's judgment call on the play.

2. The team lodging the protest won the game, so it was never formally filed. The misfortune here for fans of the game, let alone researchers, is that many of these protests, some of which involve rules violations or sticky situations that are both fascinating and unique in major league history, are forgotten as soon as the games in which they occur end and thus never reach the

152

public eye. An inimitable illustration of this is the famous "Two Balls in Play" game on June 30, 1959, between the Chicago Cubs and the St. Louis Cardinals in which home plate umpire Vic Delmore absently gave a new ball to Cubs catcher Sammy Taylor while the two were arguing without realizing there was already a ball in play. The resulting havoc ended with Stan Musial, to his shock, being tagged out at second base with the old ball even as he was leaving second to go to third after Cubs pitcher Bob Anderson had thrown the new ball wildly into center field in a vain effort to nail Musial at second. The Cards immediately announced their intention to protest the game but withdrew it when they won, 4–1.

In the early days of major league baseball successfully protested games were replayed in their entirety. Nowadays when a protest is upheld, the game is supposed to be played from the point of the protested play as corrected unless picking up the game at the point where the protest originated will unfairly impact on one of the contesting teams. However, there have also been times when the protest has been upheld, but the game has not been resumed. One shameful example was the Cardinals at Dodgers game on July 20, 1947, when both teams batted in the ninth inning and all the hitting statistics from that frame have been incorporated by current reference works even though neither team made three outs!

May 20, 1872

Place: Baltimore
League: National Association of Professional Base Ball Players
Field: Newington Park
Clubs: Baltimore versus Philadelphia Athletics
Umpire: J.S. Graham

Trouble first began brewing in the bottom of the seventh inning with Baltimore at the bat and leading 7–4. With one out and third baseman Cherokee Fisher on first base, left fielder Tom York hit a ground ball to Athletics second baseman West Fisler. Known as "The Icicle," Fisler coolly watched Fisher run back and forth between second and first bases in an attempt to distract him before he threw to first baseman Denny Mack to put out York. Fisler then moved between first and second base to position himself for the return throw from Mack in an attempt to tag out the active Fisher. Fisher, in the eyes of umpire Graham, intentionally interfered with the throw and knocked the ball awry while it was en route from Mack to Fisler. Graham immediately called Fisher out and the arguments began, Baltimore claiming Fisher was hit accidentally rather than interfering intentionally with the throw. Meanwhile the largest crowd to date in Baltimore went berserk. Order was eventually restored and the game carried on, but Graham was visibly shaken.

The Athletics took their at-bats in the top of the 8th inning with a buzz still resonating in the park. Center fielder Fred Treacey grounded to Baltimore second baseman Lip Pike and was thrown out at first. Third baseman Cap Anson worked Baltimore pitcher Bobby Mathews for a walk and went to second base on shortstop Mike McGeary's single to center field. The *Baltimore Gazette* described the final act for the day as follows:

"Mack was at the bat when Anson was apparently put out at second on a [pickoff] throw from [catcher Bill] Craver. Much confusion ensued, and for a short time nothing could be heard but yells of 'out,' 'out.' In the confusion at last, it was understood that Mack had been given a base on called balls, and Anson had gone to third and McGeary to second on a balk of the pitcher's. While waiting for the next striker, [Ned]Cuthbert, to take his place, Mathews saw McGeary far off his base and threw the ball to Pike. 'Out at second,' said the umpire. Then began a scene that defies description. [Dick] McBride and four or five of the Athletic players surrounded the umpire and tried to force him again to reverse his decision, but he refused to, and they packed up their bats, refusing to play. He ordered play, and, no striker presenting himself, three pitched balls were caught by Craver, and the striker whose turn it was was decided out. The Athletics by this time had their bag of bats in their hand and were moving off the field, when the crowd came surging around the umpire and players to see the cause of the trouble, yelling like demons, 'play the game out,' 'go on with the game,' etc. The umpire decided that, as the Athletics refused to continue the game, the score should stand as it was at the end of the 7th inning, 7–4 in favor of Baltimore."

Graham was absolutely correct in ruling Fisher out in the 7th inning. The obstruction rule in 1872, Rule 7, Section 5, was seen in all rule books dating back to the Knickerbockers' rules of 1845. The second dispute is clear cut as well and we do not understand the basis for the Athletics' complaint (although one source claimed McGeary was a victim of the hidden ball trick rather than being picked off base by Mathews). Nevertheless their protest was later upheld and the game was replayed on August 5, the A's winning 24–9 with Bill Lennon, a member of the by then defunct Maryland team that had begun the 1872 season as a member of the NA, serving as the umpire.

Because the initial successfully protested game was declared a no-decision contest Mathews lost credit for a probable win and the A's McBride escaped a likely defeat. The statistics from the game have otherwise been incorporated in the record book, however, since it went the requisite length to become an official game.

The game of May 20, 1872, was only the second official NA contest Graham, a Baltimore man with dubious credentials for the job, officiated. He umpired just one more, a June 13, 1872 affair between the Baltimore Canaries and the Brooklyn Atlantics, also at Newington Park, and won by Baltimore, 17–7.

SOURCES

Baltimore Gazette, May 21, 1872.
Charles Mears Base Ball Scrapbook, vol. II, 1872.
De Witt's Base Ball Guide for 1872.
National Republican, May 21, 1872.
New York Times, May 21, 1872.
Washington Evening Star, May 21, 1872.

September 3, 1884

Place: Baltimore
League: American Association
Field: Oriole Park 1
Clubs: Baltimore versus Philadelphia
Umpire: Al Skinner

Sporting Life said of this contest: "The game at Baltimore of the 3rd was very tame, the Athletics having a complete walkover." The final count was 12–5, with the A's' Billy Taylor besting the Orioles' Hardie Henderson and going 3-for-4 in his own cause. Umpiring the contest was the mysterious Al Skinner, about whom nothing firm is known. His speculative birth year at one time was 1846, which would have made him a 38-year-old rookie in 1884 when he purportedly played two games in the Union Association in addition to his one-game umpiring gig.

Little research has been done into the circumstances surrounding this match because AA secretary Wheeler Wikoff later threw it out "because of the clubs failing to notify him of their intentions to play a postponed game." The contest was replayed in its entirety on October 10 with Taylor again the winning pitcher, this time triumphing 9–1 over the Orioles' Bob Emslie. To our knowledge this was the first major league game that was played by both teams in good faith that it would be a regulation contest but was later washed out of the record books because it had been scheduled without proper authorization.

SOURCE

Sporting Life, September 10, 1884, and October 15, 1884.

July 16, 1885

Place: Philadelphia
League: National League
Field: Recreation Park
Clubs: Philadelphia versus Providence
Umpire: Dave Sullivan

After Providence racked up two runs in the top of the 1st inning off Quakers starter Charlie Ferguson, right fielder Jack Manning led off the bottom half of the frame against Grays starter Dupee Shaw by drawing a walk. Ferguson (a great hitter as well as a pitcher), batting in the second spot, made an out. Left fielder Ed Andrews, third in the order, ran the count to five balls and a strike—six balls were needed in the 1885 NL to walk. *Sporting Life* said at that point, "Manning was evidently unaware of how many balls had been called, or else forgot himself, and on the next pitched ball started to steal second. It was the sixth unfair ball and [Jim] Fogarty (sic) was given his base. [Con] Dailey (sic), the Providence catcher, however, seeing Manning running at breakneck speed to second base threw to [second baseman Charlie] Bassett and caught Manning, and Umpire Sullivan declared him out. Captain Manning and Manager [Harry] Wright protested against the decision as a violation of rules on the ground that Manning could not be put out, being forced to second base by Fogarty's (sic) base on balls. Umpire Sullivan, however, argued that Manning had started to steal second and was a 'base-stealer' before he had decided the sixth ball and, therefore, forfeited his exemption from being put out. Notwithstanding appeals and arguments he held to his decision, and the game was played under protest. Since then the matter has been very much discussed, Umpire Sullivan's ruling finding a few supporters, and we have been deluged with a flood of inquiries as to the correctness of the decision. Life is short and space is brief, and we can do no better than quote the League rules bearing on the case. Here they are":

Sporting Life then proceeded to quote the pertinent rules, Numbers 52 and 34, from the 1885 Spalding Guide in their entirety and said they were "very plain and it seems to us leaves but little room for argument. Umpire Sullivan banks largely upon the claim that Manning had started to steal second before he had 'awarded the batsman his base on balls' and therefore was not forced. This is the sole point upon which the umpire rests his case, and we think he is here too mistaken. The ball had to pass by the batsman before catcher Daily could get it and throw it to second base. In that case it was either the sixth ball or a strike and rule 50 declares that the umpire must count and call every 'unfair ball' or 'strike,' and it seems to us that judgment upon the ball pitched was first in order before anything else. In our judgment Umpire Sullivan's decision giving Manning out at second base was wrong and it is our belief that the protest of the Philadelphia Club will be sustained."

The following week *Sporting Life* reported that Nick Young, the NL secretary at the time, "gave (Sullivan) the cold comfort that he was all wrong" in his decision. Nonetheless Young declared that the "game now stands as played, under protest, until the meeting of the board of directors this winter, when the protest will be considered and the question finally settled, unless the Philadelphia club should withdraw the protest, which is not at all likely. Meantime the game counts for Providence in the record."

We take this as strong evidence that the National League as late as 1885 still had no firm mechanism in place to guide it in the event a protested game had an impact on a pennant race if the protest was upheld. The fact that the next protested game we will discuss apparently wrought a similar decision in the American Association two years later indicates that prior to 1888 neither league had a plan for handling protested games during the season at hand other than those that were scheduled without proper authorization.

Notwithstanding his egregious bungle during the regular season, in the fall of 1885 Sullivan was hired without opposition from either team to umpire the World's Series between NL champion Chicago and AA champion St. Louis. Game 1 ended in a 5–5 tie when Sullivan stopped play due to darkness. The following day Sullivan forfeited the game to Chicago when St. Louis manager Charlie Comiskey pulled his team off the field in the sixth inning to protest what he regarded as two rank decisions by Sullivan in the space of a few minutes that gave Chicago a 5–4 lead. (**SEE: Forfeited game of October 15, 1885.**) He was replaced as the Series umpire prior to Game 3 and never worked as a regular big league umpire again, although he officiated a sprinkling of regular-season NL games later in the 1880s.

On January 4, 1890, Sullivan lunched with three friends, one of them ex-major league shortstop Bill White, at a café owned by the former Chicago White Stockings' catcher Silver Flint and the four were waited on by another ex-major leaguer, Tony Suck, who was down on his luck. They all then adjourned to play cards. As a hand was dealt, Sullivan asked White what his best day in baseball had been and White cited a great fielding day. Sullivan recalled several other such days by players now dead and then added, "But I am too tough to die" only minutes before he suffered a fatal heart attack.

SOURCES

Nemec, David. *Major League Baseball Profiles: 1871–1901* (Lincoln: University of Nebraska Press, 2011), 2: 217.
Spalding's Official Base Ball Guide, 1885.
Sporting Life, July 22, 1885, and July 29, 1885.

June 1, 1887

Place: Philadelphia
League: American Association
Field: Jefferson Street Grounds
Clubs: Philadelphia versus Louisville
Umpire: Ned Cuthbert

Ned Cuthbert was a key figure in the first upheld forfeited game in National League history. Eleven years later, in 1887, he officiated in an American Association game that *Sporting Life*, the leading sporting paper at the time, categorically stated would be successfully protested because of the way he mishandled a batting order gaffe. Nonetheless the results of Cuthbert's actions were allowed to stand by AA president Wheeler Wikoff.

We are including this game even though it appears not to have been successfully protested, because the protest was two-pronged, the lesser prong of which was valid while the other part had at its basis a present-day rule that was so fuzzily written in its early form that it was easily open to misinterpretation. Even *Sporting Life,* the leading commentator on the game at the time, in its discussion of the case on page 1 of its June 8, 1887, issue failed to grasp that the key element of the protest was invalid.

The contest commenced with Louisville catcher Amos Cross "down on the score card to bat ninth and [Tom] Ramsey [the pitcher] eighth, but they batted just the reverse, Cross leading Ramsey. This was noticed by reporters early in the game, and the score sheets were changed accordingly." Philadelphia manager Frank Bancroft seemingly did not call attention to the discrepancy until he thought it behooved him to do so. In the 7th inning Cross singled, the first base hit or walk in the game by either him or Ramsey, and in that frame Louisville tallied the run that ultimately gave Ramsey a 3–2 win over the A's Gus Weyhing. Louisville manager "Honest" John Kelly countered Bancroft's claim that the score card was the official guide, thereupon proving his case that Cross had batted out of turn, by claiming that since Cross had batted eighth for the entire game to that point, he was entitled to bat there. "Umpire Cuthbert, after hearing both sides, finally went up to the reporters' box, and upon being assured that Cross had batted eighth from the beginning, returned to the field and called play, not allowing Manager Bancroft's point. The game was finished under protest, neither side being able to score again."

Sporting Life flatly said, "Umpire Cuthbert was wrong, the protest was good and Louisville will undoubtedly lose the game." It first of all said that "Cuthbert acted illegally when he appealed to any outsider (the reporters) for advice." Here *Sporting Life* was correct; Cuthbert needed to refute Bancroft's argument entirely on his own and opened himself to a protest when he did not. But the paper then quoted verbatim the rule that it contended underscored the complete validity of Bancroft's protest. Yet in the end Louisville's 3–2 win withstood the challenge because the rule in 1887, much as today although not nearly as clearly stated, was:

"Rule 47. *The Batsman is out*:

(Sec 1.) If he fails to take his position at the bat in his order of batting, unless the error be discovered, and the proper Batsman takes his position before a fair hit has been made, and in such case the balls and strikes called will be counted in the time at bat of the proper batsman."

As can be seen, Section 1 can be read two different ways. This is but one example of an early-day game when the rules were still in a violent state of flux and in some instances murkily written, making it difficult for an umpire who was not thoroughly abreast of them, as appears to have been the case with Cuthbert. In sharp contrast, Louisville's Kelly, an umpire by trade who officiated in five consecutive World's Series from 1884–1888, was well versed in intricacies of the playing rules. Unlike Bancroft, he recognized that after Cross and Ramsey had batted the first time in their respective wrong spots in the order without a protest being lodged it established the Louisville batting order that was to be followed for the rest of the game

Cuthbert had a long history with the city of Philadelphia. He played for three Philadelphia clubs, both amateur and professionally, for six of his first seven years in baseball. However, he lasted only 37 games as an AA umpire in 1887 before being fired for "inefficiency," a judgment he disputed. The

Philadelphia Sun announced on September 25, 1887, that Cuthbert had brought a lawsuit against the American Association for his full salary for the 1887 season.

SOURCES

Nemec, David. *Major League Baseball Profiles: 1871–1900* (Lincoln: University of Nebraska Press, 2011), 1: 524–525 and 2: 209–210.
New York Sun, September 25, 1887.
Spalding's Official Base Ball Guide, 1887.
Sporting Life, June 8, 1887.

September 23 and 24, 1887

Place: Chicago
League: National League
Field: West Side Park I
Clubs: Chicago versus Boston
Umpire: Phil Powers

Boston player-manager John Morrill and Chicago player-manager Cap Anson arranged for their clubs to play one regularly scheduled game and three postponed games in the space of two days. On September 23, Chicago won the first game of a doubleheader 9–2 behind rookie southpaw George Van Haltren. The second contest then resulted in a 4–4 tie that was halted by darkness after eight innings. The following afternoon the two clubs met again in a twinbill. Boston's Charley Radbourn bested Chicago ace John Clarkson 10–4 in the first game and the Beaneaters also won the nightcap, 9–4, behind Dick Conway.

Unhappily for Boston only its loss in the first game of the September 23 doubleheader ended up counting in the standings as an official game. The other three games had all been replays of postponed games that had been rained out earlier in Boston. In order for them to have been legitimately rescheduled for play in Chicago approval of all the other six teams in the eight-club NL was required. Five of the six agreed to the change in venue, but first-place Detroit did not. Chicago president Al Spalding opted to play the games even without Detroit's consent, believing that the Wolverines' refusal was trifling, and then planned to petition NL officials to have them count if Detroit continued to maintain its obdurate stance. But the circuit chose not to allow any of the three transferred games. The trio are now listed in the record books as no decisions, but, except for pitching wins and losses, statistics from them have been incorporated in most current reference works.

SOURCES

Boston Globe, September 24, 1887, and September 25, 1887.
Chicago Tribune, September 24, 1887, and September 25, 1887.
New York Sun, September 25, 1887.
St. Paul Daily Globe, September 25, 1887.
Sporting Life, September 23, 1887, and September 30, 1887.

May 5, 1888

Place: Pittsburgh
League: National League
Field: Recreation Park
Clubs: Pittsburgh versus Philadelphia
Umpire: Charlie Daniels

After suffering four straight losses, Pittsburgh made it five when catcher Fred Carroll had trouble handling his favorite batterymate Ed Morris's quick pitches and Philadelphia prevailed 4–3 when its ace, Charlie Buffinton, scattered eight hits and fanned 10 Smoke City batsmen. Batting last and playing second base for Philadelphia on this day was its newest acquisition, Gid Gardner, then in his last ML season. Although not particularly instrumental in his club's victory, he played a heavy role in its reversal.

Gardner had come to Philadelphia from Washington in a trade for novice second baseman Cupid Childs on May 3. The trade was rescinded, however, when Childs refused to report to the weak Washington entry and compelled Philadelphia to release him instead so that he could sign with Kalamazoo of the minor Tri-State League. Pittsburgh manager Horace Phillips protested the game of May 5 when he learned the trade had never been consummated and won his case. The game was later replayed on July 18, with Pittsburgh again losing. Numerous reference works continue to count the game of May 5 as a Philadelphia win and also to count its statistics, including those belonging to Gardner who went 2-for–3 against Morris. In any event, this is the first protested major league game that was dismissed rather than forfeited because of the use of an ineligible player.

Forced to return to Washington, Gardner played only one more game after returning before leaving the majors. Anyone reading his biography in *Major League Baseball Profiles: 1871–1900* will marvel that he was still viewed as a player of major league caliber as late as 1888. After leaving baseball in the late 1880s, Gardner seems to have never again held a steady job prior to his death in 1914.

SOURCES

Nemec, David. *Major League Baseball Profiles: 1871–1900* (Lincoln: University of Nebraska Press, 2011), 1: 244.
Sporting Life, July 18, 1888.
Washington Post, May 6, 1888.

June 10, 1888

Place: New Jersey
League: American Association
Field: Gloucester Point Grounds
Clubs: Philadelphia versus Baltimore
Umpire: Herm Doescher (aka Doscher)

This was Philadelphia's first scheduled Sunday "home" game as a member of the AA because the City of Brotherly Love refused to allow professional ball to be played on Sunday within its confines until 1933. The date had been mutually agreed upon by both teams as a make up for an earlier rained out game on April 21 in large part because it promised to draw a substantial working class crowd, which had only their Sundays free to attend games. A's second-year hurler Gus Weyhing went 3-for-5 in his own support, including a triple, and breezed to an 11–4 win over Baltimore's ace fireballer, Matt Kilroy, who was racked for 17 hits and 25 total bases.

The game was subsequently negated because it was played without the expressed approval of AA president Wheeler Wikoff. Consequently the A's first official Sunday home contest at Gloucester is now considered to have been a 6–0 win over Kansas City on August 5, 1888, but some reference works still carry the statistics from the game of June 10. The protest originated with Brooklyn president Charlie Byrne, who contended that the postponed game of April 21 had been played off earlier in the season on May 18 in Philadelphia, and Byrne's gripe was echoed by Baltimore manager Billy Barnie. Neither seems to have had anything significant to gain by it. We also find it curious that Byrne's and Barnie's protest was not registered until after the close of the AA season and that Wikoff's decision was not rendered until October 16, more than four months after the game at issue, and are including it in the hopes that our curiosity will invoke further study of how protested games in both major leagues were treated prior to 1890.

SOURCES

New York Tribune, June 11, 1888.
Sporting Life, October 24, 1888.

July 8, 1888

Place: Kansas City
League: American Association
Field: Association Park
Clubs: Kansas City versus Baltimore
Umpire: Jack Kirby and Phenomenal Smith

When Bob Ferguson went missing after umpiring the July 4 holiday doubleheader at Kansas City between the Cowboys and the Cleveland Blues, "the new system of umpiring in the absence of the regular umpire was given a trial" in Kansas City's next home game on July 6 against Baltimore. The system entailed having each team designate a player who would not be in the game that day to act as an umpire, with the choices being made by Kansas City player-manager Sam Barkley and Baltimore manager Billie Barnie. The first two games of the series, on July 6 and July 7, were conducted without any untoward incidents even though *Sporting Life* characterized them as having been umpired "with unsatisfactory results" as Kansas City won 6–3 on July 6 with Jack Kirby representing the Cowboys and Tommy Burns the Orioles and then won 13–9 on July 7 with Kansas City catcher Fatty Briody working the plate and Baltimore outfielder Joe Sommer handling the bases. The following day's game, on July 8, drew this scathing report from *Sporting Life*: "The two-umpire system with players officiating proved a decided failure in this game." Kirby and Smith, both pitchers, took turns working the plate, each calling the pitches when his side was at bat.

The game on July 8, from all accounts, went along a rocky but navigable path until the 8th inning when it began to run into a string of impasses after Kansas City took a 2–1 lead. In the 9th frame the ball and strike calls of both pitcher-umpires met with severe objections from opposing camps. "In the visitors' half of the ninth Smith called five balls on each of the first three at bat [five balls constituted a walk in the AA in 1888], his decisions being questioned. Barkley then touched the runner on second with the ball and threw to [first baseman Bill] Phillips, who touched the runner on first, Kirby calling both out [to complete a double play]. To this action Baltimore violently objected, Manager Barnie first calling his men off the field. He finally ordered them back after fifteen minutes' wrangling, and the game was played under protest." That night Barkley and a Kansas City club official went to Barnie's quarters and informed him "that while Kansas City claimed the game on its merits, they were willing to declare the game off and play it over. This was agreed to." After an off day the following day, a Monday, the two clubs met again on July 10. Bill Terry, a neutral player with the Brooklyn club which had arrived in town the night before for its upcoming series with Kansas City, umpired the game by mutual consent and with the approval of loop president Wheeler Wikoff, with Baltimore winning 12–1. Still lacking a regular umpire, the Bridegrooms and Kansas City then began their series the following day using players to officiate, and it spelled disaster. (**SEE: Forfeited game of July 14, 1888.**)

Kansas City in all likelihood agreed to replay the game of July 8 not out of the goodness of its heart but mainly out of concern that Baltimore would wreak revenge the following day by calling on someone even more biased than Smith and creating a similar debacle in which one or perhaps even both teams would once again protest the game. Conceivably Barkley and his Kansas City cohort went to Barnie only after they had wired the Brooklyn team, knowing it would arrive in town the sometime the following day after its game of July 8 in St. Louis, and gotten an agreement from them to allow Terry to umpire their game of July 10. The game of July 8, 1888, meanwhile remains the lone contest in ML history where the victorious team acceded to the vanquished club's formal protest even before it was acted upon by the league office.

SOURCE

Sporting Life, July 11, 1888, and July 18, 1888.

May 23, 1890

Place: Chicago
League: National League
Field: West Side Park I
Clubs: Chicago versus Philadelphia
Umpire: Jack McQuaid

Chicago scored two runs in the top of the 10th inning to break an 8–8 tie and seemingly won uncontestably, 10–8, when the Quakers failed to score in their final at-bats since there was no mention in any of the newspaper accounts the following day of any disputed plays or protests. Unbeknownst, however, to reporters at the game Philadelphia manager Harry Wright had lodged a protest when umpire McQuaid refused to allow him to substitute rookie catcher Bill Grey for Bill Schriver during the course of the contest. McQuaid apparently had either been unaware of or else had forgotten a new rule—Rule 28, Section 2—drafted the previous winter that substitutions as of 1890 could be made on a limited basis even for players who were not injured.

The new rule stated: "Two players, whose names shall be printed on the score-card as extra players, may be substituted at any time by either club, but no player so retired shall thereafter participate in the game."

Page 47 of the 1891 Spalding guide made it clear that the protested game was not counted in the 1890 NL standings. Nonetheless a number of reference works in the years since have credited Chicago with a win and assigned a victory to its ace, Bill Hutchison, while saddling Quakers rookie Tom Vickery with a loss.

Since the game was not included in the final NL standings, it stands as the first major league game since the National Association's lone successfully protested match in 1872 whose result was declared a no-decision during the course of a season by the directors of a league owing to an umpiring infraction. In its discussion of the matter, *Sporting Life* said on page 1 of its August 23, 1890, issue that the National League's directors had reached a unanimous decision after an interrogation of McQuaid revealed he admitted "a violation of the rules, and the presumption being that his action had a material effect on the outcome of the game."

SOURCES

Chicago Tribune, May 24, 1890.
Pittsburgh Dispatch, May 24, 1890.
Reach's Official Base Ball Guide, 1891.
Spalding's Official Base Ball Guide, 1891.
Sporting Life, August 23, 1890.

July 10, 11 and 12, 1890

Place: Boston
League: Players League (PL)
Field: Congress Street Grounds
Clubs: Boston versus Pittsburgh
Umpires: John Gaffney and Jack Sheridan

Boston won the Players League pennant with relative ease in the loop's lone year of existence. As a result, the Reds' midseason bending of the circuit's rules in collusion with the New York PL club drew little national attention at the time. During its three-game series at home with Pittsburgh on July 10, 11 and 12, Boston essentially borrowed Gil Hatfield from the New York club to fill in at shortstop while Arthur Irwin was out with an injury. The unauthorized loan immediately unleashed the ire of PL president John Ward, who was also the player-manager of the Brooklyn PL entry.

Popular with the New York Giants' dominant clique, Hatfield had shared in that club's two World's Series triumphs in 1888–89 even though he played in only 60 games during that span and hit just .183. Utilizing his Giants connections, he had then landed a coveted spot on the New York PL team in 1890. Rather miraculously, he opened the season at shortstop, but weak fielding soon landed him back on the bench until he was loaned to the Boston PL club. Hatfield was not the only player passed from one team to another illegally in the free-wheeling 1890 season, which featured three leagues and 24 clubs all struggling for survival, but his movement drew the stiffest penalty. All three games in which he appeared for Boston resulted in Boston wins and were later thrown out when the Players League as a whole shared in Ward's condemnation of his illegitimate participation. Among the statistics that were later dismissed were several home runs, including two by the Reds' Hardy Richardson, and three Boston pitching wins, one belonging to Bill Daley that would, if it had counted, have given him a .750 winning percentage, tops among qualifiers in all three major circuits that season.

SOURCES

Boston Globe, July 11, 1890, July 12, 1890, and July 13, 1890.
Sporting Life, July 12, 1890.

August 11, 1890

Place: St. Louis
League: American Association
Field: Sportsman's Park I
Clubs: St. Louis versus Brooklyn
Umpires: Wes Curry

This game is of special interest on two counts. First, it was a playoff of an earlier postponed game in Brooklyn that had been transferred to St. Louis without obtaining agreement in advance from AA officials, which in itself is sufficient reason to protest its inclusion in the official 1890 AA standings. The second reason, and the more compelling one, is that when the game is counted in the standings, 21 games were played to a decision in 1890 between St. Louis and Brooklyn (whose franchise was transferred to Baltimore after it folded following its game of August 25) when a maximum of 20 was allowed since the schedule that year in the eight-team circuit called for a total of 140 games, 20 for every club against each of its other seven compatriots. Yet the statistics for this game unaccountably are still included in most reference works including SABR's Retrosheet except for pitching decisions, which would have belonged to Tom Ramsey and Ed Daily were they registered as per *Sporting Life's* report of the game. In "a regular slugging match" the Browns trailed 7–1 in the 3rd inning when their twin ace Jack Stivetts was replaced by Tom Ramsey, who then went the rest of the way in St. Louis's eventual 15–9 triumph over the Gladiators' Ed Daily.

Had Ramsey garnered the win he would have finished with 24 victories in what turned out to be his final ML season even though he was still just 26 years old. The Browns' left fielder, Chief Roseman, also in his final ML season at age 34, was more fortunate. He went 4-for-4 on the day, stole a base and also was hit once by a pitch. Were those statistics ever to be deducted from his season totals his BA would shrink from .339 to .330.

SOURCE

Sporting Life, August 16, 1890.

April 26, 1894

Place: Brooklyn
Leagues: National League and American Association of Professional Base Ball Clubs
Field: Washington Park I
Clubs: Brooklyn versus Philadelphia
Umpire: Billy Stage

The day following Brooklyn's one-sided 13–3 loss to the Phillies, the *New York Times* wrote: "Capt. Foutz's team put up a poor game of ball against the Philadelphia team yesterday, and the result was the latter won with ease.... 'Gus' Weyhing, the old Brooklyn pitcher, was in the box for the Philadelphians yesterday, and he filled his position in good style, only one earned run being charged against him." Weyhing in fact pitched a complete game and allowed just six hits; yet, while all the statistics he compiled that day now count in all current reference works, he will never receive credit for the win, nor will his Brooklyn counterpart, Jack Sharrott, ever be tagged with a loss.

Blame it on Philadelphia manager Arthur Irwin who had an unfathomable attack of brain lock in the top of the 1st inning when his Phillies tallied three runs and in his eagerness to compile even more he sent Jack Taylor, a good-hitting pitcher (.338 in 1894) to the plate when it came Weyhing's turn to bat. After Taylor failed to deliver a hit, he retired to the bench and Weyhing, the announced starting pitcher on the lineup card Irwin handed Foutz, took the mound in the bottom of the 1st. *The New York Tribune* did not catch the error and simply printed that Taylor batted for Weyhing in the 1st inning. Apparently neither did any of the 3,500 spectators attending the game on Ladies' Day. But we surmise that someone on the Brooklyns noted that Weyhing had reentered the game after being removed for a pinch hitter, and Foutz

Sam Thompson, the winner of the 1894 National League RBI crown. The award was not bestowed on him until more than a century after the fact when Major League Baseball opted to count the previously excluded stats from protested games that season. This decision ended Hugh Duffy's long reign as the first undisputed National League Triple Crown winner.

either chose not to make an issue of it until after the game was over or else called it to Stage's attention when the incident occurred and perhaps told him to keep it under his hat until such time as Brooklyn officially lost the game. (Stage, an amateur sprinting champion of the A.A.U. of Cleveland, was making his first League appearance as an umpire.) Irwin, in any case, seemed unaware that substituting Taylor for Weyhing in the batting order and then failing to have him take the rubber in the bottom of the 1st was a flagrant violation of what was then Rule 27, Section 2, which read in effect that any player in uniform could be substituted at any point in the game by either club, but once a player's name appeared on the lineup card he could not return to the game after his name was removed from it. Had the game been at Philadelphia rather than at Brooklyn undoubtedly one of the local writers in attendance would have called Irwin's oversight to his attention immediately upon seeing Weyhing take the pitcher's position rather than Taylor. As it was, surely some of the Phillies' players ought to have been well enough versed in the substitution rule, even though it was a relatively new one, to save their skipper from embarrassment and themselves from losing a possible victory.

Brooklyn's protest of the obvious infraction was a no brainer decision for NL president Nick Young. The game was summarily thrown out and Weyhing's effort was for naught. Consequently he finished just 16–14 in 1894 and never again was better than a .500 pitcher in the majors. Weyhing, much more than most hurlers, struggled to master the change in pitching distance when it was lengthened to 60'6" in 1893. His curve ball broke too early at the increased distance, and his outing on April 26, 1894, proved to be one of the last days when he had it working to its old effect. During the preceding seven seasons Weyhing had won 200 games before reaching his 27th birthday, but he collected only 64 more wins even though, unlike many hurlers of his era, his arm did not suffer a premature demise due to overwork.

Until fairly recently none of the statistics in successfully protested games during the 1890s were counted in reference works since the custom at that time was to exclude them. That has now changed, and the Weyhing game has become pivotal. For over a century Boston's Hugh Duffy was considered to have won the first undisputed Triple Crown in National League history in 1894, but he no longer is regarded as having been the RBI leader that year. The honor now goes to the Phillies' Sam Thompson, who was involved in no less than three protested games in 1894 and collected six RBI that had previously not counted in these three games—on April 26, August 27 and September 6—to swell his total in 1894 from 141 to 147, surpassing Duffy's total of 145.

SOURCES

Brooklyn Daily Eagle, April 27, 1894.
Nemec, David. *Major League Baseball Profiles: 1871–1900* (Lincoln: University of Nebraska Press, 2011), 2: 109–210 and 216–217.
New York Times, April 27, 1894.
New York Tribune, April 27, 1894.

May 23, 1894

Place: Chicago
Leagues: National League and American Association of Professional Base Ball Clubs
Field: West Side Park I
Clubs: Chicago versus Pittsburgh
Umpire: Bob Emslie

The *Chicago Tribune* wrote of this game: "Only six innings were played at the West Side Park yesterday, but six were worse than anything.... The pitching was, on both sides, wretched, twenty bases on balls being given in the six innings." No less than six hurlers in all tried their fortunes in the contest, which was blessedly ended after six innings with Pittsburgh ahead 10–9. The affair actually went another half frame, but reverted to the 6th inning when "Chicago could effect nothing" in the top of the 7th.

At that point Emslie halted the game to enable Pittsburgh to catch a 6:45 p.m. train to Cleveland, its next destination on its western road swing, But the *Tribune* pointed out that Chicago had already decided to protest the premature stoppage in play because "there is another train at 9 every evening" to Cleveland. Though the *New York Sun* made no mention of a prearranged protest, it noted in its game recap that "the Pirates could have finished the game and left on a later train." The protest was subsequently upheld by NL president Nick Young and Pittsburgh's win was removed from the standings as was Chicago's defeat. The statistics from the game have since all been restored, however, excepting credit for pitching decisions. The chief beneficiaries of the restitution were Chicago's rookie shortstop Charlie Irwin, who went 3-for–3 that day, and one of its three pitchers in the contest, Frank Donnelly, whose ML career heretofore had ended in 1893, but he is now credited with having hurled his final game in the bigs on July 27, 1894.

Although details of this upheld protest are sketchy, one might surmise that Pittsburgh struck a pre-game agreement with Chicago to leave the ball grounds in time to catch the 6:45 train, which would bring it to Cleveland early enough that Pirates players could get a full night's sleep and Chicago officials, upon checking train schedules, learned of the 9 p.m. train that would have still arrived in Cleveland in ample time for the Pirates to still get sufficient rest before their afternoon game the following day and perhaps kept their discovery to themselves pending results of the August 27 contest.

Sources

Chicago Tribune, May 24, 1894.
New York Sun, May 24, 1894.
New York Tribune, May 24, 1894.
Sporting Life, July 28, 1894.

August 18, 1894

Place: New York
Leagues: National League and American Association of Professional Base Ball Clubs

Field: Polo Grounds III
Clubs: New York versus Chicago
Umpire: Jack McQuaid

A healthy crowd of some 15,000 came away disappointed after seeing their beloved Giants drop the first game of a Saturday doubleheader to Chicago's Scott Stratton, 6–4, and then play to a 5–5 10-inning draw in the second contest after Chicago center fielder Bill Lange made a splendid running catch of New York third baseman George Davis's long drive that saved a potential game-winning home run in the 10th frame. The day's results seemingly meant the Giants had lost valuable ground in their effort to catch the front-running Baltimore Orioles. However, later that month Giants manager John Ward induced the Cincinnati club to protest his club's defeat in the first game, because it had been transferred from Chicago to New York without league permission. When Cincinnati's protest was upheld, the lost first game of the twinbill game was thrown out.

Ward's machinations were payback for Boston's protest of the Giants' transferred game from Louisville to New York of August 25, 1894, which resulted in a New York victory. The Boston club's protest had unwittingly opened up a can of worms that it probably regretted, because, as *Sporting Life* rudely pointed out, it summoned back foul-tasting memories of the 1891 season when "the League championship was clouded by New York's peculiar action in playing off a number of postponed games in Boston with a weakened team, and a scandal ensued which unquestionably hurt the League." But unlike in 1891, *Sporting Life* did not decry the transfer of games without permission from one city to another for its potential unsavory impact on the pennant race. Rather, the paper felt the transfers were engineered "purely for commercial reasons ... merely to make for doubleheaders (in the larger Eastern cities like New York) and thereby swell the gate receipts."

When the 1894 campaign brought four such protested games, all of which were thrown out, what threatened to become a rampant practice of transferring games without first obtaining league approval was swiftly curtailed. But the practice itself continued once the larger market teams recognized that permission from the league was almost always readily forthcoming.

SOURCES

New York Sun, August 19, 1894.
New York Times, August 19, 1894.
Sporting Life, September 22, 1894.

August 25, 1894

Place: New York
Leagues: National League and American Association of Professional Base Ball Clubs
Field: Polo Grounds III
Clubs: New York versus Louisville
Umpire: Tim Hurst

The Giants won a doubleheader from the Colonels on this date, 18–6 and 5–1, but only the first game counted in the standings. Boston, coming off a string of three straight pennants and ultimately a third-place finisher in 1894, championed the protest against the lidlifter, citing the fact that the game had been transferred from Louisville, where it had been originally scheduled, without league approval. Jouett Meekin was thereby denied a win that would have brought his total that season to 34, just two behind his teammate Amos Rusie, who led the loop that season with 36 victories. Spared the loss in the protested game was George Nicol, who had hurled a 7-inning no hitter in his ML debut just four years earlier but had become primarily an outfielder by 1894.

This game was the second of four contests in 1894 to be thrown out for being transferred without league approval but the first that was acted upon by league president Nick Young. It set off a chain reaction that season but did not stop the practice of transferring games. As the 1890s wore on and economic conditions deteriorated on the national front, clubs in smaller venues like Louisville were eager to seek league approval so that they could transfer as many of their home dates as possible to the parks of their more prosperous confreres. The odious stampede to augment the coffers of the small market clubs at the expense of their fans peaked in 1899. (**SEE: Protested game of September 6, 1894.**)

SOURCES

Boston Globe, August 26, 1894.
New York Times, August 26, 1894.

August 27, 1894

Place: Philadelphia
League: National League and American Association of Professional Base Ball Clubs
Field: Philadelphia Baseball Grounds
Clubs: Philadelphia versus Cincinnati
Umpire: Tom Lynch

After 10 straight wins, the Phillies suffered a disheartening sweep at the hands of Cincinnati in a doubleheader on this date, but the first game, a 19–9 drubbing, was later erased when Cleveland initiated the protest against its transfer without league permission from Cincinnati to Philadelphia. Statistics from the game, as is true now of all protested games from the 1890s that were initially played to completion before they were thrown out, have been restored with the sole exception of pitching decisions. Kid Carsey, the Phils' starter, would otherwise have absorbed the loss and Bill Whitrock, who went the route for the Reds, had a win deducted.

SOURCES

Chicago Tribune, August 28, 1894
New York Sun, August 27, 1894.

September 6, 1894

Place: Philadelphia
Leagues: National League and American Association of Professional Base Ball Clubs
Field: Philadelphia Baseball Grounds
Clubs: Philadelphia versus Cincinnati
Umpire: Tim Hurst

Ostensibly, Philadelphia won a doubleheader from Cincinnati on this date, but the Phils' 14–7 first-game victory was later thrown out because it had been transferred from Cincinnati without league permission. As in the above protested game, the Cleveland Spiders are on record as having instigated the protest. Gus Weyhing, the victor over Cincinnati's Chauncey Fisher in the

Gus Weyhing, one of the nineteenth century's most underrated pitchers. In 1894 he became the only big league hurler to have two complete-game victories overturned via protest in the same season.

lidlifter, had his second win that season in a protested game erased when this protest was also upheld. No records are extant as yet of the number of losses or wins a particular pitcher was denied when a game in which he figured was later thrown out, but Weyhing may have been the only hurler to lose as many as two wins in a single season via protested games.

This game is also meaningful in that it too, like earlier protested games that year involving Philadelphia, padded Sam Thompson's RBI total, enabling him to now be recognized as the league's RBI leader in 1894. Some two weeks later *Sporting Life* discussed the unusual number of games in 1894 that had been transferred without league approval. The practice became increasingly common in the decade of the 1890s as the gap widened between the small market and large market teams, and permission for transferring games, heretofore given only under duress, came to be given almost as a matter of course. Game transferring from one city to another reached ridiculous proportions in 1899 when the financially strapped Cleveland Spiders played only 42 games at their home park, winning but nine, and were essentially a touring team after the season' midpoint. Although the 140-game schedule between 1893 and 1897 called for each team to have 70 home games and 70 road games and was increased to 154 games with 77 home games and 77 road games in 1898–99, in most seasons the larger market teams like New York played far more than half their games at home while teams like Louisville played far less. In 1899, the Colonels' last season as a major league entity, even though they finish with a respectable 75–76 record, they played 90 of their 156 games (including ties) on the road and just 71 at home.

We also note here that prior to 1951 there was no rule when a doubleheader that included a makeup game was scheduled with regard to which was the makeup game and which was the regularly scheduled game. In 1951, Rule 4.12 (h) was introduced, stating that the first game of a doubleheader that included a makeup game was always the regularly scheduled contest.

SOURCES

Chicago Tribune, September 7, 1894.
New York Times, September 7, 1894.
Sporting Life, September 22, 1894.

June 1, 1895

Place: Brooklyn
Leagues: National League and American Association of Professional Base Ball Clubs

Field: West Side Park II
Clubs: Brooklyn versus Pittsburgh
Umpire: Miah Murray

With Brooklyn ahead 1–0 in the top of the 3rd inning, the Pirates' right fielder and leadoff hitter Patsy Donovan doubled with two out. No sooner had he reached second base than it began to rain heavily and umpire Murray, a former ML catcher, stopped play. "After waiting about ten minutes the rain ceased and Donovan went back to second by way of a short cut. Capt. [Mike] Griffin, [Brooklyn's center fielder] came in to second and called to [Brooklyn pitcher Roaring Bill] Kennedy for the ball and touched Donovan, who was standing on the base, claiming that under the rules Donovan was out as he forgot to go to second by way of first." The *New York Sun* reported that after Murray called Donavan safe, "Griffin quickly pulled out the League rules." Cowed by the Brooklyn captain's seeming expertise, Murray, a rookie league umpire, recanted and called Donovan out, ending Pittsburgh's at-bats in the 3rd frame. Pittsburgh Manager Connie Mack, first baseman, Jake Beckley, Donovan and a motley portion of the visiting club circled Murray and argued in vain that he was interpreting the rule wrongly. The game was then played to its conclusion, Brooklyn winning 12–4 over the Pirates' Tom Colcolough.

Griffin was citing Rule 47 from *Spalding's Official Base Ball Guide, 1895*. The rule stated: "The Base Runner must touch each base in regular order, viz, First, Second, Third and Home Bases, and when obliged to return (except on a foul hit) must touch the base or bases in reverse order. He should only be considered as holding a base after touching it, and shall be entitled to hold such base until he has legally touched the next base in order, or has been legally forced to vacate it for a succeeding base runner." Common sense would lead one to believe that once a game is halted by an umpire and later resumed, the game would begin as if there were no lapse in time. Since Donovan already held second base at the time the game was stopped and was not attempting to make third or home base, he would thus not be required to touch any base in reverse order. This indeed was the thinking that league president Nick Young embraced when the protest, instigated by Pittsburgh player-manager Connie Mack, crossed his desk. Young declared the game a no-decision. His proclamation erased Kennedy's win and Colcolough's loss, but since restored were home runs by Brooklyn's George Treadway and John Anderson along with a rare four-bagger by Pirates' second baseman Lou Bierbauer, whose lone round-tripper in 1894 came in this game.

Murray's faulty reasoning in ruling Donovan out for not having touched first on his way to second after the game was resumed no doubt came from his unfamiliarity with the nuances of Rule 50. Griffin may not have known them all either, but it seems more likely that he did and was simply taking a flier that he could dupe the novice official by focusing on Rule 47 and hoping Murray would not read farther and see that Rule 50, Section 14 stated that Donovan did not need to touch first base in this case because he had attained second base prior to the game being suspended. Once the suspension was lifted all he needed to do was return as mandated to the base he held.

Whatever the case, Nick Young did not look fondly on Murray's wrong-headed action. He was not rehired by the league after working 112 games in 1895 and was never again more than a rarely employed substitute official.

The rule that Murray apparently was unaware of was first put into effect in 1881 and has been applicable in similar situations ever since

SOURCES

Brooklyn Daily Eagle, June 2, 1895.
New York Sun, June 2, 1895.
New York Times, June 2, 1895.
Spalding's Official Base Ball Guide, 1895.
Washington Post, June 2, 1895.

July, 14, 1895

Place: St. Louis
Leagues: National League and American Association of Professional Base Ball Clubs
Field: Sportsman's Park II
Clubs: St. Louis versus Cleveland
Umpires: Harry Staley and Bobby Wallace

Umpires Fred Jevne and Miah Murray had officiated St. Louis's previous home series with Philadelphia that ended on Saturday, July 13, and Jim McDonald was due to arrive sometime the following day to work the Browns' next regularly scheduled game on July 15. The July 14 game was a late addition to the schedule, meant to take the place of a game originally scheduled for September 12, and was designed to take advantage of what was anticipated would be a larger than normal crowd since it would be played on a Sunday. Following its home contest with New York on July 13, Cleveland was willing to make the trip for just a single game in part because Monday, July 15, was a scheduled off day before it commenced its series at home with Baltimore on July 16.

In the absence of a regular umpire the two clubs, as per the custom at that time, each chose a player from their own ranks to officiate. The Browns selected Harry Staley, a fine pitcher earlier in the decade who had slipped badly after he had begun putting on weight and was then in his final ML season. Cleveland picked Bobby Wallace, then in his second season and also a pitcher but slated to become a Hall of Fame shortstop once he moved from the mound to the infield. The two alternated each inning on calling balls and strikes and rendering decisions on the bases.

Going into the bottom of the 5th inning, Cleveland led 3–2 behind Zeke Wilson but trailed 5–3 by the time the bottom half of the frame ended. Meanwhile Cleveland player-manager Pat Tebeau in all probability had already stored in the back of his mind his intention to lodge a formal protest in the event Cleveland lost the game. Tebeau's grievance occurred when St. Louis's slugging first sacker, Roger Connor, while moving from first base to second, was struck by a batted ball hit by Browns shortstop Bones Ely and St. Louis left fielder Dick Cooley was allowed to score from third base on the play even though the rule then as now called for Connor to be declared out for interference as soon as the ball hit him

TEBEAU, 3d B., Clevelands

OLD JUDGE CIGARETTE FACTORY. GOODWIN & CO., New York.

An Old Judge card of Pat Tebeau as he was about to begin his first year as a member of the Cleveland Spiders in 1889. The picture of innocence here, he was the bane of every umpire in the National League while serving as the Spiders' player-manager in the 1890s and at the root of many forfeits and successfully protested games.

and the ball ruled dead with no base runners being allowed to advance. Staley, working the bases that inning, made the decision, and it was a puzzling one because, while Cooley was allowed to score from third on the play, Browns second sacker Joe Quinn, who also scored from second, was sent back to third. We can't know whether Staley slanted his decision to favor his own team or simply didn't know the rule. But one thing that was clear even at the time it happened was that the decision would lead to a protest. All the papers the next day even said as much in their recounting of the game.

When St. Louis prevailed 5–4, with the win going to its ace, Ted Breitenstein, after he set down Cleveland in the top of the 9th inning, Tebeau sent his troops back on the field, feigning that he thought the score was 4–4 and it had been decided that Cooley's run back in the 5th inning hadn't counted. When none of the Browns paid him any mind, he ordered Wallace to remain on the field and declare the game forfeited to Cleveland. Only then, when it was evident that he would not otherwise have his way, did Tebeau formally declare that he would protest the game to the league office. The contest, as anticipated, was later declared a no-decision and Breitenstein lost a win while Wilson had a loss removed from his ledger. The two clubs subsequently replayed the game in its entirety on September 15 during Cleveland's final visit of the season to St. Louis. Cleveland, then on a hot streak that would carry it to second place and a spot in the Temple Cup against the pennant-winning Baltimore Orioles, won three games in the series and tied a fourth. It would go on to win the Temple Cup, which would remain the lone postseason triumph by a Cleveland ML franchise until 1920.

SOURCES

Chicago Tribune, July 20, 1895.
Sporting Life, July 20, 1895.
Washington Post, July 15, 1895.

August 12, 1895

Place: Boston
League: National League and American Association of Professional Base Ball Clubs
Field: South End Grounds II
Clubs: Boston versus Washington
Umpire: George Barnum

The crowd of some 1,200 left South End Grounds late on the afternoon of August 12 believing that their Beaneaters had beaten lowly Washington 4–3 on a walkoff run in the bottom of the 10th inning that came home from second base with two out in the person of Hugh Duffy when Washington left fielder John Anderson muffed Tommy Tucker's deep fly ball after a long run.

Had Anderson made the catch Barnum (an actor by trade who umpired only as a side venture) in all probability would have stopped play and declared the game a tie since darkness was falling rapidly.

The game had been an unexpectedly competitive one as Washington's Jake Boyd, the owner of a career 7.20 ERA, hurled arguably the finest game of his career, allowing Boston just eight hits while Boston ace Kid Nichols scattered 11 safeties. Boston seemingly had the game won 3–1 when Washington came up for its last raps in the top of the 9th inning, but Washington second baseman Jack Crooks, who went 3-for-3 on the day, led off with a single and after shortstop Frank Scheibeck reached on an error, Washington captain Bill Joyce brought both runners home when he smashed a double off the rightfield fence. Boston shortstop Herman Long then prevented the go-ahead run by snagging Washington center fielder Charlie Abbey's pop fly after a lengthy sprint that took him deep into the territory that should normally have been the province of the left fielder, but Frank Sexton, a pitcher by trade, had been pressed into service there because Boston's regular left gardener, Tommy McCarthy, was out of action that day.

That in essence was the way the game was summarized in most of the newspapers the following day, but both the *Boston Globe* and the *Washington Post* made mention of an incident in the top of the 1st inning that ultimately expunged Boston's hard-earned victory and both Nichols's win and Boyd's defeat, although all the other statistics from the game have since been restored. Here is the *Globe's* account of Washington's first raps in the game: "'Scrappy' Joyce started the game with a high foul fly that [Tommy] Tucker took close to the fence. [Deacon] McGuire hit a hard liner against the [left field] fence for one base. [Charlie] Abbey struck out. [Kip] Selbach was given a pass to first [Win] Mercer's name was on the score card [as the next batter], but Bill Hassamaer [due up after Mercer] came up with his big club. The Boston men called the umpire's attention to the mistake, and after a careful perusal of the rules, Mr. Burnham [sic] decided that the Boston protest was in order. In fact, Mr. Burnham went further and declared Mercer out." Since the rules regarding a player batting out of turn were the same then as they are now except that a batting team today is assessed two outs instead of one, those familiar with the rule book will realize Barnum's mistake. Rule 45, Section 1 in 1895 read: *The Batsman is out: If he fails to take his position at the bat in his order of batting, unless the error be discovered and the proper Batsman takes his position before a time "at bat" recorded.*

Barnum therefore erred in declaring Mercer out before Hassamaer had not just entered the batter's box but had actually batted. Only then would Boston have had a choice whether to protest his batting out of turn, as it almost certainly would have done if he had achieved a hit or a walk or reached on an error, or to accept the result if he had made an out. By declaring Mercer out before Hassamaer actually batted and put Washington in violation of Rule 45, Section 1, Barnum opened the door for Washington manager Gus Schmelz to lodge a formal protest. Boston captain Billy Nash had of course compounded the error by calling Barnum's attention to the batting order discrepancy prematurely; and it is surprising that the Beaneaters' manager, Frank Selee, did not dissuade Nash from approaching Barnum, but Nash may have acted rashly and entirely on his own. League president Nick Young, immediately recognizing the validity of Schmelz's protest, declared the game a no-decision. It was ultimately transferred to Washington since the Senators were not slated to travel to Boston again that season and made up as part of a doubleheader on the final day of the season.

SOURCES

Boston Globe, July 13, 1895.
Nemec, David. *The Rank and File of 19th Century Major League Baseball* (Jefferson, NC: McFarland, 2012), 280–281.
New York Sun, August 24, 1895.
Sporting Life, August 24, 1895.
Washington Morning Times, August 24, 1895.
Washington Post, July 13, 1895.

May 3, 1899

Place: Pittsburgh
Leagues: National League and American Association of Professional Base Ball Clubs
Field: Exposition Park
Clubs: Pittsburgh versus Louisville
Umpires: Tommy Burns and Billy Smith

Heading into the bottom of the 9th inning Louisville southpaw Pete Dowling held a 6–1 lead and seemed to be gliding to an easy victory. Pittsburgh scored two runs to narrow the gap to 6–3 and had both second baseman Heinie Reitz and pitcher Jesse Tannehill on base with two out when Pirates left fielder Jack McCarthy, a left-handed hitter, pulled one of the mercurial Dowling's pitches down the right field line. Louisville right fielder Charlie Dexter thought it landed in foul territory, but base umpire Smith signaled that it was a fair ball. The ball hit a divot in the field and sliced to the right, heading toward a park employee who was standing outside the door to the home team's dressing room. When the employee realized the ball was in play, he opened the dressing room door and appeared to guide the ball through it with his foot. After the ball entered the dressing room reports conflict, some saying that the employee followed it inside and shut the door behind him and others that he simply made it difficult for Dexter to skirt him and open the door so that he could retrieve the ball. Still other sources say the transgressor was a small boy, which leaves it still in the realm of possibility that he was a park employee and perhaps even the son of a Pittsburgh team official.

By the time Dexter was able to reach the ball and relay it into Louisville second baseman Claude Ritchey, three runs had scored, with McCarthy's being the last of the three and the tying tally. Tom McCreery then followed with a four-bagger that gave Pittsburgh a thrilling come-from-behind 7–6 win. On McCarthy's hit, "Louisville made a great kick that it was a case of interfering with the fielder or stealing the ball, but the claim was not allowed" by Burns and Smith, according to the *Chicago Tribune*, which added, "It is understood they have protested the game." The protest was successful and the game was declared a no-decision. Statistics from this game as well as other successfully protested games in that era were not restored until early in the twenty-first century. McCarthy is now credited with a home run, the seventh in his ML career that at that time had reached its fourth season. He played eight more years in the majors and never hit another.

SOURCES

Chicago Daily Tribune, May 4, 1899.
Nemec, David. *Major League Baseball Profiles: 1871–1900* (Lincoln: University of Nebraska Press, 2011), 2: 239–240.
New York Tribune, May 4, 1899.
Sporting Life, May 13, 1899, and June 10, 1899.
Washington Times, May 4, 1899.

May 30, 1899

Place: New York
Leagues: National League and American Association of Professional Base Ball Clubs
Field: Polo Grounds III
Clubs: New York versus Cincinnati
Umpires: John Gaffney and Ed Andrews

After Cincinnati won the morning game of a Decoration Day doubleheader, 9–3, with former ML outfielder Andrews working the plate, the two officials switched places in the afternoon contest, putting Gaffney behind the dish. The second contest was deadlocked at 5-all when New York took its turn at bat in the bottom of the 8th inning. The *New York Times* reported the following day that the trouble at that point came about in this fashion.

After shortstop George Davis was retired, second baseman Kid Gleason singled and was sent to third on outfielder Tom O'Brien's double. "The enthusiasm of the crowd knew no bounds at this stage. Then followed the play that caused the row." Third baseman Fred Hartman hit a grounder to Cincinnati first baseman Jake Beckley. "Gleason started for the plate and Beckley sent the ball to Catcher [Heinie] Peitz. The latter stood across the plate and caught the ball just as Gleason came up with him, the collision with the heavy catcher sending Gleason to the ground. Umpire Gaffney declared that Gleason was not out, simply because Peitz had not touched him with the ball, as required." The entire Cincinnati club rushed toward Gaffney. The Catholic Protectory Band, which was on hand, valiantly attempted to drown out the foul language the players during the lengthy argument that ensued. It not only failed to change Gaffney's decision, but he fined Peitz and pitcher Jack Taylor. When play finally resumed, Giants first baseman Jack Doyle hit a sacrifice fly, bringing O'Brien home with another run, making the score 7–5 as Cincinnati came to the plate for its last at-bats. But when that occurred "only a few [Reds] players remained on the bench. The others marched off the field and were promptly called 'quitters' by the crowd. 'Buck' Ewing, the Cincinnati's [sic] manager said that he would protest the game, but as Catcher Peitz said that he failed to touch Gleason with the ball, it is not likely that the protest will be sustained."

The *Times* was wrong. League president Nick Young later ruled the contest a no-decision. This was an odd one. The protest was based on an umpire's judgment and Peitz appears to have admitted that he never tagged Gleason with the ball but only with his body. The piece that is missing is whether Gaffney or anyone else actually saw Gleason touch the plate. *Sporting Life* in its June 10, 1899, issue on page 6 said Gaffney claimed it "was not his place" to tell Peitz to touch his man yet offered no explanation for "why he called a run when Gleason did not touch the plate." Young, we think, made his decision when he was dissatisfied with what he heard from an umpire whose word and work had once been above reproach but had fallen off badly by the late 1890s owing to a drinking problem.

SOURCES

New York Sun, May 31, 1899.
New York Times, May 31, 1899.
New York Tribune, May 31, 1899.
Sporting Life, June 10, 1899.

May 7 and May 8, 1902

Place: Chicago
League: National League
Field: West Side Grounds
Clubs: Chicago versus New York
Umpire: Bob Emslie

After serving as president of the minor Atlantic League in 1900, Horace Fogel had returned to his regular profession as a sportswriter before he was unexpectedly pulled from its ranks when he was named manager of the New York Giants in January 1902. There was speculation that John T. Brush, who owned a piece of both the Cincinnati and the New York clubs at the time, convinced the Giants' principal owner, Andrew Freedman, to hire Fogel in order to curry favor with the hostile New York press since he was highly respected among his colleagues.

Fogel had previously served briefly as manager of the Indianapolis Hoosiers in 1887 while the club was a member of the National League. He would serve less than two months as manager of the Giants before being fired on June 10, 1902. He later was part of a group that bought the Philadelphia Phillies and eventually was elected president of the club. Fogel was banned from the NL for life in November 1912 for publicly asserting that Cardinals manager Roger Bresnahan and several loop umpires, specifically Bill Brennan, had aided the New York Giants in winning the 1912 NL flag. Though at this distance Fogel's charges seem to have had merit, at the time major league moguls dismissed them after only a cursory investigation. An earlier charge that Fogel leveled against the integrity of the game was found to have legs, however, and created two of the strangest successfully protested games in big league history.

After losing the first two games of a three-game series in Chicago, 4–0 and 10–4 on May 7 and 8, Fogel, in the words of the *Chicago Tribune* on May 10, "passed a sleepless night Thursday trying to find some way to account to [New York owner] Andy Freedman for the loss of two games to Chicago. Bright and early yesterday morning he organized a detective bureau of one and searched the West Side Grounds for "buzzers" and things, measured the base lines, the distance to the flag pole in center field, and finally discovered that the pitcher's plate was not the prescribed distance from home plate.

"With this secret carefully concealed in his breast, the New-Yorker hibernated until the hour for beginning the third game when he gleefully sprung it on Umpire Emslie and [Chicago]Manager [Frank] Selee, demanding that the trick be foiled. Two cloth tapes were tried, and although they did not agree by over four inches on the distance, neither of them made it to the necessary sixty feet and a half." With Selee looking on with a chastened expression, Emslie had the Chicago groundskeeper dig up the plate and move it back 13 inches. This bit of labor consumed over half an hour and disgruntled the already chilled spectators, but, to Fogel's chagrin, had little effect on the result that day. Chicago still won, 5–0. Fogel's only reward for his imaginative efforts was that his protestations seemingly induced the league office to throw out the first two games of the series. However, the late Joe Wayman, the editor of *Grandstand Baseball Annual*, contended in his 1988 edition that both games were included in the final official averages and compiled data for all players in these games to be added to the ICI (Information Concepts, Incorporated) official major league baseball figures.

SOURCES

Chicago Tribune, May 10, 1902.
Grandstand Baseball Annual, 1988. Joseph M. Wayman, ed. 79–80.

September 23, 1908

Place: New York
League: National League
Field: Polo Grounds III
Clubs: New York versus Chicago
Umpires: Hank O'Day and Bob Emslie

No book on protested games would be complete without in depth reportage on the only game in history that was protested by both teams, each of their protests had a sizable amount of validity, and yet neither club liked the verdict its protest engendered. The game of course is the famous—or infamous—Merkle game when Giants manager John McGraw chose seldom used sub, 19-year-old Fred Merkle, then in his second season with the club, to replace regular first sacker Fred Tenney, who was out with a bad back, on September 23, 1908, in a game against the Chicago Cubs with the NL pennant hinging on the outcome.

With the scored tied at 1–all in the bottom of the 9th and two down, the Giants had outfielder Moose McCormick on third base and Merkle on first. Al Bridwell then laced a single to center off Cubs lefty Jack Pfiester to plate McCormick with the winning tally. Upon seeing McCormick would score standing up, most sources agree that Merkle stopped on his way to second

Crabby Johnny Evers, seen here with a rare smile, no doubt wore one even wider when crew chief Hank O'Day upheld his plea to call Giants first sacker Fred Merkle forced out at second base on September 23, 1908, setting off a near riot at the Polo Grounds.

and headed instead for the Giants' clubhouse in center field. But suddenly Cubs second sacker Johnny Evers sprinted toward the second base bag and began crying for the ball.

What happened next will forever be debated. Some New York writers at the Polo Grounds that afternoon swore that Merkle made for second base at that point and got there ahead of Evers; and even if he had not, the ball Evers was thrown was not the one that had been picked up by Cubs center fielder Solly Hofman. The ball Bridwell hit, depending on whom you believed, wound up everywhere but in Evers's hands or else had somehow come into the possession of Cubs pitcher Rube Kroh, who flipped it to Evers while Merkle was nowhere in sight. Emslie, the base umpire in charge of the play at second ;conveniently claimed too many members of the crowd had immediately flooded onto the field after Bridwell's hit seemingly won the game for him to get a clear view of the play at second, and the burden fell entirely on umpire-in-chief O'Day. After a seemingly interminable delay, with the fans milling around them and trying desperately to overhear, O'Day emerged from a conference with Emslie and ruled that Merkle had been forced out at second base and the game was still tied. Since it was beyond human endeavor to clear the roiling spectators off the field and resume the contest with the Cubs at bat in the top of the 10th inning, Bruins player-manager Frank Chance demanded that O'Day award the game on the spot to his club via forfeit. Giants manager McGraw demanded in turn that a protest be registered on his club's behalf rendering O'Day's decision on Merkle's entitlement to second base ludicrous, first of all, because neither umpire had really seen whether he had touched the bag or not, and furthermore (although this was only implied in the protest), because, even if he hadn't touched it, it had been standard protocol for years not to make a base runner risk life and limb after the winning run was no longer contested by racing to the next base while threading his way among spectators who were hell bent on beating the rest of the crowd to the exits.

Both protests were denied by NL president Harry Pulliam, and the game was declared a draw. What is seldom reported is that the Cubs went as a team to the Polo Grounds the following day, arriving shortly after 12 p.m. and demanded to be allowed into the stadium. Once inside, Chance "marched" his players onto the field and had them take their regular positions, with a few of the Giants players who were there for a practice session initially looking on in silent bemusement. Chance ordered pitcher Andy Coakley to throw three pitches to catcher Johnny Kling and then stated, "We will claim the game by forfeit under rule 55 which says you must play off a tie or postponed game on the visiting team's last visit." The New York players laughed aloud once they saw the intent of Chance's production and it was not taken seriously by NL officials, although technically Chance had a case.

The game was played off on October 8 at the Polo Grounds in front of an overflow crowd after the Giants and Cubs ended their regular season schedules deadlocked. Outside the park "thousands piled upon thousands in a fearful tangle in the hollow between Coogan's Bluff and the rusty structure of the elevated railroad tracks. The police were swept aside like corks before a torrent," and a fireman clinging to a pillar on the tracks while watching the game fell to his death. "His vacant place was quickly filled." On the field, far below the bluff and the tracks, Three Finger Brown outdueled Christy Mathewson, 4–2, to bring the pennant to Chicago and the Cubs went on to beat Detroit in the World Series and capture their last World Championship in the lifetime of almost undoubtedly every reader of our book. Remarkably, the plate umpire in the played off tied game was none other than Jim Johnstone, loathed in New York ever since he had instigated a forfeited game at the Polo Grounds the year before when he had been barred from the park by the Giants after a long string of run-ins with McGraw, and on the bases was Bill Klem, renown for always working the plate in big games, especially early in his career. Several historians have commented on the odd pairing Pulliam chose for the most important game to that time in NL history, and though none have noted any umpiring decisions that impacted on the game's result, David Anderson, among others, has discussed in some detail Klem's claim in 1908 that both umpires were approached by Giants team physician Dr. Joseph M. Creamer before the game and offered a bribe, a claim that Klem unaccountably fudged about much later in his life in a 1951 interview in *Collier's Magazine.*

David Nemec in *The Official Rules of Baseball Illustrated* wrote that Merkle's almost certain failure to proceed to second base after Bridwell's hit haunted him for the rest of his life, but the real goat was McGraw for not having warned his troops that some three weeks earlier Evers had sought to have Warren Gill of the Pirates ruled out by O'Day on almost the exact same play. O'Day had ignored Evers at the time, but later that night, after debating the issue with Evers in the lobby of a Pittsburgh hotel, he realized Evers's argument not only was valid but the game for years had been fostering a lax custom in not requiring a runner while the winning run was being scored to reach the next base without being forced out if his out would have meant the third out of the inning.

Nemec noted that while Evers today is considered by some historians "to have been an ingenious groundbreaker," there were other previous attempts at the major league level to have a runner that failed to advance as necessary according to the rules declared out on a "Sudden Death" hit like Bridwell's. Nemec observed, however, that historians had "to scour minor league history to find a documented episode in which an umpire declared a runner on first forced out for failing to touch second after the supposed winning run had crossed the plate." He cited a Western League game on June 11, 1899, at Indianapolis when St. Paul pitcher Chauncey Fisher, with his team tied 12–12 with Indianapolis in the bottom of the 9th inning, found himself on first base with his catcher Harry Spies on third base. When outfielder Eddie Burke lined a one hop single to Hoosiers center fielder George Hogriever, Fisher, certain Spies would tally the winning run, detoured on his way to second to shake Burke's hand and was declared out by umpire Al Mannassau when Hogriever sprinted to second from his post in center field with the ball in hand and beat him to the bag. Perhaps it was in the making anyway, but less than a month later Mannassau was part of the first trade of a minor league umpire for a major league umpire when NL president Nick Young dealt Jack Brennan plus $350 to Western League president Ban Johnson for him.

So there was at least one precedent in professional baseball for Evers's play on Merkle, and there may have been more. Hogriever's play at the time

The National Baseball Commission at its winter meeting in January 1909. Left to right: National League president Harry Pulliam, Cincinnati Reds president and Commission president Garry Herrmann, American League president Ban Johnson, and Commission secretary John. E. Bruce, an attorney for the St. Louis Browns. After his suicide that July, Pulliam became the first person honored by baseball with all players wearing black arm bands for 30 days. It has been written that the pressure of his decision to support umpire Hank O'Day's verdict in the "Merkle Game" threw him into a tailspin that eventually drove him to put a gun to his head.

it happened was examined in depth in *The Sporting News*, whose St. Paul correspondent wrote that Fisher's maneuver was a "chump play" and there was little doubt the umpire's decision would be upheld.

And so it was. Yet nine years later Giants manager John McGraw, thought by most historians to have been among the more clever and innovative pilots in his day, still seemed unaware that such a ruling could occur. We can only marvel that no similar rulings occurred in big league games between 1899 and the Evers' decision in 1908. We have not encountered a plausible explanation as of yet for their absence but are of the view that O'Day's decision in the Merkle game was a daring one, as was Pulliam's decision to uphold it. Both were unpopular at the time, especially among Giants loyalists, but whereas Pulliam's role in the outcome of the Merkle game was a causative feature of his tragic suicide less than a year later, O'Day's probably had a fair amount of bearing on his election to the Hall of Fame in 2012.

SOURCES

Anderson, David W. *You Can't Beat the Hours* (North Charleston, SC: CreateSpace, 2013), 74–76.

Boston Globe, October 9, 1908.

Charles Mears Base Ball Scrapbook, vol. VII, 1904–1912.

Nemec, David. *Major League Baseball Profiles: 1871–1900* (Lincoln: University of Nebraska Press, 2011), 1: 145–146 and 2: 212.

Nemec, David. *The Official Rules of Baseball Illustrated,* 3d ed. (Guilford, CT: Lyons Press, 2006), 110–111.

New York Times, September 24, 1908, October 8, 1908, and October 9, 1908.

The Sporting News, June 17, 1899.

April 23, 1909

Place: Pittsburgh
League: National League
Field: Exposition Park III
Clubs: Pittsburgh versus Cincinnati
Umpires: Bill Klem and Steve Kane

Pittsburgh's Vic Willis allowed the Reds just two hits and the Pirates collected a paltry three off Harry Gaspar and Billy Campbell in winning 2–1. The Pirates scored a run in the 4th frame and another in the 6th while Cincinnati pushed across its lone tally in the top of the 9th. At issue was Pittsburgh's second run, scored by shortstop Honus Wagner. Cincinnati protested to plate umpire Klem that with a 3-and–0 count Wagner had prematurely anticipated a walk and stepped across the plate before Gaspar's delivery reached it. Cincinnati manager Clarke Griffith argued in vain that Wagner should have been called out according to Rule 51, Section 10 for crossing the plate as a pitch was on its way. Had Klem done so Wagner would never have reached base in the 6th inning, let alone scored what turned out to be the winning run. Discussion of the incident appeared in the May 1, 1909, issue of *Sporting Life* on page 5.

John Heydler, who was acting as the NL president at the time after the tragic suicide of former president Harry Pulliam, originally denied Cincinnati's protest, but his decision was appealed by the Reds and in its June 12, 1909, issue, *Sporting Life*, announced on its front page that the National League's board of directors had overruled Heydler and upheld the protest. The telling testimony came from Klem who "admitted verbally and in writing that player Wagner, of the Pittsburg[h] club, stepped from one batter's box to the other while pitcher Gaspar, of the Cincinnati club, was in the act of delivering the ball." Klem claimed that he hadn't enforced the rule at the time "because the pitcher of the Cincinnati Club, in his opinion, was clearly endeavoring to give Wagner his base on balls."

The game was replayed on September 10, 1909, and Willis again beat Gaspar, this time 4–3.

SOURCES

New York Times, April 24, 1909.
Sporting Life, May 1, 1909, and June 12, 1909.

May 30, 1911

Place: Pittsburgh
League: National League
Field: Forbes Field
Clubs: Pittsburgh versus Chicago
Umpires: Bill Klem and Jack Doyle

The Cubs lost a Decoration Day twinbill to the Pirates on May 30, 1911, but the first game was erased from the books when ex-NL umpire and now NL president Tom Lynch upheld Cubs player-manager Frank Chance's protest that an egregious umpiring gaffe had cost his team a scoring chance in the 8th inning of what initially was registered as a 1–0 Chicago loss to the Pirates' Babe Adams.

The gaffe occurred when Cubs catcher Jimmy Archer lifted a routine pop fly to Pittsburgh shortstop Honus Wagner with Cubs second baseman Dave Shean on first and one out. Wagner deliberately muffed the ball when he perceived that Archer was merely jogging to first and then threw to second baseman Dots Miller to force out Shean. But "Archer wised up in time" to get to first and seemingly thwart the double play. However, Shean had remained on first to prevent being doubled off if Wagner made the catch as expected. Former ML star Doyle, in his only year as an umpire, ruled that Archer was out because Wagner's muff was intentional and Shean was entitled to stay at first. Archer was arguing with Doyle that the reverse was true and first base was his when plate umpire Klem stunned everyone by throwing off his mask and "informed Doyle that he had made a blunder, that Shean instead of Archer was out and that Wagner did not hold the ball 'momentarily,' which was the crucial thing to be considered. At that point Shean left the bag and Archer started back toward first but was tagged out before he arrived. "Whereupon Umpire Klem declared Archer out, too, and so the side was out. Klem backed up his decision only by the argument that Archer should not have left first base since he knew he was not out and knew that Doyle was wrong in calling him out."

Klem's incomprehensible ruling made Lynch's decision to expunge not only the game but all its statistics as per the custom in the 1910s one of the swiftest he ever made while in office. The game was replayed on September 15 as part of a Friday doubleheader while the Cubs were in Pittsburgh.

SOURCES

Chicago Tribune, May 31, 1911.
Spalding's Official Base Ball Guide, 1911.
Washington Herald, May 31, 1911.
Washington Post, May 31, 1911.

October 2, 1912

Place: Chicago
League: National League
Field: West Side Grounds
Clubs: Chicago versus Pittsburgh
Umpires: Brick Owens and Bill Brennan

Dick Cotter, a backup catcher in the NL for two seasons, is listed in all reference works today as having played his last major league game on September 26, 1912. In actuality he played his last game six days later on October 2 and emerged as its hero, but it didn't count. None of it counted because the custom during the 1910s dictated that all statistics from protested games that were thrown out were permanently eradicated. And who was responsible for the game being protested? Not Pittsburgh, the losing team, though technically its secretary officially lodged the protest but only after a writer at the game brought it to his attention long after both teams had left the field that he had sufficient grounds for a protest. That nameless writer, it need be said, along with several other scribes at the game, had made frantic efforts from the press box "to put the home team next to the mistake before it was too late."

The muddle began in the bottom of the 9th inning when Cotter, a right-handed hitter, pinch hit for Wilbur Good, a left-handed hitter who had been sent up to bat for Cubs pitcher Jimmy Lavender and was called back when the Pirates replaced right-hander Howie Camnitz on the hill with southpaw Hank Robinson. Cotter ripped a single over first base that brought home Cubs outfielder Cy Williams with the run that tied the game, 5–5. Cotter then stayed in the contest, replacing catcher Jimmy Archer who had been pinch run for by Williams, while Charlie Smith replaced Lavender on the hill. After Smith held Pittsburgh scoreless in the visitors' half of the 10th frame, Chicago threatened in the home half, bringing Cotter to the plate with two out and a chance to drive in the winning run. Only Cotter this time was batting not in the ninth spot in the order, which Lavender had occupied, but the eighth spot, which had belonged to Archer. With two out and Vic Saier on second base and Frank Schulte on third, Cotter lined a single over second base off Robinson to plate Schulte with the walkoff winning run—at least insofar as everyone connected with the Pittsburgh and Chicago clubs then believed.

Umpires Owens and Brennan meanwhile had been aware that Cotter had batted out of turn when he hit in the eighth spot instead of the ninth, the spot he'd occupied when he entered the game, but looked the other way because they "thought it was up to the opposing team to claim the point, so did not declare Dick out." The *New York Sun* said both officials "waited for manager Clarke to lodge a protest, but none was forth coming, and the umpires declared that no further protests could be made, that the chance was lost when the Pirates rushed from the field." They learned otherwise before the evening was out when soon after they wired the protest on Pittsburgh's behalf to NL president Tom Lynch, Lynch read them the riot act.

Since the Giants had already clinched the NL pennant—ironically on the day that Dick Cotter played his final official ML game—the protested contest was not replayed because it meant nothing.

Except to Dick Cotter.

SOURCES

Chicago Tribune, September 27, 1912, and October 3, 1912.
New York Sun, October 3, 1912.
Sporting Life, October 12, 1912.

August 30, 1913

Place: Philadelphia
League: National League
Field: Baker Bowl
Clubs: Philadelphia versus New York
Umpires: Bill Brennan and Mal Eason

The Giants kayoed Phils ace Pete Alexander early in the game and jumped out to a quick 6–0 lead but were trailing 8–6 when they came to bat in the top of the 9th inning against Dut Chalmers, who had held the New Yorkers hitless since coming on in relief in the 4th frame. Giants manager John McGraw chose outfielder Moose McCormick to pinch hit for the heavily battered New York starter, Christy Mathewson, who was due to lead off in the

New Yorkers' last at-bats. After Chalmers fanned McCormick, McGraw complained to Brennan that some of the fans in the center field bleachers had been waving their glistening white and yellow straw hats and reflecting the sun directly into the eyes of McCormick, impairing his ability to see Chalmers's pitches. Brennan appealed to Phils captain, shortstop Mickey Doolan, to move the spectators out of the centerfield area. Doolan consulted with player-manager Red Dooin, who had been ejected earlier in the game. When Dooin claimed he could do nothing, the police were summoned to move the crowd. However, the stands were packed, leaving little room for the offending spectators to change their seats. Dooin then suggested to McGraw that they play the game under protest, but when McGraw refused Brennan forfeited the game to the Giants.

"As soon as the word had been spoken, the New York players made a rush across the field to the clubhouse." But some were not quick enough and were impeded by angry spectators who pelted them with seat cushions and other missiles. The umpires likewise were beleaguered when they tried to get safely off the field. The trouble magnified when the umpires and the Giants later tried to leave the grounds. Both parties needed a police escort to get to the North Philadelphia Station of the Pennsylvania Railroad, four blocks from the park. On the way several men tried to attack McGraw but were held at bay by a policeman who drew his revolver. The umpires were similarly besieged before they reached the station and scrambled aboard a 6 o'clock train bound for New York along with the Giants' players.

That night Dooin sent in a protest to NL president Tom Lynch, claiming that his club "was powerless to move the spectators because they had paid their money and were entitled to occupy the seats." He also stressed that they had been in those seats since the start of the game and there had been no place for them to move. On September 2, Lynch reversed Brennan's decision, stating "that the umpire plainly went beyond his authority in declaring a forfeiture, for which he had neither the protection of the regular playing rules nor of any special ground rule." The game was awarded to Philadelphia, 8–6. The Giants, to no one's surprise appealed Lynch's reversal. On September 15 the Board of Directors of the NL overruled Lynch, declaring that the game would be resumed on October 2 prior to a doubleheader in Philadelphia that day "with the same men on the field and the same status existing that existed" on August 30. Since the Phillies were challenging the Giants for the NL pennant at the time, comparisons were drawn to the protested Merkle game in 1908 as well as other imbroglios that invariably seemed to go the Giants' way.

But by October 2, the Giants had already clinched the pennant and the resumed game was anticlimactic. It took only a few minutes to complete as

Red Murray grounded out for the Giants' second out in the 9th frame and then, after Fred Merkle singled for the lone hit off Chalmers in his six innings in relief of Alexander, he was forced at second by catcher Larry McLean, who pinch hit for center fielder Fred Snodgrass. The lone point of interest beyond Merkle's hit was that it was not strictly true that the same men were on the field the day the protested game was completed. In addition to Brennan and Eason were Bill Klem and Al Orth, who were scheduled to umpire the doubleheader that followed. Their presence made for the first time in ML history that four umpires worked in the same regular-season game, Brennan behind the plate and the other three on the bases.

It merits mentioning that the previous year, when Phils president Horace Fogel was banned from the NL for leveling accusations that certain NL umpires were suspiciously amicable to McGraw and the Giants, Brennan was high on the list of those he named. David Anderson has pointed out that in addition this protested game "had far reaching concerns for both Brennan and Lynch. Lynch was out as president of the National League [after the 1913 season], while Brennan jumped to the Federal League and was [its] Umpire-in-Chief in both 1914 and 1915." After the Federal League folded, however, Brennan had to drop all the way down to the Class C South Atlantic League to find an umpiring job in 1916, and he subsequently spent five years officiating in the minors before returning to the NL in 1921 for one final season in big league blue.

SOURCES

Anderson, David W. *You Can't Beat the Hours* (North Charleston, SC: CreateSpace, 2013), 230.
Boston Globe, August 31, 1913.
New York Times, August 31, 1913, September 7, 1913, September 16, 1913, and October 3, 1913.
New York Tribune, August 31, 1913.

May 14, 1914

Place: Buffalo
League: Federal (FL)
Field: Federal League Park
Clubs: Buffalo versus Chicago
Umpires: Ed Goeckel and Steve Kane

If nothing else, the details of this protested game suggest that the quality of officiating in the rebel Federal League left a lot to be desired.

After the Chicago Chifeds scored four runs in the top of the 8th inning to tie the count at 4-all on a soggy and chilly day, the game entered the bottom of the 9th still tied. With one out and Buffalo catcher Walter Blair on first base, Buffalo pitcher Fred Anderson attempted to sacrifice his batterymate to second but popped his bunt try into the middle of the diamond. Chifeds pitcher Max Fiske set himself to make a routine catch while Blair properly hugged first so as not to be doubled off. But the ball dribbled through Fiske's fingers. Meanwhile Anderson had turned away in disgust at his miserable bunt effort and started toward the Buffalo bench. Fiske retrieved the ball and flipped it to Chifeds first sacker Fred Beck, who in due order tagged Blair who was standing near the bag and then tagged the bag. Had he tagged the bag first, Blair of course would not have been forced to vacate it. "By this time Mr. Anderson had reached the bench and was crawling into his sweater."

To the amazement of player-manager Joe Tinker, umpires Goeckel and Kane ruled that only Blair was out, "claiming he was forced out when tagged." Upon hearing this, 'the wise fellows on the Buffalo bench had dragged Anderson out and stood him on first base" where he was allowed to stay when Goeckel insisted that Beck had not tagged the base but only Blair. Even if true, Goeckel's decision was counter to a Federal League rule that mandated "a batter must run out his hit or take a chance on being doubled should an infielder drop the ball." After Fiske came unraveled following Goeckel's blunder and walked home the winning run in the person of Anderson, Tinker, who had already announced his intention to protest should his team lose, made good on it. FL president James Gilmore threw out the game of May 14 as soon as the protest came to his attention.

SOURCES

Chicago Tribune, May 15, 1914.
Sporting Life, May 23, 1914.

June 19, 1915

Place: Baltimore
League: Federal League
Field: Oriole Park V
Clubs: Baltimore versus Chicago
Umpires: Jim Johnstone and Lee Fyfe

The actions of the officials in the second and last successfully protested game in the Federal League's brief history were also of a quality that could not have pleased league president James Gilmore, especially since he was present in a private box at the Baltimore park to witness them.

The breakdown in officiating occurred in the top half of the very first inning and resulted in three Chicago runs that soon helped to turn the game into an 8–1 route. The former Chicago Chifeds, now known as the Whales, loaded the bases with only one out. Third baseman Harry Fritz, the fifth hitter in the order, then fanned on a George Suggs breaking ball for the second out, but the pitch (which may have been a spitter) eluded Baltimore backstop Frank Owens. Chicago shortstop Jimmy Smith, who was on third, started for home, but Owens reached the ball in time to throw it to Suggs covering the plate. Believing he was forced out, Smith stopped in his tracks and headed for the Chicago bench while Max Flack and Bill Fischer, the other two runners, moved up a base. In the supervening confusion Smith sprinted out from the bench and touched the plate, and umpire Johnstone, a veteran official with several years of experience in the NL who should have known better, called him safe since no one as yet had tagged him and he was not a force-out at home. Baltimore player-manager Otto Knabe, who was out of the lineup that day, "contended Smith was automatically out for running to the bench" and that his club had thus escaped the inning without allowing a run.

Gilmore's decision in this instance was nearly as simple as the only other protest decision he had to make in his short reign as FL president. Since all statistics from the game vanished as soon as he rendered it, Claude Hendrix, the Chicago starter that day, lost not only a win but a home run that would otherwise have been his fifth of the season and led all pitchers in the majors that year, including Babe Ruth.

Johnstone had come out of a two-year retirement from umpiring to work one final season in the 1915 Federal League, but his contributions to his craft were not finished. That season he began refining the catcher's mask that was then in use. In 1921 he first marketed a mask of his own design through the A.G. Spalding & Bros. Company. By 1924 some five thousand of his masks were in circulation. David Anderson has written that big league "catchers and umpires obtained the new mask because it permitted freer and more unobstructed vision and because it was made from aluminum casting, it was lighter in weight than the regular professional wire mask." Versions of Johnstone's mask are still in use today, though mostly at the amateur and recreational level.

Sources

Anderson, David W. *You Can't Beat the Hours* (North Charleston, SC: CreateSpace, 2013), 119.
Chicago Tribune, June 20, 1915.
Sporting Life, June 26, 1915.

August 17, 1915

Place: Pittsburgh
League: National League
Field: Forbes Field
Clubs: Pittsburgh versus Chicago
Umpires: Bill "Lord" Byron and Mal Eason

The Cubs and Pirates seemingly split a doubleheader on August 17, 1915, with Pittsburgh corralling the first game 3–2 behind the lefty slants of Rube Benton. However, no sooner had Benton taken the mound in the top of the 1st inning than Chicago player-manager Roger Bresnahan filed a protest to be taken under advisement in the event his club lost. Bresnahan's protest was a simple one. Benton had been put up for sale by Cincinnati the previous week and the Giants had placed a verbal option of $3,000 on him that was not due to expire until Monday, August 15. Meanwhile Pittsburgh owner Barney Dreyfuss had offered $4,000 on Friday, August 12, and Cincinnati had accepted the offer, disregarding its pledge to John McGraw and the Giants. The Cubs felt—rightly, as it turned out—that they should not have "to battle a New York hurler on a Pittsburgh field," while "Dreyfus [sic] simply told Manager [Fred] Clarke to use Benton and let the National League go t'l."

NL president John Tener did not take that remark kindly when he read it in the *Chicago Tribune*. He sent Benton to the Giants and threw out all record of his ever having pitched for Pittsburgh. Disappearing along with Benton's Pittsburgh statistics were a double by Bresnahan on his first day back in action behind the plate after suffering a broken toe in Boston.

SOURCES

Chicago Tribune, August 18, 1915.
New York Sun, August 18, 1915.
New York Tribune, August 18, 1915.
Sporting Life, August 28, 1915.

September 3, 1915

Place: Chicago
League: American League
Field: Comiskey Park
Clubs: Chicago versus Cleveland
Umpires: Billy Evans and Ollie Chill

The first column on the front sports page of the September 4, 1915, *Chicago Tribune* shrieked: PRIZE BONER BEATS SOX IN SECOND GAME. The bug line beneath it was: Failure To See Umpire's Error Kills Chance For Double Victory.

"The skull stuff," as the *Tribune* snidely put it, came in the 4th inning of the second contest of a doubleheader with Chicago ahead 2–0 behind the sharp slab work of Eddie Cicotte. The Tribe tied the count in that frame on a two-run single by Elmer Smith. Then, with Smith on first and only one out, Cleveland first sacker Jay Kirke fanned on a pitch "so wild that [catcher Wally] Mayer could not reach it, and the pill went right along to the grand stand." Kirke wound up on second base and Smith on third; both later scored, giving Cleveland its third and fourth runs in what ended, at least temporarily, in a 6–5 Tribe victory.

Incredibly, both umpires drew a blank on what was then Section 6 of Rule 31, which stated that a batter was automatically out on a third strike with first base occupied and less than two out. This rule had been on the books in all professional leagues since the start of the 1887 season. Even more incredibly, Chicago manager Pants Rowland and none of his charges seemed aware of the rule either. Not until the end of the inning was Sox captain Eddie Collins apprised by Rowland, who had been clued in by members of the Chicago press, to play the game under protest. Plate umpire Evans freely admitted his goof as soon as it was called to his attention, but the Chicago papers were still doubtful that the protest would be successful because there had been a similar instance in the American League earlier in its history where a protest had been disallowed. In this case, however, AL president Ban Johnson ruled on the Sox behalf, saving the Pale Hose and Cicotte a loss. The game was made up as part of a doubleheader later in the series between the two clubs.

SOURCES

Chicago Tribune, September 4, 1915.
New York Times, September 4, 1915.
New York Tribune, September 4, 1915.

April 17, 1917

Place: Philadelphia
League: National League
Field: Baker Bowl
Clubs: Philadelphia versus Boston
Umpires: Hank O'Day and Kitty Bransfield

In the first extra-inning contest of the 1917 season, Braves catcher Hank Gowdy went 4-for–5 and his teammate, shortstop Rabbit Maranville, made a brilliant running catch of a deep foul fly, to help spur manager George Stallings's club to a 6–5 win in 12 frames—but all to no avail. Phils manager Pat Moran protested a decision by rookie umpire Kitty Bransfield, who had been on the job scarcely a week, that was later upheld by John Tener, who had taken over the NL presidency, replacing the controversial former umpire Tom Lynch during the course of the 1913 season.

Bransfield, a solid ML first baseman for over a decade and a former teammate of Moran's, sparked the grounds for protest in the top of the 3rd inning. Phils pitcher Jimmy Lavender, the first batter up in the frame, walked. Leadoff hitter Dode Paskert then hit a hot grounder to Braves third sacker Red Smith, who rifled the ball to rookie second sacker Mike Massey, looking to start a double play. But Massey, in his haste to get two, hopped off the second

Former big league first baseman Kitty Bransfield was working only his fourth game as a National League umpire in 1917 when he rendered a successfully protested decision on a base runner running out of the line that will forever remain a mystery as to exactly what transpired.

base bag before he got the ball and then threw wild to first baseman Ed Konetchy. Lavender, supposing he was out, walked off second base and headed for the Phils' dugout. Tipped that he had been safe, he did a quick about face "and beat it across the diamond to third base and got there before the ball thrown by Gowdy," who had chased down Massey's wild throw, reached Maranville, who was covering third. "Bransfield then declared Lavender out for running out of the line."

"Lavender did not run out of line," the *Boston Globe* admitted, "and

Moran appealed to O'Day," the plate umpire that day, expecting O'Day to reverse the decision based on his contention that a base runner could not legally be retired for leaving the base line unless he did it to avoid being tagged. Faced with this unique point of view, O'Day, a Hall of Fame umpire, seemed confused but nevertheless refused to overrule his colleague. It was left to Tener to pick up the pieces, and he declared the game a no-decision, which eliminated all the statistics that were compiled by both teams that day. The game was later made up as part of a doubleheader in Philadelphia on August 30.

Bransfield's decision was in fact correct if Lavender wandered more than three feet from a direct line between second and third base, as per Rule 56, Section 7 of the 1917 Spalding Guide. The retrospective answer to whether Lavender ran out of the base line lies partly in knowing the location of the Phillies' dugout in their home park in 1917. If it was on the first base side of the diamond, then Lavender certainly violated the three-foot base path rule. If the report stating that he had to run across the diamond to third base was accurate, he was unquestionably out of the base line regardless of where the Phillies' dugout was situated. Indeed, it is hard to imagine a scenario in which he did not have to run out of the line to reach third base. Yet we have the *Boston Globe's* admission that Lavender, a player on the Boston team's rival that day, was not guilty of running out of the line. Will we ever know what actually happened here? Not likely now that every participant in the play is long since dead.

A footnote of interest: Massey, whose double error initiated the trouble, was gone from the majors by the end of June and Bransfield, whose decision compounded it, was not rehired by NL president Tener after he completed his rookie season in blue.

SOURCES

Boston Globe, April 8, 1917.
Nemec, David. *The Rank and File of 19th Century Major League Baseball* (Jefferson, NC: McFarland, 2012), 92.
New York Sun, April, 8, 1917.
Spalding's Official Base Ball Guide, 1917.

August 19, 1917

Place: Washington
League: American League
Field: Navin Field
Clubs: Detroit versus Washington
Umpires: Tommy Connolly and George Hildebrand

We would be remiss if we did not comment at various junctures in this book on the extraordinarily large number of successfully protested and forfeited games in major league history emanating either from boneheaded decisions or else an unfamiliarity with the rules that were perpetrated directly or at the very least abetted by a future Hall of Fame umpire. Here is yet another one.

In a taut pitchers' duel between Washington's Doc Ayers and Detroit's Howard Ehmke, the Senators and Tigers were deadlocked at 1-all at the start of the bottom of the 9th inning. First baseman George Burns led off for Detroit by singling sharply to center field. The ball eluded Senators center gardener Clyde Milan and rolled all the way to the deepest part of Navin Field. Milan, still a speedster even though he was in the twilight of his long career in Washington, chased down the ball in time to make a play on Burns. But as Burns reached third base he appeared to hesitate for an instant and was then pushed along by Tigers star Ty Cobb, who was coaching third at the time. The *Washington Herald* reported, "Immediately the entire Washington club swarmed around umpire Hildebrand, with a demand that Burns be called out because Cobb had touched him." But Hildebrand, the base umpire, ruled that Burns's game-ending run counted even though Cobb had aided him illegally in his course around the bases (as per Rule 56, Section 17), and future Hall of Famer Connolly did not contradict his partner.

Washington manager Clark Griffith filed a protest before leaving Detroit. While admitting that Burns would have scored anyway even if Cobb had never laid a hand on him, he felt that Burns "should have been called out for the assistance Cobb rendered him in pushing him from third." AL president Ban Johnson agreed and threw out the game and with it all of its statistics. The game was later made up in Washington as part of a doubleheader on Monday, September 24, since Washington did not travel again that season to Detroit. Johnson's decision aided the main culprit, Cobb, who had gone hitless that day, in what would be his successful quest for his eighth AL batting title.

SOURCES

New York Times, August 20, 1917.
Spalding's Official Base Ball Guide, 1917.
Washington Herald, August 20, 1917.
Washington Post, August 20, 1917.

April 29, 1918

Place: Cincinnati
League: National League

Field: Crosley Field
Clubs: Cincinnati versus St. Louis
Umpires: Hank O'Day and Bill "Lord" Byron

The Cards and Reds were knotted at 3-all when St. Louis came to bat in the top of the 8th. Reds starter Mike Regan retired St. Louis center fielder Jack Smith but then weakened, allowing second sacker Bert Niehoff to double and giving a free pass to third baseman Doug Baird. Hod Eller came on in relief to face the Cards' cleanup hitter, shortstop Rogers Hornsby, and walked him to load the bases. Left fielder Walton Cruise then lofted a deep fly to Reds center fielder Edd Roush, and Niehoff tagged up at third base, expecting to score the go-ahead run after Roush made the catch. But the *Cincinnati Enquirer* reported that "just as [Roush] reached the ball he stumbled and fell to the ground. The sphere bounced out of his glove as he fell, but Edd twisted around and caught it in one hand as he hit the sward."

Niehoff meanwhile had left third base the moment Roush first touched the ball and scored standing up. Upon rising, Roush relayed the ball in to second baseman Lee Magee who fired it to third where Reds hot corner man Heinie Groh was hollering for the ball. Groh tagged the bag and then appealed to umpire-in-chief O'Day, who ruled that Niehoff had left third before the catch was completed and was thereupon the third out rather than the go-ahead run. The *Enquirer* said, "Hank's decision on this play was a most unusual one, but eminently correct under the rules." The *St. Louis Post-Dispatch* was not so sure, especially after Cards skipper Jack Hendricks announced he was playing the game under protest when he failed to convince O'Day's partner, Byron, that Niehoff had every right to vacate third the instant the ball first touched Roush's glove. It concluded: "It was a peculiar tangle, one that is now up to President Tener to decide which is right, Manager Hendricks or Umpire Hank O'Day," upon learning that Hendricks had followed through on his threat and filed a formal protest immediately after the Reds tallied a run with two out in the bottom of the 9th off Cards starter Lee Meadows to win 4–3.

On Sunday, May 12, Tener notified Cardinals president Branch Rickey that Hendricks's protest had been allowed and the game of April 29 would have to be replayed in its entirety. Tener's decision was based in large part on O'Day's frank admission that Niehoff had waited until the ball first touched Roush's glove but continued to maintain that "he should have remained on the sack until Roush entirely completed the catch."

Yet neither O'Day nor his partner on April 29, Byron, should be castigated too severely, for the rule at that time still stated that a base runner had the right to advance after returning to his original base as soon as a fly ball had settled into the hands of a fielder. O'Day and Byron were not the first pair of umpires for whom the phrase "settled into the hands of a fielder" spelled confusion and who construed it to mean the ball had to be firmly secured before the runner was free to tag up and advance. Some outfielders as a result took advantage and challenged an umpire's interpretation by becoming adept at juggling fly balls in order to hold a runner to his base while jogging toward the infield until they were close enough to throw the runner out if he attempted to advance. Not until 1920 was the rule on tagging up on a fly ball finally rewritten so that it clearly allowed a runner to advance without risk of being doubled off base as soon as the ball made contact with any part of a fielder's person regardless of whether or not it was held secure.

As for Roush, researcher and writer Tom Ruane has noted that his protested catch and assist on the inning-ending double play on April 29 may have cost him the

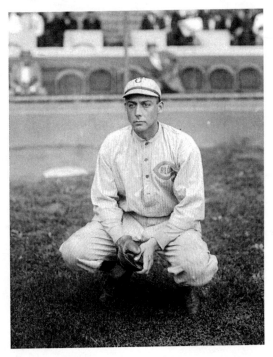

Edd Roush, the lone man to still be denied a batting title because Major League Baseball continues not to recognize statistics from some successfully protested games. Roush lost the 1918 National League crown to Brooklyn's Zach Wheat largely because he juggled a fly ball. Had he caught it cleanly or even dropped it he would have won.

NL batting title. He went 2-for-3 in the disallowed game. When it was replayed as the second game of a double header on August 11, he got only one hit in four at-bats. Had the protested game not been thrown out he would have finished with a .336 BA, one point ahead of the actual crown wearer, Brooklyn's Zach Wheat and five points ahead of Wheat if the protested game that follows this one in our book (in which Wheat went 0-for–5) had also not been thrown out.

SOURCES

Cincinnati Enquirer, April 30, 1918.
Denver Post, May 1, 1913.
Nemec, David. *The Official Rules of Baseball Illustrated,* 3d ed. (Guilford, CT: Lyons Press, 2006), 107.
St. Louis Post-Dispatch, April 30, 1918, and May 13, 1918.

June 3, 1918

Place: Brooklyn
League: National League
Field: Ebbets Field
Clubs: St. Louis versus Brooklyn
Umpires: Cy Rigler and Charlie Moran

In a game between two early-season tail enders that the *New York Times* deemed "the most weird of the season," the Cardinals compiled 23 hits in topping manager Wilbert Robinson's Brooklyn Robins 15–12 in 12 innings and Cards second baseman Marty Kavanagh had his career day, going 5-for–7 and tallying three runs. Conversely, Brooklyn gardener Zach Wheat went 0-for-5.

None of it counted.

In the Cards' half of the 6th inning, with third sacker Doug Baird on second, right fielder Walton Cruise ripped a low liner that Brooklyn center fielder Dave Hickman got his glove on but failed to capture. Baird had reached third base, convinced Hickman had no chance on Cruise's shot, before he looked back and saw Hickman holding the ball aloft. Thinking Cruise's hit had been caught, he started rushing back toward second base. After going about 20 feet he heard teammates shouting that the ball was in play and wheeled around and cut across the diamond, beating Hickman's throw to the plate. Brooklyn shortstop Ivy Olson was ejected by Rigler when he complained too loud and too long that Baird should be declared out for not retouching third base before heading home. Realizing that Olson was correct in his argument, Robinson announced that he would protest the game to NL president John Tener in the event St. Louis won. When he was victorious in his protest, it moved Brooklyn temporarily out of the NL cellar and into seventh place ahead of the Cardinals.

Rigler's partner that day, former ML catcher Charlie Moran, probably knew Rigler was wrong in awarding Baird a run but may have kept his mouth shut as was the wont of many rookie ML umpires in the pre-TV replay era when their thinking was in conflict with their elders. Moran went on to a 22-year career as an ML umpire and also served for a time as both a college and a pro football coach. Rigler also survived his gaffe to officiate for another 17 years in the NL. Among the many other statistics that his blunder caused to be expunged forever from the record books was his ejection of Olson. As for Kavanagh, he may have lost five hits—more than he sometimes collected in a month—but he will forever be remembered for hitting the first pinch-hit grandslam homer in AL history on September 24, 1916, while with Cleveland when his bounding ball reportedly squirted through a hole in the fence in Cleveland's League Park.

SOURCES

Boston Globe, June 4, 1918.
Nemec, David. *The Official Rules of Baseball Illustrated,* 3d ed. (New York: Lyons, 2006), 93.
New York Times, June 4, 1918.

July 5, 1920

Place: New York
League: National League
Field: Polo Grounds IV
Clubs: New York versus Philadelphia
Umpires: Barry McCormick and Pete Harrison

After dropping the morning game of an Independence Day twinbill, 5–1 (which was played on Monday because the holiday fell on Sunday and New York was not yet receptive to Sunday ball, especially on a National Holiday) to the Phils' Eppa Rixey, the Giants seemingly earned a split on the day when southpaw Art Nehf blanked Philadelphia 6–0 in the nightcap. However, in the top of the 7th inning the Phils had Casey Stengel on second base and Art Fletcher on first with one out when Russ Wrightstone hit a towering pop fly to short left field. Giants shortstop Dave Bancroft and left fielder George Burns both gave chase. At the last moment Bancroft dropped to the ground, thinking Burns had called for the ball, and it "dropped unmolested. Meantime, Stengel had gone to third, and Fletcher was on his way to second." Burns quickly retrieved the ball and threw it to Giants second sacker Larry Doyle. Umpire Harrison ruled it was a double play and the side was out. Wrightstone was pronounced out because he had hit an infield fly and Fletcher was out because umpire McCormick, a former ML infielder, said Doyle had tagged him. The Phils argued that Doyle hadn't tagged Fletcher but had only put his foot on the bag, thinking it was a force play, which it could not have been if the infield fly rule was in effect.

When the arguing had ceased for the moment, Stengel was allowed to stay on third base and Wrightstone was sent to first after McCormick prevailed over Harrison's decision to call a batted ball that would have been a tough catch an infield fly. The Phils then played the game under protest, saying Harrison's infield fly call should have been allowed to stand and they should have runners on second and third rather than first and third. NL president John Heydler sided with the Phils, and the game was resumed prior to the regularly scheduled game between the two teams on September 4, with Fletcher on second base and Stengel on third in the top of the 7th.

The Phils failed to score again in the resumed game, but the Giants tallied seven runs in the bottom of the 8th and the final score now officially read 13–0 as several New Yorkers fattened their batting averages. However, Nehf, who was not rested enough to work in the resumed game, was deprived of a shutout when Poll Perritt was called on to finish the contest.

McCormick that same season was behind the plate on May 1 in Boston for the longest day game in major league history, the 26-inning 1–1 tie between the Braves and the Brooklyn Robins that he finally had to call on account of darkness. His partner on July 5, Harrison, was behind the plate in the last triple-header in major league history on October 2, the closing day of the 1920 season, when Cincinnati took two of three games from the Pirates at Forbes Field.

SOURCES

Brooklyn Daily Eagle, July 6, 1920.
Nemec, David. *Major League Baseball Profiles: 1871–1900* (Lincoln: University of Nebraska Press, 2011), 1: 241.
New York Times, July 6, 1920, and September 5, 1920.

May 28, 1921

Place: Pittsburgh
League: National League
Field: Forbes Field
Clubs: Pittsburgh versus Cincinnati
Umpires: Bill Brennan and Bob Emslie

This was a game right out of the nineteenth century when balls were still in play when they rolled through open doors and came flying out of nowhere.

With his club leading 3–2 in the bottom of the 8th inning, Reds pitcher Dolf Luque thought he had tagged out Pittsburgh pinch runner Carson Bigbee in a play at the plate. When umpire Brennan called Bigbee safe, Luque became so enraged that he fired the ball into the Reds' dugout. Pittsburgh third sacker Clyde Barnhart, certain that he would be allowed to advance at least one base since the ball had gone out of play, started to move up, but suddenly the ball came flying out of the dugout from an unknown hand into the mitt of Reds' catcher Ivey Wingo. In the ensuing rundown, Barnhart was nabbed and the inning ended with the score knotted at 3-all. Once Cincinnati won 4–3 on a run in the 10th inning off Babe Adams who had come on in relief of Whitey Glazner after Glazner had been removed in the 8th for pinch hitter Ray Rohwer (the man Bigbee ran for), Pirates manager George Gibson filed a formal protest, claiming that the ball Luque heaved into his own dugout in the 8th frame should have been declared dead and Barnhart should automatically have been awarded a base without a play being made on him.

NL president John Heydler agreed with Gibson that the assistance from a player in the Reds' dugout on the wild throw should not have been permitted and ordered that the game be resumed from the point when the disputed play occurred the next time the teams met in Pittsburgh. On June 30 the last inning and a half of the May 28 game was replayed, and this time Pittsburgh won on a 9th inning homer by first sacker Charlie Grimm. On this occasion Adams was credited with a win rather than a loss, and Luque, who had been replaced by Rube Marquard on May 28 after his tantrum, remained on the hill and took the defeat.

We can offer no reasonable explanation for why Brennan and Emslie did not automatically allow Barnhart to freely advance not just one but two bases thereby enabling him to score when Luque's wild heave flew into his own team's dugout. In 1921 Rule 72, Section 3 read: "In all cases where there are no spectators on the playing field, and where a thrown balls goes into a stand for spectators, or over or through any fence surrounding the playing field, or into the players' bench (whether the ball rebounds into the field or not), or remains in the meshes of a wire screen protecting the spectators, the runner or runners shall be entitled to two bases. The umpire in awarding such bases shall be governed by the position of the runner or runners at the time the throw is made."

SOURCES

Boston Globe, May 29, 1921.
New York Times, July 1, 1921.
New York Tribune, May 29, 1921.
Washington Herald, May 29, 1921.

July 15, 1924

Place: Chicago
League: National League
Field: Cubs Park (later Wrigley Field)
Clubs: Chicago versus New York
Umpires: Bill Klem and Frank Wilson

When the Giants defeated the Cubs 9–4 on Tuesday afternoon, July 15, practically everyone in the park left believing that the New Yorkers had made a clean sweep of the four-game series between the two teams, but Chicago president Bill Veeck, Sr., was already preparing a protest to NL officials even as the park was emptying.

His grievance sprang from an umpiring decision reversal in the bottom of the 2nd inning. With the game still scoreless and none out, the Cubs had Hooks Cotter on second base and Bernie Friberg on first, both via walks after Giants starter Wayland Dean had encountered an early wild streak. Dean then ran the count to full on the next Cubs batsman, outfielder Denver Grigsby. The *Chicago Tribune* reported: "Naturally the men on the bases were on the go with the pitcher's arm on the next delivery." Dean's pitch was low and outside; Grigsby started to swing at it but then, in Klem's judgment, yanked his bat back in time. As Grigsby started to jog to first, Cotter pulled up in his dash toward third base and also downshifted to a jog. But Giants catcher Pancho Snyder felt that Grigsby had swung at the pitch and fired the ball to third, where Heinie Groh took the throw and tagged Cotter. The Giants then charged at Klem and claimed they had made a double play. "Klem finally appealed to [base umpire] Wilson who ruled that Grigsby had struck out and that Cotter was out stealing."

Cubs manager Bill Killefer then protested "that no player can be put out for doing exactly what the umpire's ruling called for and therefore Cotter must have been safe at third when compelled to advance to third by the umpire's first ruling." *The Sporting News* informed its readers in its August 14, 1924, issue that NL president John Heydler had upheld the Cubs' protest. The game was replayed at Chicago on August 25, with the Cubs winning 3–2.

SOURCES

Chicago Tribune, July 16, 1924.
The Sporting News, August 14, 1924.

July 28, 1924

Place: St. Louis
League: American League
Field: Sportsman's Park II
Clubs: St. Louis versus Boston
Umpires: Brick Owens, George Moriarty and Pants Rowland

After the Browns scored a single run in the bottom of the 9th inning to tie the score 5–5, Boston tallied five runs in the top of the 10th to win 10–5, but even before the teams left the field observers were aware that St. Louis player-manager George Sisler intended to protest the game on the grounds that Owens, the umpire-in-chief that day, had not properly followed the substitution protocol when he refused to allow substitute infielder Norm McMillan to bat in what Sisler contended was his correct spot in the order in the bottom of the 9th inning. Owens's failure to do so Sisler felt had robbed his club of a full opportunity to win the game in regulation length.

McMillan had entered the game in the 8th inning to pinch run for catcher Hank Severeid and then had remained in the contest at shortstop, replacing Wally Gerber. Since Severeid had been batting seventh in the order, Sisler maintained that McMillan now belonged in that spot and Tony Rego, who had replaced Severeid behind the plate at the beginning of the 9th inning, should take over Gerber's eighth spot in the order. Umpire Owens ruled otherwise, thereupon depriving McMillan (.279), a better hitter than Rego (.220) in 1924, of an at-bat that offered a better chance of delivering a game-winning hit in the bottom of the 9th. Since Owens was wrong in not allowing McMillan to bat in the seventh spot in the order, the spot occupied by the player he replaced, the protest was subsequently upheld by AL president Ban Johnson and the game was declared a no-decision. Statistics from the game except for pitchers' decisions are now included in all reference works.

SOURCES

Boston Globe, July 21, 1924.
The Sporting News, July 31, 1924, and August 28, 1924.

August 1, 1932

Place: Detroit
League: American League
Field: Navin Field
Clubs: Detroit versus New York
Umpires: Dick Nallin and Roy Van Graflan

It is sometimes a difficult decision for a league president who decides to uphold a protest whether to replay the protested game in its entirety or resume it at the juncture when the point under contention occurred. An example of the former is the July 15, 1924, contest between the Cubs and the Giants. Here the disputed play developed so early in the contest—in the 2nd inning of a game that was still scoreless—that NL president John Heydler met with no opposition from either club when he handed down his ruling that that game had to be started over from scratch.

A somewhat different set of circumstances in the Tigers-Yankees game of August 1, 1932, delivered a decision from AL president Will Harridge to start the game afresh. In this case there was an inability to duplicate the situation when the protest arose without putting one team at a disadvantage. The dilemma began in the top of the 2nd inning when Yankees second baseman Tony Lazzeri stepped up to the plate under the assumption that he had been listed on manager Joe McCarthy's lineup card as the fifth man in the order, following cleanup hitter Lou Gehrig. Plate umpire Nallin corrected Lazzeri, informing him that right fielder Ben Chapman was listed as the fifth batter in McCarthy's lineup. When McCarthy pleaded that he'd made a mistake in filling out his lineup card and stressed that Lazzeri always hit in the fifth slot, Nallin forgave McCarthy's error and allowed Lazzeri to bat fifth.

Detroit manager Bucky Harris remained silent on the issue until Lazzeri singled and then immediately appealed to Nallin, showing him the lineup card McCarthy had given to the home team as required before the game, which

Left to right: Bob Hart, Billy Evans, Hank O'Day and Dick Nallin, the abettor of a batting order snafu that resulted in a game between the Yankees and the Tigers having to be played and replayed three times in 1932, his final season as an American League arbiter.

listed Chapman hitting after Gehrig. Harris demanded that Nallin call Chapman out for not having batted in his proper turn. Nallin refused, stating that Lazzeri had batted in the fifth spot with his permission. Harris then revised his protest to one that asserted that Nallin had no right to change the batting order that had been given to the home team and especially not after the game had started and informed Nallin that he would formally protest the game if Detroit lost. For the remainder of the game Lazzeri batted fifth and Chapman hit sixth even though their positions were the reverse on the lineup card Harris had on prominent display in the Tigers' dugout.

After the Yankees won the game 6–3, with Lazzeri going 3-for–5, Harridge upheld Harris's protest and ordered the contest replayed in its entirety since Lazzeri's first illegal hit had been made in the 2nd inning and had led to a Yankees run. The two teams replayed the game on September 8 on the Yankees' next visit to Detroit. It was rescheduled as the second half of a doubleheader and ended in a 7–7 tie that was called after seven innings on account of darkness. The following day the game was replayed for yet a third time, again as the second half of a doubleheader. Detroit won 4–1 to put to rest the gargantuan amount of work that had been required to undo the chaos that Nallin's effort to accommodate McCarthy's lineup card snafu had created. At the finish of the 1932 season Nallin's 18-year tenure as an AL umpire came to an end, though we have found no connection between his departure and the lineup card misadventure. Nallin worked in four World Series during his career and was behind the plate for Charlie Robertson's perfect game on April 30, 1922.

SOURCES

Nemec, David. *The Official Rules of Baseball Illustrated,* 3d ed. (Guilford, CT: Lyons Press, 2013), 65.
New York Times, August 2, 1932.

July 2, 1934

Place: Chicago
League: National League
Field: Wrigley Field
Clubs: Chicago versus St. Louis
Umpires: Bill Klem and Cy Pfirman on July 3 and Ernie Quigley, Dolly Stark and George Barr on July 31

After scoring one run in the bottom of the 7th inning, the Cubs led 4–1 and still had the bases loaded and only one out with their top slugger, Chuck Klein, stepping to the plate. Klein popped up a fastball from Cards rookie

Paul Dean. "The ball, driven into the wind, sailed into fair territory just to the right of the plate and eluded Catcher [Bill] DeLancey who, before the play was completed, erred on a throw to the plate. The Cards immediately swarmed on Umpire Klem and claimed Klein should be out under the infield fly rule. Mr. Klem's answer was that the rule did not apply because no one was in position to catch the ball. That didn't suit the Cardinals." And before the Red Birds had finished arguing the point, player-manager Frankie Frisch, Dean's brother Dizzy and player-coach Mike Gonzalez had all been tossed from the game. Before departing, Frisch announced the Cardinals were playing the game under protest.

The Cubs went on to score two more runs in the 7th frame and led 7–1 at that point. They ultimately won 7–4 after St. Louis tapped Cubs starter Lon Warneke for three runs in the 8th inning. NL president John Heydler, who was at the game, slapped Frisch and Gonzalez with fines of $100 and $25, respectively, for their clash with Klem but nonetheless agreed that the Cards had a valid protest. At least one paper in reporting Heydler's decision said it was the first time that Klem had ever been proven wrong. Readers who have examined our discussions of forfeited and protested games in chronological order will know by now that this testament to Klem's infallibility is not even remotely true. Klem in actuality may have been involved in more overturned and controversial contests than any other umpire in history. Even after making allowances for his long tenure as an official, he seems to have courted far more than his fair share of disputes.

When the game was resumed on July 31 at the point where the quarrel arose, Klein was declared out on an infield fly but the Cubs' runners on base were each allowed to move up a sack, making the score 5–1. The Bruins added no more runs in the 7th inning but scored two in the 8th. Meanwhile Warneke, who had pitched what he thought at the time was a complete-game 7–4 win on July 3 finished the protested game by holding St. Louis scoreless for a 7–1 victory and then hurled the entire regularly scheduled game that day, topping the Birds 7–2. Warneke, a future longtime NL umpire, thus in essence received credit on July 31 for pitching two complete games and winning both, though the first victory was a belated one. The double win put the Cubbies in second place 2½ games behind the front-running Giants and 2½ ahead of the third-place Cards, but it was the Cards who eventually won the NL flag that year and with it their enduring sobriquet: The Gas House Gang.

SOURCES

Chicago Tribune, July 3, 1934, and August 1, 1934.
New York Times, July 3, 1934.

August 6, 1937

Place: New York
League: American League
Field: Yankee Stadium
Clubs: New York versus Cleveland
Umpires: Charlie Johnston, Brick Owens and George Moriarty

First baseman Hal Trosky's second homer of the game, a solo shot, put Cleveland temporarily ahead 6–5 in the top of the 10th inning. When Yankees outfielder Myril Hoag led off the bottom of the frame with a single, Cleveland manager Steve O'Neill replaced his young fireballer, Bob Feller, with veteran reliever Joe Heving. Yankees pinch hitter Jack Saltzgaver fouled off two bunt attempts to sacrifice Hoag to second base and then singled to right field, Hoag stopping at second. Yankees shortstop Frank Crosetti followed by sacrificing both runners along, putting the potential tying run on third and the potential winning run on second.

At that point the game began to disintegrate. Yankees third baseman Red Rolfe appeared to pull his bat back in time on a 2-and–2 count, but Johnston, working the plate, said Rolfe had swung and called him out when Cleveland catcher Frankie Pytlak plucked the ball out of the dirt and tagged him. The Yankees protested that Rolfe had not swung at the pitch. Johnston then shocked them by saying he'd tipped the ball and was out on a tipped third strike. Reminded that Pytlak had picked the ball out of the dirt, an embarrassed Johnston changed his mind again and said the count was now 3-and–2. That brought O'Neill out of the Cleveland dugout. "The harried Johnston consulted Brick Owens, the umpire at second base, who said it was a foul-tip Pytlak caught."

That ended one argument, but a larger one loomed. With two on, two out and the count full, Yankees center fielder Joe DiMaggio ripped a line drive at Cleveland third baseman Odell Hale. The ball caromed off Hale's glove and rolled into foul territory as Hoag and Saltzgaver scored the tying and winning runs. "Meanwhile Umpire Johnston was frantically waving a foul signal at the plate," thus nullifying the runs. "That brought another storm. Finally Johnston shook himself free of the debaters, consulted [umpire] Moriarty at third and, upon being advised the hit was fair, reversed himself." O'Neill immediately announced his plan to protest, claiming that it was Johnston's call to make, he was in the best position to make it, and he made it, calling the ball foul. O'Neill also contended that Cleveland left fielder Moose Solters could have cut down the winning run at the plate if he had not been given to think DiMaggio's hit was a foul ball. On the last day of August, AL president Will Harridge ruled that the umpires should have sent Saltzgaver back to third base and allowed Yankees cleanup hitter Lou Gehrig to bat with two outs and the score tied 6–6. Since they had not, Harridge ruled that the game was a no-decision. New York columnist Dan Daniel thought it was a foolish verdict because there was no way that Solters could have thrown out DiMaggio at second base trying for a double, let alone Saltzgaver, even if he had known at the outset of the play that the ball was fair. All were agreed on only one thing: Johnston had been guilty of bad umpiring. He was not rehired after the 1937 season.

SOURCES

Cleveland Plain Dealer, August 7, 1937.
New York Times, August 7, 1937, and September 1, 1937.

May 14, 1938

Place: St. Louis
League: National League
Field: Sportsman's Park II
Clubs: St. Louis versus Cincinnati
Umpires: Ziggy Sears, Lee Ballanfant and Bill Klem

Reds lefty Johnny Vander Meer, just a month away from pitching two consecutive no-hitters, sailed along through eight innings, allowing only one run, and held a 5–1 lead going into the bottom of the 9th frame. But in their last at-bats the Cards drove him from the mound by exploding for four runs and tying the game at 5-all. At the close of the inning Reds skipper Bill McKechnie announced that he was formally protesting the game in the event his club lost in overtime. His grievance stemmed from a drive in the 6th inning by Reds left fielder Dusty Cooke with two on and two out that struck the edge of the pavilion roof in deep right field, which went for only a triple rather than a home run as was called for by the park rule that any ball hitting the roof was good for an automatic four-bagger.

The ruling became crucial when the Cards tied the score, because Cooke had been left stranded on third after his triple. Had he nailed a homer McKechnie argued the Reds would have won 6–5 in regulation length. Instead they lost 7–6 when reliever Gene Schott coughed up two runs in the bottom of the 10th on an Enos Slaughter homer with Joe Stripp on base after the Reds had tallied a single run in their half of the frame. McKechnie's contention that Cooke's blast had struck the pavilion roof met with support when NL presi-

dent Ford Frick investigated the incident and discovered that base umpire Ballanfant initially signaled the ball was a home run but then backed off his original ruling when plate umpire Klem, who had failed to see his signal, halted
Cooke at third. Upon gathering testimony from all three umpires that day
Frick decided that the game should go into the records for the season as a 7–
7 tie and ordered it to be replayed in its entirety. Frick's verdict saved Cincinnati's Schott from a loss but cost Cards reliever Bob Weiland a win. Happily,
it didn't also cost Ballanfant his job. The junior umpire in the crew had in
essence "swallowed his whistle" when senior crew member Klem signaled that
Cooke's blast was in play.

SOURCES

Cincinnati Enquirer, May 15, 1938.
Milwaukee Journal, July 25, 1942.
New York Times, May 15, 1938.

September 12, 1939

Place: Washington
League: American League
Field: Griffith Stadium
Clubs: Washington versus Chicago
Umpires: Eddie Rommel, Cal Hubbard and Lou Kolls

A mere four hours after losing a 3–2 battle to the White Sox, Washington
pilot Bucky Harris learned that AL president Will Harridge had sustained his
protest and ordered the game to be replayed in its entirety the following day
as part of a doubleheader since it was Chicago's last visit to Washington.

The dispute revolved around a double play the Sox had perpetrated in
the Washington half of the 6th inning. With Senators center fielder Johnny
Welaj on first base and one out, left fielder Taft Wright lifted a short fly to
Sox left fielder Gee Walker. Walker appeared to drop Wright's fly intentionally
before throwing the ball to Sox shortstop Eric McNair, who tagged out Welaj
before he could reach second base. After calling Welaj out, Kolls "then ruled
Wright was also out, despite the fact that Wright had reached first with no
play being made on him." When Harris argued that Wright was safe Kolls
rather lamely attempted to justify his decision by maintaining that Walker
held the ball long enough to constitute a catch, which Harris also took violent
exception to. "Harris cited Rule 24 of American League regulations, which
permits an umpire to call a batter out on an intentionally dropped outfield fly

only when two are on base at the time." There followed a brief conference among the three umpires, and it appeared at first that Hubbard and Rommel might overrule Kolls, "but they took no action beyond accepting Harris's protest officially."

Harridge ultimately allowed the protest because it appeared that not only Kolls but perhaps his two colleagues as well had "misinterpreted the rule, which prohibits the deliberate dropping of a fly ball." The rule was a new one and had been adopted only the previous winter "after several clubs, notably Cleveland, had made frequent use of the fly ball ruse" and intentionally dropped routine flies in the hope of perpetrating an easy double play if the batter loafed to first base.

It may surprise the reader that what was then Rule 24 was not adopted until 1939. Research unearthing how many double plays originating from deliberately dropped fly balls teams like Cleveland actually performed in the years immediately preceding 1939 would no doubt prove illuminating.

SOURCES

Chicago Tribune, September 13, 1939.
Washington Post, September 13, 1939.

June 20, 1940

Place: Chicago
League: American
Field: Comiskey Park
Clubs: Chicago versus New York
Umpires: Eddie Rommel, George Pipgras, Bill Summers and John Quinn

After copping their fourth straight pennant in 1939 to set a new AL record, the mighty Yankees seemingly left Chicago reeling on the evening of June 20, 1940, having just been swept in a three-game series by the lowly White Sox that extended their hapless offensive slump to 20 straight scoreless innings. Earlier in the day Chicago outfielder Bob Kennedy's "towering fly against the left field stand which George Selkirk almost caught but couldn't hold" had doubled home catcher Mike Tresh for the lone run of the game in the 11th inning to give Johnny Rigney a hard-earned 1–0 victory in which he allowed only five hits. The lone blemish from the Sox angle, if it could even be called that, was a rumor that Yankees skipper Joe McCarthy announced that he was protesting the game based on his complaint about a call made in the 2nd inning by umpire Quinn on a foul fly hit by Yankees catcher Bill Dickey and caught in Quinn's judgment by Sox left fielder Moose Solters after Quinn had first ruled no catch. The rumor of a protest was so nebulous, however, that it went unmentioned the following day in both the *Chicago Tribune* and the *New York Times*, although it was picked up by the *Washington Post*.

So matters stood until July 2, 1940, when AL president Will Harridge decreed that the game of June 20 was a no-decision contest and would have to be replayed. Harridge's proclamation was:

"From statements made by [Sox] Manager Jimmy Dykes over the recent finding in the Chicago-New York game of June 20, there seems to be a misunderstanding as to the facts of the case. The American League office, under the rules, cannot entertain any protest involving umpire judgment. The protest of the New York club was registered in the belief that Dickey's foul fly, handled by Solters, was not a caught ball under what was then Section 3 of Rule 44.... My decision, allowing the protest, was based strictly on Umpire John Quinn's misinterpretation of this rule."

SOURCES

Chicago Tribune, June 21, 1940, and July 4, 1940.
New York Times, June 21, 1940.
Washington Post, June 21, 1940.

June 5, 1943

Place: St. Louis
League: National League
Field: Sportsman's Park II
Clubs: St. Louis versus Philadelphia
Umpires: George Barr, Lou Jorda and Jocko Conlan on June 5 and Bill Stewart and Tom Dunn on July 29

In front of a slim crowd of 1,678 and under threatening skies the Cards took over first place in the NL when Howie Krist blanked the Phillies' promising rookie southpaw, Jack Kraus, 1–0 in a contest abbreviated to seven and a half innings when rain began to fall heavily before the Birds came to bat in their half of the frame. "Bucky Harris, manager of the Phillies, protested the game because he said the Cardinals had made no effort to keep the field in proper condition for play during the time out."

NL president Ford Frick upheld the protest, but unlike AL president Will Harridge who had forfeited a game to Boston in 1941 under similar circumstances (**SEE: Forfeited game of August 15, 1941**), Frick ordered the game to be resumed on July 29 at the start of the home half of the 8th inning.

After Kraus held the Cards scoreless, left fielder Jimmy Wasdell led off for the Phils in the 9th inning by homering off Krist and Merrill May singled home Babe Dahlgren with the go-ahead run later in the frame after Red Munger had replaced Krist. In the bottom of the 9th inning Wasdell saved the 2–1 victory for Kraus when he gunned down Cards pinch hitter Danny Litwhiler at the plate as he tried to score from second on Whitey Kurowski's two-out single. After a short delay, Munger then took the hill for the Cardinals in the regularly scheduled game that day, and the Birds took their revenge, winning 13–5.

The ground crew at Sportsman's Park came under similar fire some nine years later for their plodding efforts to protect the field during the second game of a Labor Day doubleheader on September 1, 1952, between Cleveland and the St. Louis Browns. With his club ahead 2–1 in the top of the 5th inning, Satchel Paige, a notoriously slow worker, "speeded up" enough to get three quick outs and make the game official before umpire Jim Duffy stopped play due to rain for an hour and 12 minutes. Bob Lemon retired the Browns in their half of the 5th and Cleveland then set upon Paige for three runs in the top of the 6th frame before rain began plummeting again as the Browns were about to come to bat. The field, already saturated after the ground crew took its time covering it during the first delay, soon became unplayable in Duffy's estimation when the tarp was again slow in being put down. He called the game after only a few minutes, erasing Cleveland's three runs in the top of the 6th and causing the score to revert to 2–1, where it had stood after five frames were completed.

Upon learning the Tribe was protesting the affair, Cleveland papers harkened back to AL president Will Harridge's decision to allow a similar protest by Boston in a game at Washington in 1941 when the Senators' ground crew had been laggard, but their hopes were dashed when Harridge denied the Indians' argument. His verdict was crucial as the Indians finished a mere two games behind the Yankees in the 1952 AL flag race. That winter an amateur Cleveland pantomime troupe received numerous bookings in the Forest City area just to don St. Louis Browns caps and jackets and do a two-minute imitation of the Browns' ground crew in action—or perhaps more accurately, inaction.

SOURCES

Chicago Tribune, June 6, 1943.
Cleveland Plain Dealer, September 2, 1952.
New York Times, September 2, 1952.
Washington Post, June 6, 1943, July 30, 1943, and September 2, 1952.

June 13, 1943

Place: New York
League: National League
Field: Polo Grounds IV
Clubs: New York versus Philadelphia
Umpires: Beans Reardon, Larry Goetz and Lee Ballanfant

After losing the first game of a doubleheader 6–2 to ancient Carl Hubbell, the Phils began their last at-bats in the second contest trailing 3–2. They then chased Giants starter Bill Sayles and also relief specialist, the aptly nicknamed Ace Adams, in the process of tying the score and forcing New York player-manager Mel Ott to beckon Ken Trinkle in from the bullpen. Trinkle walked Phils first sacker Glen Stewart with two out to load the bases and bring Babe Dahlgren to the plate. Normally a first baseman, Dahlgren had been the Yankees' sub that had ended Lou Gehrig's then record consecutive games played streak four years earlier but was playing third base that day.

"Trinkle's first pitch to Dahlgren was a called strike. The Babe didn't like the decision and an argument with Reardon ensued. Suddenly Trinkle pitched and just as quickly Dahlgren stepped across the plate and directly into the ball." Ott later protested the game on the grounds that Dahlgren, "in crossing the plate and going out of his way to be hit by the ball, should have been called out and the side retired" with the game deadlocked at 3-all. Reardon appears to have professed that "he was talking to Earl Whitehill, the Philly coach, at the time, and was not in position to call the play, so it was 'no pitch.'" When play resumed after Reardon's ruling, Dahlgren took Trinkle's next pitch deep against the right field wall to clear the bases and was thrown out by Ott trying to stretch his hit into a triple.

The game seemingly ended with the Phils winning by a 6–3 count when the Giants were scoreless in their half of the 9th, but NL president Ford Frick voted to honor Ott's protest. However, for reasons that remain incomprehensible to this day he decided to count the Giants' half of the 9th inning rather than resuming the game from the point where Dahlgren was ruled out after the fact for illegally stepping into Trinkle's pitch. The game was thus picked up in the 10th inning prior to the regularly scheduled game of August 6, with the same trio of umpires but Rube Fischer on the mound for the Giants in place of Trinkle, who had been traded to Jersey City after the protest was made. Fischer retired the side without incident and then bagged a quick 4–3 win when Phils reliever Newt Kimball walked the bases loaded with two outs and then walked home the winning tally after his catcher, Dee Moore, extended the frame by dropping a routine pop foul.

SOURCES

New York Times, June 13, 1943, and August 7, 1943.
Washington Post, June 13, 1943.

July 20, 1947

Place: Brooklyn
League: National League
Field: Ebbets Field
Clubs: Brooklyn versus St. Louis
Umpires: Jocko Conlan, Larry Goetz and Beans Reardon

In the top of the 9th inning, with the heart of their order due up, the Cards led 2–0 behind rookie right-hander Jim Hearn, who had been invincible to that point. After Stan Musial fanned and Enos Slaughter flied out to center fielder Pete Reiser, the Cards' rotund right fielder, Ron Northey, belted a pitch by Dodgers relief ace Hugh Casey to deep right center. Reiser gave chase and leaped as high as he could reach at the wall but couldn't catch the ball and after "a lapse of a couple of seconds" it dropped back on the field. Right fielder Dixie Walker quickly retrieved it and rifled it in to second baseman Eddie Stanky whose relay throw to catcher Bruce Edwards nailed Northey at the plate as he tried for an inside-the-park homer.

But while base umpire Goetz "who ran out toward the outfield instantly called 'No!' as the ball hit the wall, or the top of the wall, the Cardinals claimed that Reardon, the other base umpire, had waved Northey home as he approached third base "with the statement that it was a home run." Northey then slowed his pace. *New York Times* writer Roscoe McGowen contended, "Had the pudgy outfielder run at full speed he would still have beaten Stanky's throw. As it was, he was out by a slight margin."

St. Louis pilot Eddie Dyer immediately announced he was playing the game under protest if his club lost, and such turned out to be the case. In the home half of the 9th Reiser greeted Hearn's first pitch with a double off the centerfield wall and Walker followed with another double high off the scoreboard in right. At that point Dyer brought in lefty Al Brazle, who got pinch hitter Carl Furillo to ground out, and then followed by calling on righty Murry Dickson when Dodgers manager Burt Shotton sent righty swinger Cookie Lavagetto to bat in place of his left-swinging third baseman Spider Jorgensen.

Dickson ultimately took the loss a few minutes later when pinch hitter Eddie Miksis singled home Pee Wee Reese with the walkoff winning run.

On July 25, NL president Ford Frick upheld Dyer's protest that Northey had been deceived by Reardon and would have scored if he had not slowed down. So far, so good. But Frick than baffled everyone with even a nodding acquaintance with baseball's rules when he did not resume the game in the top of the 9th inning with the Cards ahead 3–0 and two men out, which would have been the rightfully expected decision. Instead he allowed the Dodgers' three runs in the bottom of the 9th to stand and declared the game a 3–3 tie. No one will ever know what decision he would have conjured up if Brooklyn had scored four runs in the 9th. Another vexing question is a photograph of the play on Northey at home, which shows him sliding into Edwards's tag. Why would he have slid if Reardon had told him he had homered? One possibility is that it may have occurred to him that Reardon was wrong, another is that he feared he'd misheard what Reardon had said when he saw the Dodgers were making a play on him. In any event, he was credited with a homer on the ball he hit and all the statistics counted except Dickson's loss and the win that would have gone to the Dodgers' last pitcher in the 9th frame, Casey.

Retrosheet's Dave Smith wrote an excellent article about this bizarre game, which has more juicy details and also includes photographs, in the Society for American Baseball Research publication *The Baseball Research Journal*, Number 33, (2004).

SOURCES

Brooklyn Eagle, July 21, 1947.
New York Times, July 21, 1947.

August 17, 1947

Place: Philadelphia
League: National League
Field: Shibe Park
Clubs: Philadelphia versus Brooklyn
Umpires: George Barr, Jocko Conlan and Lou Jorda

With the second-place Cardinals looking ever more closely over the Dodgers' shoulders in the 1947 senior league race after the weird tie between the two teams less than a month earlier, the Dodgers were blanked 4–0 in the first game of a Sunday doubleheader by the Phils Dutch Leonard and were hoping to achieve a split on the day when they took a 5–4 lead in the 7th inning of the nitecap. But at the time a Pennsylvania curfew law required that all Sunday major league baseball games had to end no later than 6:59 p.m.. Once the Dodgers scored the go-ahead run on outfielder Dixie Walker's single there were only five minutes left to play. Dodgers base runners and batters tried to deliberately allow themselves to be put out by getting caught between bases and swinging wildly at every pitch. But nothing could force the Phils to end the top half of the 7th inning until Dodgers gardener Gene Hermanski meandered toward home from third base and Phils catcher Don Padgett had no alternative but to stand at the plate and wait for Hermanski to "move against the ball."

With the Phils slated to come up, "Harry Walker [Dixie's brother] couldn't find his bat and Hugh Casey had time to pitch only two balls and one strike to him when time ran out and the score reverted to the sixth inning," which had ended tied at 4-all. At that juncture "thousands of the 32, 220 spectators poured onto the field, some pleased that the Phils had gained a tie after winning one but many obviously disgruntled."

It is unclear whether the Dodgers formally protested the Phils' actions, but they hardly needed to, because the following day NL president Ford Frick angrily proclaimed that the game had to be resumed on September 25 when the Dodgers were next in Philadelphia with Walker at bat with a 2–1 count and none out in the bottom of the seventh. He based his ruling largely on umpire-in-chief Barr's report that "the Phils made no attempt to put out Brooklyn base runners, and otherwise employed means of 'beating the clock.'" His official statement added that "it was a farcical exhibition which was a disgrace to baseball and a complete travesty of all the rules of sportsmanship." Frick's jaundiced assessment of the affair was based in large part on a remark by Phils manager Ben Chapman that Barr had overheard. Chapman had told Dixie Walker before he drove in the lead run that he, Chapman, didn't care if the game ended in a tie because the replay was likely to draw another 30,000 or so, which could only benefit Chapman who had an attendance clause in his salary. Those who saw the 2013 Jackie Robinson bio-pic learned in the event they didn't already know that Chapman resorted to other means as well to insure there were large crowds in Shibe whenever the Dodgers came to Philadelphia that year.

On September 25 prior to the regularly scheduled game at Shibe Park that night, the Dodgers won the completed game, 7–5, behind Casey. Harry Walker, whose missing bat, had a large role in the travesty on August 17, sat out the night with an injured shoulder but had already all but wrapped up the NL bat crown with a .363 mark.

SOURCE

New York Times, August 18, 1947, August 19, 1947, and September 26, 1947.

August 25, 1948

Place: Pittsburgh
League: National League
Field: Forbes Field and Ebbets Field
Clubs: Pittsburgh versus Brooklyn
Umpires: George Barr, Jocko Conlan and Lou Jorda on August 25 and Bill Stewart,
   Butch Henline and Jocko Conlan on September 21

A day that had already been marred by a brawl in the Dodgers' dugout in which *Associated Press* cameraman Danny Jacino was mauled and later filed a trespass suit against the Dodgers and in particular infielder Tommy Brown finished in a protest by Pirates manager Billy Meyer which the *New York Times* admitted that NL president Ford Frick "cannot avoid upholding."

The Pirates entered the bottom of the 9th inning trailing Brooklyn 11–6 with Hugh Casey on the hill in relief of starter Erv Palica. With two out and second baseman Danny Murtaugh on third, Pittsburgh suddenly rallied for three runs and had catcher Ed Fitzgerald on first base and third sacker Frankie Gustine on third. When Carl Erskine came out of the pen to replace Casey, Meyer sent up infielder Eddie Bockman to bat for pitcher Woody Main. Bockman worked the count to 3-and-1. Brooklyn manager Burt Shotton then sent in Hank Behrman to relieve Erskine, forgetting that what at the time was Rule 17, Section 4 clearly states that a pitcher must face at least one batter until he is either retired or reaches base, the lone exception being if a pitcher sustains an injury that in the umpire-in-chief's judgment calls for him to be replaced. Shotton's blunder was shared by the three umpires who failed to realize their oversight until they had conferred among themselves and then with Shotton after Bockman grounded into a force at second base on Behrman's first pitch to him to seemingly end the game.

The unfinished contest was transferred to Brooklyn since the Dodgers did not visit Pittsburgh again that year and completed prior to the regularly scheduled game between the two clubs on the afternoon of September 21. Identical lineups for both clubs were used except for Brooklyn's third base slot where Tommy Brown, the main malefactor in the dugout brawl with a cameraman on August 26, replaced an injured Billy Cox. The substitution proved lethal to the Dodgers' chances. Erskine, back on the hill to face Bockman with a 3-and–1 count, walked him with his first pitch. Now Shotton was legally allowed to replace Erskine with Behrman if he so chose, and he did. After Behrman ran the count to full on him, Pirates shortstop Stan Rojek slammed a hot shot between third and short. Brown got his glove on it, but it bounded away into left field. With the runners off on the pitch, all three scored to saddle Erskine with a 12–11 loss while Main earned his first career win nearly a month after he had thrown his final pitch in the game for which he received it. The *New York Times* deemed Rojek's hit a "fluke double" when the scorer elected not to credit Brown, a disaster in the field throughout his career, with an error. (In his nine seasons in the majors, which began when he was 16, Brown, who was nicknamed "Buckshot" due to his scatter arm, posted a career fielding average of .931.) Consequently Rojek came away with five RBI in the protested game and added another in the regular game that night, which the Pirates also won, 6–3, to all but completely scorch Brooklyn's final chance to catch the front-running Boston Braves.

SOURCES

New York Times, August 26, 1948, and September 22, 1949.
Pittsburgh Dispatch, August 26, 1948.

September 22, 1954

Place: Milwaukee
League: National League
Field: County Stadium
Clubs: Milwaukee versus Cincinnati
Umpires: Hal Dixon. Bill Jackowski, Lee Ballanfant and Al Barlick

Holding a slim 3–1 lead at the top of the 9th inning, Milwaukee brought its top starter, Warren Spahn, out of the pen to close out the game. Spahn walked Reds outfielder Gus Bell, then induced slugging first sacker Ted Kluszewski to foul out to catcher Del Crandall before walking Wally Post. Cincinnati manager Birdie Tebbetts sent up Bob Borkowski to bat for speedy left fielder Lloyd Merriman, a star running back at Stanford who was nicknamed "Citation" after the Triple Crown winning horse. Borkowski fanned on a pitch in the dirt and the ball skipped past Crandall. He threw too late to Braves third sacker Eddie Mathews to get Bell at third, but Mathews then fired the ball to first baseman Danny O'Connell (normally a second baseman who was playing out of position that day) to nail Borkowski, who was running even though he was automatically out since first and second base had been occupied with less than two out when he whiffed. The throw struck Borkowski and rolled into right field, allowing both Bell and Post to score. The umpires conferred for some 18 minutes and then ruled Bell was out for the third out of the inning because Borkowski was guilty of interference for having drawn the throw after he was already out. Umpire-in-chief Dixon said they were basing their ruling on Section 7.09, subsection E.

Tebbetts immediately announced he was protesting the ruling, saying, "If Borkowski was supposed to know he was not entitled to run, then Mathews should have known it, too, and not thrown to first trying to get him."

The following day NL president Warren Giles upheld Tebbetts's protest both because the rule, in his estimation, was fuzzily written and needed to be refined and because the result of the game had potential implications on the final standings and the World's Series shares of five different clubs.

On September 24, Milwaukee became the first major league team since 1899 to defeat two different teams on the same field on the same day when the Braves whipped the Cardinals 4–2 in the regularly scheduled game after surviving a Cincinnati comeback in the protested game to triumph 4–3. The protested game was resumed with Bell on third, Nino Escalara running for Post on second and two out, with Dave Jolly on the slab in place of Spahn and Reds second baseman Johnny Temple at the plate. Temple singled to score Bell and Escalara came home too with the tying run when Braves center fielder Billy Bruton momentarily fumbled Temple's hit. After Cincinnati catcher Andy Seminick fanned to end the Reds' threat, the Braves tallied the winning run in their half of the 9th on a single by right fielder George Metkovich that plated left fielder Jim Pendleton.

SOURCES

Chicago Tribune, September 23, 1954, September 24, 1954 and September 25, 1954.
Milwaukee Journal, September 23, 1954.

August 1, 1971

Place: Philadelphia
League: National League
Field: Veterans Stadium
Clubs: Philadelphia versus St. Louis
Umpires: Stan Landes, Mel Steiner, Satch Davidson and Shag Crawford on August 1 and John Kibler, Bruce Froemming, Al Barlick and Paul Pryor on September 7

The Cards and Phillies finished the 9th inning of their Sunday afternoon game deadlocked at 3-all. Neither team threatened to break the tie until the visitors' half of the 12th when Lou Brock singled off Bill Wilson, the Phils' third pitcher in the game, stole second and went to third on a passed ball. After second baseman Stan Javier was hit by a pitch, play was then interrupted by an hour and forty-nine minute rain delay. When action resumed the Cards tallied three runs and still had only one out before rain stopped play again for 31 minutes.

While the field was being readied for a second resumption of play, the Zamboni machine used to remove the standing water broke down. Upon determining that the Zamboni could not be repaired, umpire-in-chief Landes called the game because the field was unplayable, and the Cards' three runs were erased, the score reverting to 3–3, where it had stood at the finish of the last completed inning.

Cards skipper Red Schoendienst protested Landes's decision to revert the score due to the home team's defective equipment, and NL president Chub Feeney agreed. The game was finished on September 7 in Philadelphia with a new set of umpires before the regularly scheduled game that night. After the Cards were retired in the 12th inning without doing any further damage, the Phillies retaliated with three runs of their own in the bottom of the frame. St. Louis then posted three more runs in the top of the 13th inning, and this time the Phillies could not answer back. Stan Williams, the Cards' sixth and last pitcher in the game, bagged the win and Manny Muniz took the loss.

SOURCES

New York Times, August 2, 1971.
The Sporting News, September 18, 1971.

May 15, 1975

Place: Montreal
League: National League
Field: Parc Jarry
Clubs: Montreal versus Atlanta
Umpires: Nick Colosi, John McSherry, Chris Pelekoudas and Paul Pryor on May 15 and Jerry Dale, Shag Crawford, John Kibler and Dick Stello on July 20

The Braves got to Expos starter Steve Renko early and were leading 4–1 with the Expos at bat in the bottom of the 4th inning when rain began to fall heavily. After an hour wait, umpire-in-chief Colosi called the game on account of rain. Braves manager Clyde King complained that the umpires hadn't waited long enough before terminating play and in addition hadn't physically tested the field to see if it was still playable at the time the game was canceled. NL president Chub Feeney upheld King's protest.

The game was resumed at the point where it was stopped on July 20 with a new crew of umpires prior to the Expos' regularly scheduled game that day with the Braves. Heading into the bottom of the 9th, Braves starter Phil Niekro led 5–2 and seemed to be coasting to victory. But two successive doubles put him on the ropes, and Max Leon had to hurry in from the pen to get a save and the third out to preserve the Braves' 5–4 win.

SOURCES

New York Times, May 21, 1975 and July 21, 1975.
The Sporting News, August 2, 1975.

August 21, 1979

Place: New York
League: National League
Field: Shea Stadium
Clubs: Houston versus New York
Umpires: Frank Pulli, Andy Olsen and Doug Harvey

With two out in the top of the 9th and the bases empty, Mets starter Pete Falcone seemed to have a shutout locked down when Astros outfielder Jeffrey Leonard flied out to Mets' center fielder Lee Mazzilli. The Mets were racing off the field when third base umpire Doug Harvey began waving his hands and shouting that Mets shortstop Frank Taveras had asked for a time out before Falcone delivered his final pitch to Leonard and Harvey had granted it.

After the Mets had taken their places in the field again, Leonard singled through the box. No sooner was he on first base than Mets manager Joe Torre called attention to the fact that his first sacker Ed Kranepool was not on the field and argued that the game could not legally resume without a full complement of defensive players. The umpires agreed and summoned Leonard back to the plate as Kranepool trotted out to take his spot in the field. Astros manager Bill Virdon immediately bounced out of the Houston dugout to argue that if Leonard's at bat was to be a do-over, the count should revert to 0–0. Plate umpire Pulli disagreed and Virdon then announced he would protest the game if the Astros lost. After he returned to the dugout, Leonard flied out to left fielder Joel Youngblood, this time enabling the Mets to leave the field secure in their feeling that Falcone had tossed a nifty complete-game shutout.

However, NL president Chub Feeney, who was at the game, approximately one hour after the teams had gone to their respective dressing rooms upheld Virdon's protest and furthermore ruled that Leonard's single had been legal because it had been Torre's own fault that he had allowed the game to resume with his first baseman absent. The following afternoon, before the regularly scheduled game between the Mets and the Astros that day, Kevin Kobel officially recorded the last out of the previous night's game when he induced Jose Cruz to ground out to second baseman Doug Flynn to preserve the Mets' 5–0 win. Apart from the Astros, the biggest loser in the hodgepodge was Pete Falcone, who in effect had notched 28 outs and allowed no runs on the night of August 21 yet was credited with neither a complete game nor a shutout.

Sources

New York Daily News, August 22, 1979.
New York Times, August 22, 1979, and August 23, 1979.

July 24, 1983

Place: New York
League: American League
Field: Yankee Stadium
Clubs: New York versus Kansas City
Umpires: Tim McClelland, Drew Coble, Joe Brinkman and Nick Bremigan on July 24 and George Maloney, Tim Welke, Dave Phillips and Rick Reed on August 18

This game to date is the only one of its kind in major league history in that a league president upheld a protest even though his umpiring crew had enforced the rule that triggered the protest to the letter.

In his 2006 book, *The Official Rules of Baseball Illustrated,* David Nemec wrote: "Beyond any doubt the most famous violation ... of Rule 1.10 (c) [as it was constituted in 1983] was the "Pine Tar Incident" in 1983, which began on July 24 ... but echoed deep into the off season and did not culminate until late December when Commissioner Bowie Kuhn fined the Yankees $250,000 for 'certain public statements' made by Yankees owner George Steinbrenner about the way American League president Lee MacPhail handled the incident."

Nemec went on to say the incident had been instigated by Royals third sacker George Brett's two-run homer off Yankees closer Goose Gossage with two out in the 9th frame to put the Royals ahead, 5–4. As Brett started for the dugout after circling the bases, Yankees manager Billy Martin, perhaps alerted to the infraction by catcher Rick Cerone, asked the umpires to check

Brett's bat for excessive pine tar. Plate umpire McClelland looked at the bat, and upon realizing that the pine tar on it might extend beyond the 18-inch length allowed from the end of the handle, then consulted with the other umpires for a full minute. Crew chief Brinkman measured the pine tar on the bat handle against the 17-inch width of home plate and decided that it exceeded the 18-inch limit by at least an inch. The umpires then ruled Brett out for using an illegal bat, thereby nullifying his home run and ending the game with the score reverting to 4–3, New York. As McClelland turned to the Royals dugout and gave the out sign, Yankees third baseman Graig Nettles celebrated and pounded his glove as he sidestepped away from McClelland. The crowd exploded with delight. At that point Brett lost it and charged the umpires like a crazed lunatic. Video of the incident shows that he was cut off just before he got to McClelland by the three other umpires along with several Royals players but not before he had reeled off a string of choice expletives. During the melee around home plate Royals pitcher Gaylord Perry furtively snatched up Brett's bat. He apparently threw it to someone standing near the on-deck circle who then threw it over the railing into the Royals' dugout. The bat was then rushed down the runway to the Royals' locker room by a bat boy. A scene out of the Keystone Kops unfolded as players, coaches, an umpire, New York City policemen and a suited Yankees security representative ran down the dugout steps and though the narrow passage way leading to the locker room chasing the bat boy who probably felt that he was running for his life.

Four days after Royals manager Dick Howser lodged an official protest, MacPhail announced he was upholding it, the first time in his 10 years as AL president that he had overturned an umpire's decision. But MacPhail made it clear the fault lay not with his umpires but rather with the rule, which needed to be revised to establish that a bat coated with excessive pine tar was not the same as a doctored bat that had been altered to improve the distance factor or to cause an unusual reaction on a batted ball.

"With the protest upheld," Nemec wrote, "the score once again became 5–4, Royals, with two out in the top of the ninth. When MacPhail ruled the game had to be finished at Yankee Stadium on August 18, an open date for both teams, Steinbrenner at first said he'd rather forfeit. The completion of the game eventually took place as ordered by MacPhail. But not before there was an attempt by Yankees fans to get a court injunction" barring the game, followed by a last-ditch effort by Martin to have Brett declared out.

With Howser, Brett, Perry and Royals coach Rocky Colavito suspended from the game, the Yankees took the field on August 18, and Martin immediately had his infielders try appeals at first and second bases. One of the infielders was lefty Don Mattingly, normally a first baseman, who was put at second base by the rebellious Martin while another lefty, pitcher Ron Guidry, occupied center field. When the umpires—not the original crew—gave the safe sign at both bases, Martin filed a protest, claiming that the four umpires that day could not know if Brett had touched every base on his home run trot since none of them was in Yankee Stadium on July 24. But Martin's imaginative ploy had been anticipated. Crew chief Phillips whipped out a notarized letter signed by all of Brinkman's crew that not only Brett but also U.L. Washington, the runner that scored ahead of him—had touched all the bases. Nemec wrote that the game itself then "took only 12 minutes to complete, as the Yankees meekly went down in order in the bottom of the ninth" to seal the Royals' win. "None of the various court orders the Yankees subsequently launched to quash the result came to anything much, but over the winter Rule 1.10 (c) was revised to stipulate that a bat with too much pine tar shall call for the bat's ejection from the game but not for nullification of any play that resulted from its use."

The entire game, coupled with the protested completion of it, is available on YouTube.

SOURCES

Nemec, David. *The Official Rules of Baseball Illustrated,* 3d ed. (Guilford, CT: Lyons Press, 2006), 8–10.
New York Times, July 25, 1983 and August 19, 1983.
www.youtube.com.

June 16, 1986

Place: Pittsburgh
League: National League
Field: Three Rivers Stadium
Clubs: Pittsburgh versus St. Louis
Umpires: Bob Davidson, John Kibler, Bruce Froemming and Randy Marsh

Fittingly perhaps the last successful protested major league game to date could not have occurred in baseball's infancy when the home team had sole control of at what point, if at all, to resume play after a weather delay. With the Cards leading 4–1 in the top of the 6th inning, two rain delays occurred. The first lasted only 17 minutes before the tarp was removed. But before play could resume the rain began again. This time the umpires decided after waiting just 22 minutes that it was a lost cause and called the game, erasing two Cardinals outs and a walk by Willie McGee that had come before the first rain stoppage. Pirates manager Jim Leyland protested, claiming the rule demanded that the umpires wait a full 30 minutes after the second stoppage, not a combination of time that equaled 30 minutes as they apparently believed when they halted the game. The following day NL president Chub Feeney announced that he concurred with Leyland's interpretation and the game was resumed in the Cards' half of the 6th before the regularly scheduled game between the two teams that night.

The action following the resumption was uneventful. In the 8th inning the Pirates scored a run off reliever Pat Perry on Lee Mazzilli's sacrifice fly to bring the score to 4–2, St. Louis, and that was how it ended.

SOURCES

New York Times, June 17, 1986.
The Sporting News, June 23, 1986.

Bibliography

BOOKS

Anderson, David W. *You Can't Beat the Hours*. North Charleston, SC: CreateSpace, 2013.

Browning, Reed. *Baseball's Greatest Season, 1924*. Amherst: University of Massachusetts Press, 2003.

Epstein, Dan. *Big Hair and Plastic Grass*. New York: Thomas Dunne Books, 2010.

Jordan, David M. *The Athletics of Philadelphia*. Jefferson, NC: McFarland, 1999

Miklich, Eric. *Rules of the Game*. North Babylon, NY: privately published, 2002.

Nemec, David. *The Beer and Whisky League*. New York: Lyons & Burford, 1995.

_____. *The Great Encyclopedia of Nineteenth-Century Major League Baseball*, 2d ed. Tuscaloosa: University of Alabama Press, 2006.

_____. *Major League Baseball Profiles, 1871–1900*. 2 vols. Omaha: University of Nebraska Press, 2012.

_____. *The Official Rules of Baseball Illustrated*, 3d ed. New York: Lyons, 2006.

_____. *The Rank and File of 19th Century Major League Baseball*. Jefferson, NC: McFarland, 2012.

Orem, Preston. *Baseball, 1845–1881*. Aldena, CA: privately published, 1961.

Ryczek, William. *Blackguards and Red Stockings*. Wallingford, CT: Colebrook Press, 1999.

NEWSPAPERS

Baltimore Gazette
Boston Globe
Brooklyn Daily Eagle
Buffalo Commercial Advertiser
Chicago Times
Chicago Tribune
Cincinnati Enquirer
Cleveland Plain Dealer
Denver Post
Hartford Courant
Los Angeles Times
Louisville Courier-Journal
Milwaukee Journal
National Republican
New York Clipper
New York Daily News
New York Daily Tribune
New York Evening Telegraph
New York Herald
New York Sun
New York Times
Pittsburgh Dispatch
St. Louis Post-Dispatch
St. Louis Republic
St. Paul Daily Globe
Toronto Star
Troy (NY) *Whig*
Washington Critic
Washington Evening Star
Washington Herald
Washington Post
Washington Times

MAGAZINES, JOURNALS AND OTHER PUBLICATIONS

Grandstand Baseball Annual, 1988. Edited by Joseph M. Wayman.

Proceeding of Convention of the National As-

sociation of Professional Base Ball Players.
Beresford, 1871.
The Baseball Research Journal, Number 33,
2004.
Sporting Life, 1883–1917.
The Sporting News, 1886–1995.

Baseball Guides

De Witt's Base Ball Guide, 1871 and 1872.
De Witt's Base Ball Umpire Guide, 1875.
Reach's Official Base Ball Guide, 1882–1891.
Spalding's Official Base Ball Guide, 1876–
1996.
Wright and Ditson's Base Ball Guide, 1884.

Manuscripts and Archives

Charles Mears Base Ball Scrapbooks 1871–
1884; 1906–1920. Cleveland Public Library, Cleveland, OH.

Web Sites

www.19cbaseball.com.
www.RetroSheet.org.
www.youtube.com.

Index

Numbers in **bold italics** indicate pages with photographs.

235